THE
PAST STILL
BREATHES

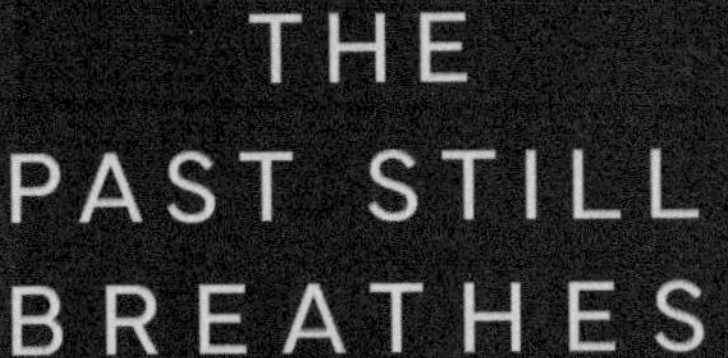

THE PAST STILL BREATHES

A MEMOIR OF SURVIVAL, REINVENTION & GLOBAL ADVENTURE

KIRSTYN LEWIS

The Past Still Breathes
Copyright © 2026 by Kirstyn Lewis
All rights reserved.

Cover and interior design by Laura Duffy Design
Cover photograph by: Kian Kanani

Paperback ISBN: 978-1-7645405-1-3
E-Book ISBN: 978-1-7645405-0-6

There are times when
We firmly believe that by controlling things
And events, we can escape the pain,
The repetition of patterns that have marked,
Frustrated, and bent us in the past …
As we build intricate fortresses and castles of
Cards that momentarily separate us from the truth …
We try to distance ourselves
And look away from our wound
Instead of facing it with compassion and
Courage, telling it that it is a part of us and,
Therefore, can be loved.
What we run from is simply destined to
Become a déjà vu of the future …
It will return to our doorstep to settle its
Accounts with us and, if we choose,
To set us free.
—Francesca Gobessi

PREFACE

I BEGAN WRITING THIS BOOK ON 12 January 2025, at 7:12 am, not knowing exactly where it would lead me, only that I could no longer ignore the pull of my own story. What followed was a year of writing and rewriting, of laughter and tears, of doubt, frustration, courage and clarity. This memoir is the result of that journey, a deeply personal account of the experiences that have shaped me, challenged me, and ultimately strengthened me.

The Past Still Breathes is not about perfection. It's about resilience. About the stories we carry, the histories that live in our bodies, and the quiet determination it takes to keep moving forward in a world that hasn't always been designed for women to thrive.

Along the way, I have been supported, inspired and held by extraordinary women—women who lift each other, who change the narrative through dedication and who remind us of the power of community. Their presence echoes throughout these pages.

I share this story not to seek approval, but to offer connection. To the women who have survived, rebuilt, and dared to imagine more. To those who understand that the past never truly disappears, but that it doesn't have to define our future.

This is my story. And perhaps, in some small way, it is yours too.

BREATHE.

It was 5 pm on Sunday when I realised my apartment key no longer fitted the lock. I tried again and again, listening for the zip of metal. The lock refused to budge.

I looked up and checked the apartment number. No, it was definitely hers. She had moved from 5G to 5F, so for a moment I was confused. For so many years I had only known the place overlooking Third Avenue.

I became desperate, I was already cold. *Try faster, then slower.* I tried every speed. Nothing. Not only did the key not move, I was beginning to think it didn't fit.

The light at the top of the stairs flickered. A damp chill clung to the air outside. Manhattan was quickly starting to dim.

Susu had gone out East for a few days. My calls had gone unanswered and I couldn't be sure my texts had gone through. Silence.

A knot tightened in my stomach. Dread started to creep in, slowly and heavily, as if it had been waiting for the right time. I stood staring at 5G etched in brass for far too long.

Don't cry.

I reached into my purse, pulled out my wallet and counted the notes. Barely a hundred dollars. Not enough for comfort. Only enough for survival, at least for one night. I would need to head back down to Midtown.

I looked down again at the lock. It held no answers. I trundled my bag back down the stairs and headed back out to the street in Upper East Side.

Drizzle is the most pointless of all weather. A little too light to justify an umbrella, and too cold to ignore. Its misery works its way into your bones. I was unsurprised that millions had left to enjoy their evening in. It was only me still out in it, or that's how it felt. The shopfronts glowed behind their glass, indifferent to me, the only passerby. So too were the streetlights and deserted commercial spaces. They had already made their minds up about me. New York had that effect.

I let the heavy white door fall shut behind me, and for a moment the blast of warmth felt almost protective. I'd never stayed at the YMCA before. Even the single bed, white sheets pulled tight, corners folded with the kind of military precision Tom would've inspected with a nod, seemed to be trying its best to behave like a home.

There wasn't much to take in; just a small wooden desk with outdated handles pressed against the window, and a mid-century chair recovered in earnest blue, which performed as an upgrade. I set my bag beside it. The room felt larger than I'd ever need. The bathroom, they said, was down the corridor, past the drinking fountain. Not that I would ever know.

I lifted the phone on the desk and dialled Lifeline. I expected someone to answer in a kind voice. Someone elderly, patient and wise. A grandfather or grandmother; someone who understood the perils of life. With a few measured words, they would soothe the sobs that had begun to rise in my chest.

An irritated operator picked up.

'Who are you looking for? What are you saying? I can't understand you. Lifeline? Do you want me to connect you to emergency?'

Without warning, my voice broke into jagged gasps. My desperate words collapsed into unintelligible sounds. I clawed for air.

Like the city's drizzle, my tears blurred the room. Defeated, I hung up.

In that moment, a familiar sensation returned: a feeling of spinning uncontrollably through a vortex of white, so soft in its composition that it fills every cell of my being. I imagine it is much like it feels when one passes over. A strange cocoon of weightlessness and nothing.

It is a place where my past still breathes. Strangely comforting and familiar, it's a place I feel loved. A place where I am not required to be brave and endure the ordeal of being human. Heaven.

Psychiatrists would no doubt interpret it differently. They'd flatten the experience as they scribbled into their notepads, ready to diagnose it as a mental breakdown. *Dissociation, retreat, overwhelm, hallucination, stabilisation required, medication needs urgent review.* They'd risk liability and blame if they leaned in and tried to understand my version of spiritual coherence. A generation of practised, older, white male psychiatrists had always been dismissive. Their discipline erred on the side of scientific caution and far from more visionary states, those shaped by more mystical experiences. They still weren't ready for a broader conversation. Not in America, anyway.

I had written to Martina that evening, not that I remembered. My rambling missive reached her inbox as she was reaching for another sip of her morning coffee while scrolling through her emails. She skimmed the first few lines and caught her breath.

This isn't the girl I know. How did it get to this?

She set her cup down and dialled Susu.

'Something is wrong with Kirsty. Where are you?'

The concern in Martina's voice was unmistakable. Susu knew something had gone terribly wrong. She told me she had sprung from the lounge chair to find her handbag. Papers, lipstick, hairbrush – she tossed them aside as her fingers fumbled around for her car keys, and without a coat, without a word of explanation, she left the house.

As the operator was referring my distressed call to emergency services, Susu was already on the freeway from Long Island. Rain hammered the glass in relentless sheets. Her wipers were already thrashing back and forth at full speed, barely keeping pace with the water on her windscreen. Oncoming headlights smeared her view, as every passing truck obstructed the lines on the road. She drove on, her knuckles white on the wheel, until she reached Manhattan, now bleary and deserted. It was almost Monday.

Susu followed nothing more than her hunches, crisscrossing the blocks she knew I'd be familiar with, and where she thought I may have gone. She even checked a venue I had booked the week prior to see Diane von Furstenberg speak, but with doors already locked, under no circumstances would visitors be admitted until morning.

It had become a race against time.

Several black NYPD uniforms with their glossy gold badges now crowded my doorway as they made their way in, followed by paramedics. I was puzzled. They were too big to be policemen. Did they recruit the night patrol from a pool of former linebackers? I couldn't be sure. I only knew they were far too big and immovable to be in my room.

With practised precision, an officer reached for the plastic orange CVS prescription bottles. How many pills had I taken? I didn't know. I had taken as many as I could, but I'd run out of water.

Another moved to my bag sitting on the ground by the blue chair, unzipped it and flicked through its contents, filing a mental note of its inventory before taking it. An overwhelming tiredness had started to drill down upon me. I wanted to close my eyes.

'Is there anyone we can contact?' The question sounded more procedural than curious.

The two paramedics had moved quickly, strapping a monitor to me while they checked my pupils.

I hadn't been thinking straight, as most of my medication was designed to release consistently over a twelve-hour period. My mistake was their gain. They now had time.

The paramedics' quiet concern extended into triage, before they signed me off in a place where sirens most famously converged after 9/11. Stabbings, gunshot wounds, broken bodies and broken minds would be funnelled through the same fluorescent corridors that smelt of bleach and despair. Clinicians here wore their residency as a badge of honour.

To 'end up in Bellevue', one of the busiest and most scrutinised hospitals in the United States, commonly meant one thing: madness.

BEHIND THE GLASS

IT WAS JUNE IN 1965 WHEN MY BIRTH mother, Sharon, stood alone at the nursery glass in the dim corridor, bare feet cold against the linoleum, her hospital gown slipping at the shoulder. It wasn't the first time she had pleaded to see her daughter. She didn't know what was worse: postnatal exhaustion or the shame of being branded a teenage mother. Either way, she would have to pay her penance. Sins were sins, and the Catholic institution had its processes to follow.

When she fell pregnant as a teenager, her family spirited her away to a novitiate before the neighbours could start talking about her belly. No one had told her how swiftly a woman's body conspires to bond with the child inside her, nor how oxytocin would flood her system. I was lifted from her tender young breasts just after my first feed, before the nurse's tea had cooled at her station.

Placed alongside all the other babies in a special room where mothers were forbidden to see or cradle their newborns, I was blissfully unaware of the teenager standing only feet away for the next several days, hollowed by loss.

'It's better this way, dear,' the nurses told her, their voices firm but gentle.

'Why won't you show me my baby? Why? What have I done wrong?' Sharon whispered as her eyes dropped to the floor, either out of respect or fear of repercussion.

One should, after all, respect one's elders.

SCORPIO SEASON CAN BE CHALLENGING. A time governed by sex, death, rebirth, and what is hidden. Her journey had been written in the stars. It spoke heavily of family secrets. A child born into illusion and sexual deception, who would live a life of love and loss.

It was on 6 November, 2024, when I heard Sharon's name again. It was difficult to grasp that more than twenty-five years had flown by since we had last spoken.

The timing was exact that day. Scorpio is not sentimental about endings. Sharon would have understood that more than most.

'Nick is trying to find you. Can you call him?' A text on Instagram. It was from my cousin's wife, Vali, an uncombative woman of gentle persuasion.

Sharon's nephew Nick and I had kept in contact over the years, partly because I was a new addition to his extended family, and partly because we enjoyed each other's easy, cousinly company.

I knew this was about her as I picked up the phone and dialled New Zealand.

'Nick? I had a message to contact you.' I needn't have said more.

'Kirstyn … I'm so sorry to be the one to tell you.' Nick's voice carried that soft, steady patience he saved for difficult moments. 'The Turkish Embassy has contacted our family to tell us that Sharon has passed away. We don't have the full details yet. Let me set up a WhatsApp group so we can share what we know. We'll work everything out together. And … just to let you know, the family don't want to repatriate her. The Embassy has told us she can't be cremated in a Muslim country.'

I sat cross-legged on my sofa, staring aimlessly at the television, then past my balcony glass into the mid-morning desert haze of Dubai. My gaze then settled on the residential tower next door that blocked my view of the racecourse. Its mirrored grey windows concealed the lives within; strangers I would never meet. Sometimes I caught them watering their plants on their balconies, most of which would die in the fierce heat of summer or when they left for vacation. It's crazy what goes through your mind when someone dies.

I tried to catch my breath, but it became ragged and stuttering, before turning into convulsions that arrived in waves I couldn't control. It was as if something unseen had taken hold of me.

I reached for the phone to call my dad. Most know him as Pete. It's a strange feeling to tell your father that your birth mother has passed; I didn't want to sound disrespectful as he quietly listened.

'You'll never regret doing the right thing,' he said.

My father had always been a very kind man.

At eighty-seven, Pete knew a thing or two about life. He had grown up in a broken home during the Second World War, the eldest child from one of his mother's four husbands.

Dad had already lost the mother I grew up with. He had nursed his wife, the love of his life, at home through several years of emphysema, a chronic and irreversible lung disease. Not only had he buried Dawn, but he had also buried my little brother in tragic circumstances.

Life hadn't been easy or fair for him. Pete had brought me up to weather life's storms with the knowledge that he had of the world, as only a good father could do.

For those of us who live in Dubai, Turkey may be seen as a city break. I had never been a person to travel like that. Nor have I ever been in a hurry to reach my final destination, or to return multiple times to the same place.

Despite being well-travelled, this time I had inadvertently forgotten to book a seat.

I am of small stature, so I can agreeably sit in an economy seat on relatively short flights. This time I needed more space to protect my energy, so I packed my noise-cancelling headphones to ensure no one spoke to me.

'I can do this,' I told myself as I shuffled down the aisle.

Check-in had given me the middle seat.

45B. Perhaps I had a seat either side to myself? My luck quickly changed as my fellow passengers arrived. A well-dressed Nigerian man now sat to my left. Like me, something must have weighed heavily on his mind, as he stared into the clouds for the entire flight.

The Sudanese fellow seated to my right had arrived swathed in a red shawl. He fidgeted nervously, then added a grey airline blanket on top of his shawl before proceeding to theatrically fling the blanket open like bat wings as he readjusted his position. He did this regularly throughout the flight, almost as if he, too, was preparing to take off.

Five hours into the flight, I sat in restless silence, unable to decide on morning tea or a film. I ordered a Blood of Christ instead. Why not? The Church serves red wine not long past seven-thirty on Sunday mornings. With Batman flapping about beside me, I quietly feared the worst the moment my merlot arrived.

In the end, I closed my eyes and listened to Cat Stevens. It reminded me of her.

A flight from the US had arrived at the same time as my Emirates flight. I had cleared customs quickly so hadn't noticed the familiar American twang of tourists at the conveyor belt. With only a black Samsonite carry-on, I followed the directions on my phone to the black Mercedes waiting at the kerb. The drive from the airport seemed far longer than I remembered.

The reception of my old town hotel was pleasing enough after its recent renovation – so much so, a group of well-dressed, middle-aged American tourists had also chosen to stay there.

'Would you believe we just travelled ten hours? It's a long way,' one of them drawled, 'but we've always wanted to visit since our son came in 2020. He's in the military, you know.' They went on and on and on, so I waited.

Ahmet had drawn the short straw. I caught him nodding, waiting for the perfect moment to divert the conversation so he could offer them a welcome drink.

'Welcome back, Miss Lewis.'

Hotel rooms never quite look like their appealing photos. Four floors up, my room was defined by a wall of faux tree ferns and a narrow sliver of afternoon light that peeked through the architectural feature above. I supposed the designers intended it as a privacy measure should the guest wish to keep the curtains open for raunchier moments.

The weather would favour my visit, as was usually the case. What could be more miserable than a grey, rain-soaked farewell? Sharon, unless revelling in her hasty departure, wouldn't have wished for me to stand outside, shivering in the elements. Not when I had made a special visit to see her.

Maybe that's why people opt for a cremation. It's quicker and more efficient, and the urn can take pride of place in the car ride home before being placed on the mantle. Mum still sits in Pete's office upstairs. He says it's so she can spot the dust and watch him work.

It was now late afternoon. I headed to the rooftop to watch the Bosphorus slowly swallow the skyline of gleaming golden domes and minarets as the sun started to set.

I stayed until the moon rose in the distance over the flickering lights. It was a reminder that the world turns whether we're in it or not. I thought about how quickly the shock of death dissolves into diaries, details and duty. Even in grief, people remain perpetually busy. The procedures and paperwork around death astonished me. I hadn't expected it to be like this.

The WhatsApp group between my cousins and me had agreed it was best to lay her to rest in the city where she had drawn her final breath. It felt right. A place as exotic, spiritual and mysterious as we knew her to be.

So that is how I came to be in Istanbul. I was there to bury the woman who gave me life. Her DNA ran thick through my veins, though for most of my life I knew her to be scattered, unwilling to settle and estranged. She was more than a little different from most mothers.

Sharon had been a lot of things, most of which I would never know about. Pieces of her story suggested she was a risk-taker, bi-sexual and bohemian. She carried a quick intelligence and a restless charm, the kind that drew strangers into her orbit and kept them there, those curious for more, anyway.

The time had never been right to reconnect, because the space between us was worth more than my knowing. It had been chal-lenging to find the right way of doing things, and, like her son, I no longer had the energy to deal with her debt or her drama.

We filled the gaps between time zones with photos, and tidbits about her family and what little we knew about her life.

That's what grief does. It makes us piece together the fragments of generations. Over a group chat, our conversations about nature versus nurture were shaped by what we knew: jawlines, eyeshapes and hairlines. Those family photos made it clear: we all swam in the same gene pool.

Despite Sharon's known propensity for poor choices, we tried to grasp the extent of what had happened and how she had ended up in Turkey. Her condition, based on a hospital report, was written in Turkish. Another cousin working in neuroscience would take a stab, making deductions from those words she recognised.

I wondered what had gone through Sharon's head in the hours before death, when she was at the finish line, alone. In my heart, I believed she would have apologised for all the grief she had caused over the years. She wasn't a bad person; her judgement was just a little skewed. We all agreed it couldn't have been easy being her.

She was so far from everyone she had ever really known or loved. At what point had it all gone wrong? It likely started at the glass of the nursery wondering why they hid her baby from her.

Lewis would say, 'Mum, you're becoming your mother', or, 'You're just like Sharon.' I said thank you and hoped he didn't mean it.

My mother had given birth to me nine days after her sixteenth birthday. She said it was because the nuns forced her to eat Weet-Bix with hot milk. She swore they did it on purpose.

I was a healthy seven pounds two ounces, popping out just in time for a morning cup of tea on a cold winter's day in June. But there was nothing remotely celebratory about my arrival. She only made a weary telephone call home.

'I had a little girl, Mum. I'm sore, but okay. It was the Weet-Bix that did it.'

I was taken from her after my first feed.

To confuse those who stood at the nursery glass in search of their newborn, they placed the same colour baby card above every bassinet with each baby's date and time of birth and weight.

It was a place where a baby's cries would neither speed nappy changes nor a bottle of formula. Babies like us would have to wait. Rules were rules.

I was, in many ways, a broad stroke of the sixties.

My life, like my mother's, would unfold like a one-thousand-piece puzzle scattered across the floor, with bits always missing.

MALACHITE

THE FUNERAL DIRECTOR ARRIVED looking exactly as she chose to be seen – in tight leopard-print trousers, with lashings of red lipstick applied with the ease of a woman long finished with apologies. Hattie's long dark hair had been teased into a crown of defiance, and her wing-tipped kohl and black mascara had been laid on with precision, and a somewhat heavy hand. I shouldn't have been shocked.

When you've worked in funerals for twenty-two years, when you've dressed the dead, laid them to rest and seen the living come undone beside them, you earn the right to show up however you please. She was unapologetically herself because she understood, better than most, how little our appearance matters in the end.

'You are one of the very few who have come for a relative.' Her throaty rasp, which told you everything you needed to know, softened nothing between her regular cigarette breaks. 'Most leave them here for only us to bury; they don't care unless there is money involved. This is common today.'

I fell silent, struck by how calculating people can be.

Sharon had been living in Cyprus and had apparently travelled to Turkey for cancer treatment.

'Prior to her admission to the hospital, she often spoke of a third husband, an Afghan, whom she had since divorced.' It was another whiplash moment from Hattie.

My shock was palpable, even though she offered no further

details. Sharon had apparently shared this snippet with someone in the hotel she had been staying at. It was another secret that went to her grave, a little like the brand-new iPhone she carried (along with another phone), the one with only four contacts listed in it, one voicemail, and photos of little consequence.

I told Hattie she could keep both phones, knowing she could probably do with an extra phone in her line of business. My brother didn't want to take any calls from those Sharon likely owed money to.

Her suitcase had been neatly packed prior to our arrival at the hotel. Inside, the last fragments of her life, among all her freshly laundered clothes. We rifled through it briefly, as if we didn't want to disturb her privacy. A Qur'an, a beginner's guide to Arabic, a Bible. The bag was more full of letters, unfinished and unsent, and half-formed thoughts that trailed off mid-sentence, than of her clothes. It was the only clue we had about her last days, and of the faith and hope she was searching for in the end.

The contradictions were staggering.

As if on cue, the call to prayer across the road started. The city was moving on, and so was faith, indifferent to another story that had just come to a close.

Sharon's hospital was a short distance away, and we still had to 'collect' the body for the funeral. Hattie accelerated through roundabouts, narrowly missing a dent or worse, and pushed the timing of red lights. It wasn't the only jolt to my senses.

'She was green throughout when they opened her up.' The news was delivered casually as we crossed the hospital grounds from administration towards the area where the bodies waited. Most would never pause to consider what loomed above them as they drove underground to the visitors' parking. I realised how easily we go about our business, not knowing we could be parking beneath the weight of the dead.

I was still trying to process how her body had turned the colour of malachite.

In the utilitarian '70s brick structure lay the stainless-steel refrigerated chambers of those recently departed. Here, the living and the dead shared the same space with quiet indifference.

The atmosphere was thick and unmoving, as one would imagine but not fully expect. Fluorescent lights had stripped everything of its warmth, including ours, revealing only the cold mechanics of life's finality.

Along a wall in reception a group of women in black abayas and headscarves swayed and wailed, their grief unfiltered, raw. Their guttural cries reverberated off the tiled walls, filling the sterile space with something painfully more human. The staff moved around them with unfazed efficiency.

Death was routine here. And a transaction.

The undertaker, a tall, grim figure with the gravity of someone long acquainted with sorrow, sat in a small room at the end of the corridor. His long, spidery fingers hovered and twitched, scanning each cubbyhole before plucking a black plastic bag. Its sagging weight was out of proportion to Sharon's meagre belongings inside. Hattie ruffled through it briefly. The usual for an overnight hospital stay. We took only her debit card and passport to send to the embassy for cancellation.

Along the hallway back to reception, my eyes had caught two rooms on the right and left, both empty except for a smooth, silvery table above which hung an enormous overhead light. It was here that morticians worked to reconstruct and clean the deceased, methodically taking out their organs to weigh them and dissect them under a microscope. They would then collaborate on the forensic report before putting the body back in the drawer, ready for dressing.

The wailing of the women had become longer and louder as

loved ones had gathered around them. The administrator didn't appear to notice as he ran his finger down the page of his leather-bound ledger, stopping near the bottom at Sharon's perfectly handwritten name. A card machine sat next to him, clinical proof that debts still had to be settled. He didn't look up as he requested payment. He simply made a note in red ink next to her name.

BLACK DOG

WE HAD ALMOST REACHED THE car park when I spotted him. A black labrador, slightly arthritic, looked up briefly. He rose stiffly from his spot and trotted as best he could down the small embankment towards us. He stopped on the other side of the fence and poked his nose through a familiar hole. He continued, as we did, along the wire fence, before hobbling down the concrete steps.

Hattie, an animal lover, crouched down with a warm smile and extended hand. She expected him to come to her. Instead, he came to me, and with his entire body weight pressed himself firmly against my leg.

His brown eyes gazed softly up into mine, not so much in a greeting, but in something far more deliberate. He lingered against me longer than he needed to. I think he understood that the final part is always the hardest.

It was an extraordinary thing for him to do at that moment. No doubt the other homeless dogs who lived outside on the grassy knolls at the Dr Lütfi Kırdar Hospital did the same thing. They had assumed their position in life as unofficial service dogs for those who needed them the most.

BUREAUCRACY THRIVES ON FORMS. The Ministry of Foreign Affairs needed them signed, stamped and notarised in order to bury Sharon. It was already late in the afternoon, ten days after her passing, and Sharon was scheduled to be buried the following day. And we still didn't have a death certificate.

From the moment I stepped inside the police station, I knew it had its own agenda, with its ticketed queues and Baltic languages.

A burly female officer sat behind the desk we had been directed to. She was sorting through a towering pile of files with complete disinterest. Occasionally she would swivel towards her computer screen and tap on her keyboard.

She barely looked up at Hattie or me as she reached into a red plastic bag of sweets open on her desk. I'm sure it gave her some momentary pleasure, unlike the documents we had slid across her desk for her to look at.

'Proof of relation?' Officer Ayşe exhaled loudly.

I offered my Australian passport as Hattie explained I was the daughter of the deceased. My family name would betray me. It had never been hers.

'Not possible,' the officer said flatly. She was already reaching for the next file and another sweet.

We waited a minute, then another. The silence stretched, so we watched and listened to everyone else.

Beautiful young girls from Russia, Ukraine or neighbouring

countries were huddled around, waiting to be freed, or trafficked to the Middle East. Hattie didn't know which. Nothing was happening in a hurry, if at all.

Officer Ayşe finally told us we would have to come back on Monday. There was no reasoning with her.

Hattie turned to me. 'Leave it to me, I'll sort it out.'

Fresh air and the Bosphorus would recalibrate me. I wandered down the hill from the historic district towards its silvered edge, past the fat and fluffy Persian street cats who had retired outside the cafés. Cutting across to the Blue Mosque, I tried to catch a half-decent selfie in the dark.

The local man who offered to take my photo followed quickly with, 'Are you single?'

'No, I'm on vacation with my husband. I'm waiting for him to finish a meeting up the road.' I pointed in the general direction of a hotel.

I felt bad for telling him a white lie, but solo travel will do that to a woman.

THE WEIGHT OF SOMEONE WHO CARES

WHAT I WAS LOOKING FOR WASN'T far from the Hagia Sophia: a small café just off İstiklal Caddesi that was rated for its excellent flat whites. On the opposite side of the single-lane road, a handful of two-seater tables sat alongside a wall, at the top of which lay a small park where the street cats slipped like secrets between the wrought-iron railings.

There is no right way to begin the day you bury someone, especially one who gave birth to you. It felt oddly right to sit there and drink coffee: Sultan Suleiman ruled his country not far from this spot. A history tour had told me that the black pearl, also known as coffee, was treated with suspicion. It had been forbidden by law as treasonous and punishable by death. Naturally, I ordered a second cup in honour of the free thinkers and political types who, like me, would not know what the day ahead would bring.

Coffee creates both a habit and a moment of solace for me. The familiarity of this small, private ritual would settle me before I followed the smell of warm börek, past minarets and old hammams, down the hill and back to the hotel.

If Sharon were ever to choose a place that mirrored her spirit at the end of her life, Istanbul would have answered the call. A city of thresholds and contradictions, it was not the worst place for a bohemian to pass. It felt persuasive to those who knew her.

I was to meet Hattie on the far side of the Galata Bridge in Karaköy, at another coffee shop. As I walked past mid-morning fishermen trailing their lines from the rails, I pulled my black coat closer to warm myself against the chill now whipping across the Bosphorus. At least it wasn't raining.

Hattie was a woman who didn't waste time. I noticed it in the way she drove into the street where I stood waiting.

No sooner had she stopped and flung open my door, than my eyes had caught the flash and dazzle of her sizeable diamond ring and varnished nails. A relic from a past love, she said, as my eyes steadied upon the enormous carats as she hastily reached for her phone.

'Do you want to see Sharon?' She showed me a photo she had taken that morning anyway.

Sharon looked at peace, and much younger than I had imagined.

Her breasts were still unnaturally proud, and distinctively defiant in the photo taken that morning. Her hands were purple and blue. They had never looked like mine. They were so swollen, they wouldn't have looked out of place on a man. My shocked silence must have been obvious, so Hattie reached for her black horn-rimmed glasses clipped to the gold chain around her neck to expand the screen with her thumb and forefinger and take a closer look.

'Likely multiple catheters.' She peered at me from over the frames before putting the car into first gear and roaring off down the street. Even the dead had a schedule to keep.

It should have been an hour or two to the Black Sea coast cemetery, instead we had managed to miss the signpost and detour a hundred kilometres off course, trebling the time. Not that delays were anything new. We managed to pull into the cemetery just before three in the afternoon. A car in front of us was navigating its way through a canine roundabout. The dogs lounged about as if by assignment at the entrance to slow the traffic.

Higher up the hill, the street dogs kept vigil. They lay along the edges of the smallest graves, but closest to three fresh mounds of earth. The children's section was restless. Rainbow windmills stuck into the soil spun themselves. They went wild, whipped by a wind that touched nowhere else on the hillside. It was as if the air gathered only for them.

Watching them turn, I couldn't help but think that the little ones were still at play. Perhaps their spirits stirred the air with a laughter that their parents could no longer hear.

The dirt fell in soft thuds, final and absolute, upon her simple casket. As it closed in around her, Hattie whispered, as everyone tends to do at gravesites, 'Would you like to say a few words?'

I didn't.

There was nothing I could have said to Sharon that would have sounded sincere. My comfort lay in believing she was finally at peace, and that at the end I was there for her. Sharon had always been too otherworldly to really fit in to life on Earth.

In time, when land becomes more of a premium, the cemetery will no doubt release her plot in the international quarter to another. Unless we are famous, or beautifying the cemetery with an impressive marble crypt, in four generations we are forgotten, and no one really cares.

Nature would now do its work until only her bones remained.

Nevertheless, a beige marble tombstone would be crafted to read:

Mother, Daughter, Sister, Traveller
Lived life her way.

After paying the gravediggers their gratuities, we drove back down the hill in silence. At the gate, my eyes met those of a furry black and white dog to the left of the gate. Like the black labrador at the hospital, he understood the gravity of my day.

Would he take the meaty bone we had given him earlier and

carry it away from the others, up the hill? Would he know to go to the left, then along the winding country road to the end, and onward to the last plot, the one in the top left-hand corner? Would he sense later that night, in the still, that in her solitude she could probably do with some company?

I hoped he would lie on her grave long enough so that she would finally feel the weight of someone who cared. I hoped he would bury his bone nearby so he could visit her again when it was warmer, when the wildflowers bloomed again.

MĀORI FOLKLORE HOLDS THAT HUMAN longing and the divine are never far apart. From such longing was born Auckland Harbour's largest and most distinctive volcano, a forbidden love so fierce it split the earth and formed Rangitoto Island.

By September 1964, that ancient rupture had become little more than scenery. The USS *Archerfish*, dark, sleek, and already mythologised in its own way, sliced past Rangitoto on its way into port. The island's ancestral wound would have meant nothing to the randy appetites of the so-called 'Playboys of the Pacific'. Towards the end of the Second World War, their submarine had sunk the world's largest aircraft carrier, *Shinano*, a feat that secured its place in military history, even as it passed indifferently through a harbour shaped by love.

During the Cold War it had been retrofitted and redeployed from Pearl Harbour. On board would be navy personnel and civilian scientists, who would conduct deep-sea research. The bachelor-only vessel would visit 129 ports during Operation Sea Scan, with extended stays in New Zealand and Australia.

Sharon had stood wide-eyed at the water's edge. She knew that her father, who had served in the Second World War, would have approved of the Americans' military precision. Sharon understood the power of military uniforms and clipped commands, the scent of boot polish and the slap of leather as her father walked purposefully across the kitchen linoleum.

In New Zealand, Americans were seen as war heroes. With their confident swagger and Southern drawls, she wouldn't have sensed any danger when they opened the hatches and let her look inside. She would have trusted them, just like she trusted the uniform her father wore.

With her schoolbag in hand she had skipped down the stairs that morning, waving goodbye as she left the house. She was thrilled to go, but not to school. She waited at the park until it was safe, then she ran down to the wharf in time for their arrival.

I'm sure she wasn't the only one. Girls always turned up when the American military came to town.

His time in Auckland would be just under two weeks: a few nights of beer with the boys, submarine excursions for the public and an official event at the Northern, a club for foreign dignitaries. There would have been dancing, some sneaky hands and plenty of laughter.

Pretty young girls like Sharon would have hung on their every word as they embellished their heroism and stories of exotic places where the palm trees swayed softly at sunset.

For him, she was just another fleeting port story. For her, he was something else entirely.

Sharon had invited him home for dinner. He liked roast pumpkin and classical music, and he played the violin – or so he claimed. How could she be sure, when he was weeks beneath the ocean?

Each port would be a potent cocktail of confidence, danger and theatre. With his handsome face and quiet smile, he wouldn't need to chase. Women enjoyed feeling part of his fantasy.

Sharon was one of seven children. She was bright, funny and athletic. If any of them were going to make it in life, it would be her, so her parents agreed, after their daughter's incessant pleading, that they would apply for a scholarship to Auckland Girls'

Grammar. First they would need a copy of her school reports.

Nana made an appointment, but not for the reason the principal believed it was being made.

'Is everything okay at home? We haven't seen Sharon here for the past three months.'

Nana's face had drained of colour. 'But she leaves every morning in her uniform and with her schoolbag.'

Sharon had only just started menstruating at fifteen, so was confused why she could no longer hide her growing belly. No one had explained the birds and the bees to her.

No one knows where Sharon went in those months, or how she spent the days before coming home; perhaps her confusion was too much too bear.

In the quiet, rigid world of her family and Catholicism, sexual consent was neither spoken of, nor taught at home or in schools. With her father's ruler-straight back and sharp tongue, he made it known that whether Sharon's mistake was by choice or by force, her sin would leave a stain on the family's reputation.

What happened to pregnancy outside of marriage was a judgement that belonged to God. The Church dictated what was right and wrong. Before long it would be whispered between the pews.

It would handle her indiscretion with a one-way ticket to the novitiate. There she would polish balustrades, mop floors and scrub her soul clean.

Nana and Grandad had considered keeping me, but with seven children already, a Royal Air Force flight engineer's salary couldn't stretch to one more. Her brothers and sisters would be told she had simply left to become a nun.

She was effervescent, far too alive for a life of silence and obedience, so no one expected Sharon to last in a sacred profession. When she finally arrived home, the space I had occupied was already empty.

OUT OF THE MOUTHS OF BABES

WHEN I WAS BORN, LIFE FOLLOWED a predictable rhythm. People married young, had children and got on with things.

Somewhere in New Zealand, my new parents were waiting.

At twenty-seven, my dad was already supporting his wife and raising a family. Mum had lost her second baby not long before I was born.

'We heard it was a little girl,' Dad said. 'Mum and I were both looking forward to having a daughter.'

After her miscarriage, my parents had decided to adopt a sister for Shaun. Dad told me later that at the time baby girls were in high demand. The pill might have arrived, but most married couples still chose to start their families the old-fashioned way. Adopting a child was easy, but even by 1965 the waitlists stretched on for months, as people could afford to pick and choose.

It was a Saturday morning late in August when the phone call came from the maternity hospital.

'We have a baby girl looking for her forever home. I hope you don't mind, she's not a newborn; she's a couple of months old. We're hoping you'd like to meet her.'

If my parents had hesitated they might have missed a rare opportunity. Fate, Dad said, had intervened.

Dad said he had shut the boot of his Holden EK with a firm push and checked it twice, making sure the white cane bassinette didn't fly out onto the road on their journey north. Inside lay the symbolism of another turning point in life: folded cloth nappies, a striped pastel blanket, the knitted one my Nana had made for the baby they no longer had. He made sure the baby bottles were also tucked in tight.

Their two-hour drive was a mix of half-finished sentences and silence, broken only by the crackle of the AM radio, the ham sandwiches Mum had made for the trip and the hum of the road beneath the tyres.

The smell of floor polish and hospital disinfectant hung in the air as they arrived at St Helens and made their way up the stairs to the second floor with their almost-three-year-old son in tow.

'I believe there is a little girl in your nursery looking for a family,' Dad said, smiling.

'Oh, yes!' The Matron's face visibly softened. 'We've been expecting you. How lovely of you to come up from Kawerau so quickly. Would you mind taking a seat?'

Dad remembers them being particularly organised. I suppose they needed the space in the nursery.

He said I was sleeping when they carried me out, swaddled in a hospital-issue baby blanket and blissfully unaware of the gravity of the moment.

Shaun was the first to peer over the white cotton wrap edged in pink. He inspected my face with the authority that only a toddler could possess, and grinned.

'That's my Kirsty.'

Out of the mouths of babes. I had just met my forever family.

THE WILD AND THE SACRED

(Whispers of Papatūānuku)

I WAS ADOPTED, AND THAT MADE me special, or so my dad said.

At bedtime he would read *Mr Fairweather and His Family*, a story of a man who visited Sunshine House to find a child his family had longed for.

I always knew I didn't come from a pet shop, like the other kids from school would tell me.

As a toddler, a little on the round side with a mop of bright blonde ringlets, I had a voice that didn't quite match the rest of me. Dad said I sounded like a middle-aged man trapped in a little girl's body. By two, I had become 'the middle child' with the arrival of an even chubbier little brother. Klyn was the apple of my mother's eye for as long as I could remember.

Nothing particularly set me apart from others, except maybe my handwriting. I could write in cursive not long after I learnt to tie my shoelaces and spell big words like *umbrella* and *telephone*. Uncle Barry always seem so pleased when he quizzed me. He also gave us the best Christmas presents as kids. They usually came from London – like the telephones with the wire between them. We ran them from the lounge room to the bedroom, but my brothers got sick of going to the other room to listen to me talk for the sake of talking.

I particularly liked to run. Fast. Peter Snell, a New Zealand

Olympic gold medallist, once handed me a little gold medal for sprinting twenty-five metres in bare feet on our grassy playing field. Dad told me that over a mile, Snell could run faster than any man alive. He said it was his last name that made him the fastest.

Our family home was filled with food from the back garden and my mother's strong moral compass. Even though my parents weren't practising Catholics, we never ate meat on a Friday. Instead, Mum would send Dad down to the local fish and chip shop before six o'clock, because she wanted a rest from boiling vegetables.

Mum always sat on my left at the table, nearest to the kitchen, where the disciplinary bamboo cane was kept.

Sit up properly. Don't drop it down your lap. Elbows in. Eat your peas. Finish what's on your plate before you leave the table.

It didn't stop there.

Finish what's in your mouth before you speak was quickly followed by *It's not your turn to talk.*

It was endless. *Don't leave the table until everyone has finished. Take your plate. Wipe the table. Dry the dishes with your father.*

My brothers rarely got a bollocking. I was certain Mum made the rules up only for me.

She used to be an Air Force nurse, although the only medicine I remember in the cabinet was a tin of zinc and castor oil ointment in blue and gold. It had been in the house for years, and I remember its lid had a dent in it, as did the rim from being prised open with a butter knife.

When we were sick with something contagious we would be confined to our bed. Under no circumstances should I ever get out of it if I was home from school sick. That was no fun, so I don't remember getting sick with anything but chicken pox and the measles.

A lawn full of clover turned our backyard into a war zone of bee stings over summer. On more than one occasion my foot swelled up to the size of an elephant's. I had to stay in bed for that, too.

My older brother, Shaun, farmed ants. He liked to feed them to the massive black spiders that lived in the webs covering the fence at the end of our yard. I never went down there for fear he'd push me in and I'd be eaten alive.

Then there was the Murder House, a twice-yearly compulsory visit to the dental clinic, starting in our first year in school. The smell of antiseptic would hit us as soon as we arrived, but I loved the smell; it felt like home.

The nurses, stiff in their starched white uniforms, looked like angels of mercy until they picked up their drills. We'd all have to line up and go in one by one and sit in the oversized leather chairs in a long row. The whimpering would start once we were all seated, and the screaming would soon follow.

Not me, I trusted them. With the big bright lights, trays of fluoride and stainless steel tools, they went into my little mouth with their whirring drills, filling my teeth top and bottom. I suppose they passed their internship based on the number of fillings they had done.

The nurses told me I ate too many sweets, which is why I needed so many fillings. I wasn't prepared to give up a bag of lollies for a filling.

Later, my teeth got so big that Mum said I had to go to the orthodontist to get braces. She said it was because I didn't chew my peas properly.

Winter in New Zealand usually brought chilblains. They made my toes burn to death. They would itch and swell so badly I was not allowed to sit next to the fireplace. I thought she wanted me to freeze to death.

I spent most of my time in my playhouse, the one Dad had built just for me. He also built a treehouse, which I had to share with my brothers – which was just a deck up a dead tree he 'planted' in concrete. The ladder, which he also built, reached up through a hole so we could sit more than a storey off the ground without railings. It was the place we read *Archie* and superhero comics and ate homemade iceblocks whilst Mum cleaned the house or Dad mowed the lawn. We knew we'd break a leg if we ever fell off so we all sat slightly back from the edge just in case. In the '70s, there was always a fine line between fun and catastrophe.

When it rained, I would spend the day on my crimson Singer sewing machine making outfits for my Barbie dolls. It was the kind you had to turn by hand. Everyone said I was so good, I should be a dress designer, although this wasn't the path I would later choose.

My mother was so strict, I often found myself on the receiving end of the belt, the fly swat, or the dreaded bamboo cane, which always left a welt on the back of my legs, she'd hit me that hard. These implements of torture lay silently in wait down the right-hand side of the fridge.

With the threat of violence ever present at home, it wasn't surprising it translated to the school ground. I was often called up before the headmaster for landing a well-aimed punch on a boy. It usually resulted in a bloody nose. I was often fighting my own war, marked by a curated collection of bruises and scratches – if not from school, then from the razor-sharp leaves of the Prince of Wales bush the boys shoved me into on my way home.

When I wasn't fighting, I skipped, played hopscotch or hunted for the chewiest huhu grubs with the Māori kids. They claimed the fat, wriggling white worms were a real treat. Sweet, juicy and yummy, they would say. They were definitely chewy.

My older brother Shaun made all the decisions about how

games were played. Some Saturday afternoons, we'd spread out on the lounge room floor to play Warship, Snakes and Ladders, Chess or Monopoly. He'd run the bank with a suspicious level of success and whilst we squabbled, mum would bake cheese scones, biscuits, and sometimes pink lamingtons.

On November 5, Guy Fawkes night, Jean Batten Primary would host their annual fair. The Māori, Samoan, Fijian and Tongan dads would prepare the school hāngi. Barefoot and wrapped in brightly patterned sulus that shifted with the breeze, the men bent low over the ground, lifting hot stones into the pit for the hāngi before placing sides of pork, cabbage and potatoes on top. Nothing tastes better to me than food that has been cooked underground all day. There was always more than enough food for the entire school.

After sunset, the more responsible fathers would light the fireworks.

'Stand back, kids,' said some of the dads as they spread out their arms so wide we couldn't see properly.

It was clearly dangerous work. We'd watch in awe as the night sky ignited with a whoosh, hiss, bang or boom.

The highlight of the evening was the torching of life-sized teacher effigies on a series of huge bonfires.

This too was men's work, as one would set the great piles of dried branches ablaze after pouring petrol atop to 'get it going'.

We'd all cheer as our teachers went up in flames.

Māori and Pasifika culture were woven throughout my school life. My brothers told me I had a Māori nose, so that's why I thought I belonged with them and my friends from the Cook Islands.

The first song we ever learnt to sing at school was 'Pōkarekare Ana', New Zealand's unofficial national anthem. It was a song of a man who loved a woman so much that if she didn't come back to him, he might die. We all knew it so well that Dame Kiri Te Kanawa, who had sung at King Charles's first wedding, would sing it to bring in the Millennium. Mum said the reason Dame Kiri sang so beautifully was because she was taught by the nuns.

We knew that our Land of the Long White Cloud, or Aotearoa, as we called it, was God's own country. At school they said it was because he left the best for last so he wouldn't make any mistakes.

At school I learnt what the Māori had always known, that our land and sea were alive with guardians and that whales and dolphins were never just creatures of the ocean; they carried our ancestors across vast waters, guided us to safe shores, and rescued those lost at sea. They should be honoured and protected. That is how they became part of my spiritual belief system.

Our school would take us on an adventure excursion once a year, sometimes to the caves where we could see the sparkles of tiny blue-green lights from millions of glow worms. I then realised that stars weren't only in the sky; they were also under the ground. Everything we needed to heal, nature had created for us and that was why we had to look after our planet.

My first crush was Rangi, a Māori boy from school. His brown skin and long dark lashes drew me in. In my young mind, I believed Rangi was meant to meet me because he knew more about life than the other boys. He was not only handsome, but very confident for a ten-year-old.

The air was thick with sulphur, and our sneakers heavy with mud the day Rangi turned to me and looked me straight in the eye and said, 'I love you.'

I'm convinced the Earth Mother Papatūānuku had whispered in his ear that day during our school trip to New Zealand's most active volcano, Mt Ruapehu.

Our romance was over before it began. It never went further

than that day, but it didn't need to. He was the first to say the words I didn't know I longed to hear. If anyone would know how to love, it would be my Māori boy, Rangi.

From that moment on, those who walked like warriors became part of a much bigger problem.

PEAS AND PERFUME

THE SPEAKERS ABOVE MY SEAT crackled awake. A man's voice pushed through the static, thin and buzzy. He sounded like he was talking from inside a tin can.

'Good afternoon, ladies and gentlemen. We are now ready for take-off …' His words drifted down from the ceiling with the same authority as my grandfather. 'We will have you in New Plymouth before you know it, so sit back, relax and enjoy your flight.'

With my nose pressed against the window, I watched a man on the ground jump-start the propellers. I waited to see if his hand would be chopped off.

Then, with a deep whirring growl that built to a sharp whine, the engines finally settled into a steady hum before the Fokker Friendship roared down the runway and up into the sky.

Looking out the window, I couldn't believe how the cows turned into dots and the paddocks that I had only ever seen from the ground were now quilted together in various shades of green. The billowing cumulus clouds sat in the sky like dollops of cream. I kept staring at them, trying to decide if I was in Heaven, because that's how it looked in my picture books.

My first solo flight was more than thrilling. Before landing, a stewardess led me into the cockpit to meet the captain and his first officer, their hats firm and proud on their heads. I knew at that moment I was in the safest hands in the sky.

Nana and Poppa were there at the airport to meet me and drive me to nearby Hāwera, where they lived. It was an unremarkable town, except that in days gone by it had been the largest dairy-producing town in the world, and it was where I learnt to squeeze the teats of a cow.

Their weatherboard house was painted the latest shade of Dulux green, the same colour as the peas Nana shelled around three in the afternoon on her wide front veranda. Hardly anyone passed by on the pavement, which sat unusually high from the road. Only the man delivering bottles of milk and fresh cream, or a neighbour heading to the corner shop with the clear view of Mt Taranaki.

Like most Nanas at the time, mine wore her hair mauve. Her hair also matched her hand-knitted cardigans and it became my favourite colour for a while. In yoga, hypnotherapy and clairvoyant work, mauve is the colour that disentangles us from past attachments. I think my Sagittarian Nana secretly knew it to be the spiritual colour of intuition and feminine intelligence.

I slept in the front room, an unused master bedroom at the cold end of their house. It was opposite the black dial telephone, which sat on a small shelf high on the wall and directly connected to the party line. I wasn't allowed to touch it.

On the wall of my designated room hung a hand-carved mahogany box. Inside it, behind a small glass door, stood a porcelain Virgin Mary nearly a foot high. She wore pale blue and white robes edged with gold leaf; her hands were open, her gaze calm, untroubled. She watched over everything.

Only later was I told it was a communion chest, traditionally used for the sick and the dying – though I'd never heard of anyone holding a church service at home. At the bottom of the cabinet was a wooden drawer for the crucifix. Ours held a chalice for the wine, or Blood of Christ as we always called it, along with a very delicate embroidered linen napkin. A solid silver plate for the wafers sat beneath it, and Nana's glass rosary beads were tucked neatly on top, as if she liked things kept in order. I also wasn't allowed to touch them without asking.

A bottle of 4711 eau de cologne sat on the vanity, always just to the left of the mirror on a lace doily. It sat there as long as I could remember. I don't know whether she ever used it, because it was always full and familiar to smell.

Nana was one of eleven children, and was expected to enter the postulancy. Instead of becoming a nun she met Poppa Jim, and he obviously changed her mind. She had been raised on the west coast of the South Island, where no one went on vacation because it rained all the time. Poppa Jim had Scottish roots that were firmly placed in Dunedin, which was another place our family never visited. Apparently it was too cold.

On the opposite side of the hallway was the 'other front room', the formal lounge that no one used. It was where my brothers and I would unroll our sleeping bags and place them on top of our canvas camp stretchers during school holidays. They were the kind that sank in the middle, or collapsed if you weren't careful.

We had to be in bed early even when we weren't tired, because our parents needed a rest from us and wanted to watch telly that we weren't allowed to see. Shaun would entertain us with British radio comedy when the lights were off.

'Oi 'ave a plan so cunnin', you could put a tail on it an' call it a wee-zul!' 'You rotten swine! You have deaded me!' I had no idea what it all meant. It was no surprise that later he would turn into the smartest person our family had ever known.

Above the fireplace, which never worked, sat two little Chinese dragon lamps and a silver Schwarzkopf trophy engraved with 'Winner'. Everything belonged to Uncle Barry. Below sat a brown leather pouf with pharaohs and camels that he had sent especially from Egypt. It was my favourite piece of furniture in the entire house after the communion chest.

On Saturday mornings Poppa would switch on the wireless, an enormous and beautifully crafted mahogany radio. Poppa would twiddle with the dial until he had the perfect reception. With his form guide he would settle in for the day to listen to the horse races, his pen poised ready to note the final result. Sometimes he would head down to pick up his winnings, and other times he would go and watch the races live at the local track. If I behaved, I could go with him. Nana always stayed home because Saturday was laundry day.

We always had the cleanest, freshest and crispest sheets in New Zealand, pegged side by side on the washing line propped up by a sturdy wooden eight-foot pole, so they could dry quicker in the wind, because cleanliness was next to godliness.

Nana used to tell me that whites should be washed and hung in the moonlight, especially when it shone bright.

I was in charge of collecting the eggs from the chicken coop at the far end of the block, past the clothes line, the glasshouse filled with tomatoes and grapes and the vegetable patch that extended either side of the path.

I reached into the wooden hatch to see if an egg had been laid. Sometimes I would peer in through the hole and have a chat to the hens. I wasn't allowed to open the wire door to the coop in case the hens made a dash for it. The only ones allowed in were Nana with an enamel bowl of vegetable peelings, or Dad or Poppa, and they usually had an axe.

Mr Brown's coop a few doors down was more profitable. He'd count the eggs I found before pressing five cents into my palm for every one.

I would stay at Auntie Millie's house next door. She was only three well-worn wooden steps out the back door and through the gap in the hedge. She didn't drink, so she never came over for a glass of McWilliam's sherry with Nana and Mum.

Her husband had gone to war in the 1940s but had been killed in action, leaving her a widow from an early age. She never remarried, and their wedding photo remained on the wall for as long as she was alive. I always looked at it in the living room she never used, above the turntable where I played the Kinks records.

Auntie Millie didn't appear to need a man. She drove a dusty-pink post-war Austin A40, much like the one from *Driving Miss Daisy*, a car so oversized she could barely see over the steering wheel with her horn-rimmed glasses. Even though she only drove it to church, she was the only woman I knew who could drive.

After lunch, when Poppa needed to rest in his sun room, we weren't allowed to run, scream or go near him or he'd get grumpy.

It was under the bed where he napped that I found an issue of *Cosmopolitan*, at eleven years old. With it my first encounter with adult mystery. Inside, Hollywood actor Burt Reynolds lay reclined on a bearskin rug, armed with nothing but a cigarette and a smile.

Beyond the peas in their porcelain bowls, the scent of 4711 cologne and Nana's laundry glowing under the moonlight, another world shimmered just out of reach. A world of fur, kaftans, music and glamour; a world that felt as if it belonged to me already.

BEHIND THE BLINDS

I WAS SURROUNDED BY MY OWN version of international glamour from a young age. My uncles had both travelled the world. Uncle Bill and Auntie Margaret had then become teachers in Tokoroa. She wore her hair in a soft afro and floated about in flowing kaftans. Neil Diamond's *Jonathan Livingston Seagull* and *Love at the Greek* played loud and often on the turntable. Mum only liked Shirley Bassey, Tony Bennett and Herb Alpert, and that was no fun for a kid.

Uncle Barry offered more of a theatrical contrast to the family when he returned to New Zealand from New York or London, either by ship or DC-10. One time he arrived dressed like a film star, in a full-length fur coat, matching fur cowboy hat and gold-rimmed glasses with his initials monogrammed in gold in one corner. He worked as a hairdresser and makeup artist, coiffing Princess Margaret and Dame Joan Collins, and bought me Mary Quant makeup and bottles of Miss Dior perfume. Uncle Barry always frosted my hair a lighter shade of Schwarzkopf blonde before teasing it, for Hollywood glamour.

Then there were the Hare Krishnas with their drums banging, cymbals clashing and that lilting chorus *Hare Krishna … Hare Rama …* Their saffron robes and wooden beads seemed to dance to something wild and free as they made their way down the street towards our house.

As soon as Mum heard them coming she would race to shut the

venetian blinds and close the front door.

'Stay down. We're not home,' she'd hiss as we would giggle, hidden behind the lounge.

We always pretended to not be home, although the scattered bikes on the lawn and Dad's car in the driveway made it obvious that we were. But the real danger didn't look like a stranger at all. It lived much closer than anyone imagined.

TALISMANS, TUTUS AND TITLES

CHRISTCHURCH HAD ITS OWN KIND of discipline – colder, stricter, carved into daily life. I had been enrolled at a girls' school run by the Sisters of Mercy, where order and tradition framed every day. I would keep up my ballet schedule under the sharp, exacting eye of my teacher Miss Peters at the Southern Ballet Company, which added another pillar that would shape me. Home, school and dance class: they all insisted on precision, posture and restraint.

To be honest, it was more about keeping me pure and not pregnant.

This wasn't difficult, especially in winter. At Villa Maria College, the long and heavy dark-green tartan kilts, under which I wore witches' britches, would be firmly fastened with a Scottish grouse claw. Set with garnet for strength, resilience and passion, it became my first talisman. I felt like a Highland huntress with my mum's dead bird's foot, my kilt, and red thermal undies.

Classical ballet lessons demanded the same rigidity as the Catholic education system. 'Stand straight. Tuck those hips under. Squeeze your buttocks. Shoulders back, ladies. Do not lean on the barre.'

Any fingers gripping too tightly were rapped with a snooker stick, as were any elbows that drifted downward in second, third or fourth position. The pianist sat at the upright with one foot already hovering over the pedal, ready to clink out the next exercise on cue. Everywhere I went, I was dodging that stick.

'Un, deux, trois, quatre, répétez. Merci.' With every count her voice grew slightly louder and more demanding. As my ballet classes relentlessly tried to perfect my poses, the nuns sought to perfect my soul.

My education was mapping me out for one of three acceptable careers – secretary, nurse or teacher. Only the dozens of Mills & Boon romance novels I borrowed from the school library gave me a small break from how life was quickly shaping up, and they set an unrealistic precedent around what I thought intimacy would look like when I finally got there.

How love and sex happened was still very much rose-tinted in my imagination. School offered no real practical advice, only pencilled drawings and later a disturbing film on abortion.

All I knew was that kissing led to pregnancy. What I needed to know was waiting in my parents' bedroom.

'If you're bored, read a book,' Mum would say.

'I've read everything.' (None of them being school books.)

'Choose something else,' she would yell from the kitchen and a stove of boiling vegetables.

Sliding open the mirrored wardrobe door, I would scan the piles stacked in a disorderly way on the shelves next to her clothes. I wasn't interested in science fiction paperbacks, and I'd read *The Godfather*, but not the saucier novelists like Harold Robbins, Sidney Sheldon and Jacqueline Susann.

It's hard to imagine Mum reading such sprawling, racy Hollywood sagas full of sex, ambition and intrigue. Then again, not much happened in Christchurch.

Valley of the Dolls, The Love Machine, Once Is Not Enough. I raced through one after another of scandalous stories of women undone by barbiturates, betrayed by lovers and caught in a spiral of glamour and ruin. As I devoured desire and devotion, the stories became addictive. I was also learning how the promise of riches could quickly turn into peril.

Did 'happily ever after' even exist? I wanted to think so.

Outside, the universe, and the millions of stars that we could see from our porch, offered another kind of education, one that spoke of wonder, mystery and the pull of something far larger than my closeted world. Dad said if we could find the Southern Cross in the sky, without the telescope he had set up, we would always be able to find our way home.

I never imagined that those same stars would witness the confusing tenderness of my first kiss.

AT EIGHTEEN, HE WAS BETTER KNOWN as a second-row rugby player from a boarding school in the North Island. Sean's father ran a hotel in Christchurch, I knew this because it's where we used to hang out together when he was home for the holidays. He had a smile that disarmed parents and a body that made girls dizzy. For a brief time, whilst he was in his last year of school, he was mine.

Our beige dial-up telephone would spring to life, usually on a Thursday evening, after Sean had finished his homework and sports training. It was obvious it was him because no one else would ever call at night.

'It's for me! Don't touch it,' I screamed, tearing from my room into the hallway for fear the only phone in the house would ring off too soon.

'How do you know?' Klyn was always flippant.

Because you have zero friends. The thought wasn't worth saying out loud.

He mumbled under his breath to everyone, like little brothers tend to do when they want the last word, before turning his attention back to watching *Space: 1999*.

I pulled the curly cord as far as it would stretch, trying to put a few precious feet between me and my mother's listening ears in order to have a very private conversation with my new love.

Sean would pull into the driveway with the confidence of someone who expected a yes, before he asked my dad's permission to take me out. Somehow, my parents let their fourteen-year-old daughter spend the afternoon with him at the hotel in town, the one where his father was a manager and Sean had his own room.

Our first kiss should have been sweet although in the back of my head was always my mother's voice. What if I 'ended up like my mother'? Apparently then I would have to go and live with the strictest religious order my mother knew, the Carmelites. I didn't understand at the time why she would threaten to send me to live with the nuns.

I was fourteen and still without a period when Sean swept me up in his arms, leaning closer towards me than he ever had before. His lips were, without warning, on mine, and his prying tongue suddenly and unexpectedly inside my mouth.

I wasn't sure if it was supposed to feel like Mills & Boon or *Once Is Not Enough*.

Sean never pushed for more. I couldn't give him what he ultimately would want.

Our last date was during the next school holidays when he was back from boarding school in Wellington. I wanted to see a Woody Allen film about an older man's affair with a teenage girl. *Manhattan* was, at the time, nothing more than an artistic piece set in New York, but life was already breadcrumbing.

A week later a Par Avion letter arrived, the kind written on very fine paper to save on postage.

I'm dropping you.

I read it again and again until his words blurred and a chill started to seep through me. The boy who wrote *I love you* was now breaking up with me. I regret that one by one, all the Par Avion letters he had sent me about his rugby games, those signed with *Love Sean* and a kiss, were fed into the fire.

The thin blue paper curled quickly as I watched the ink bleed and disappear forever up the chimney and into the night. His voice, his affection, everything that had felt safe in my world had vanished into wisps. By the time the last letter dissolved into ash, I had burnt him out of my life.

The following month I still didn't have a period. I was now fifteen. Panic set in. Mum must have suspected something, as she dragged me to the doctor. This was, after all, the 'dangerous age'.

As it turned out, nature was simply taking its time.

AUGUST NIGHTS

THE SUN WAS ABOUT TO SET ON MY idyllic childhood. What had once felt secure would soon shift underfoot. Dad was transferred back north for work, and Mum and my younger brother Klyn followed.

Shaun and I would stay behind in Christchurch, boarding with separate families. After that, we barely saw each other again.

I lived with the Paulsons, their house always full of friends, laughter and music.

Like Auntie Margaret, they were devoted to Neil Diamond. 'Hot August Night' made the lounge room speakers shudder, and Donna Summer's 'Last Dance' drifted all the way out to the hot tub in the backyard. You didn't need to be told that music mattered in that house.

The Paulsons were close to the Camerons, a family I'd babysat for since I was twelve. Their house had always felt like a second home to me; I often slept in the spare room after tucking their two children into bed after a night of games and stories. Without my parents' ever-watchful eye, small things started to become more noticeable in the most unsettling of ways.

Most conspicuous were the glossy, explicit *Penthouse* magazines with their covers as bold as they were bare. No one moved them. No one reached for them. No one spoke of them.

Mr Cameron's BMW was less of a car and more of a statement: low-slung, gleaming and unapologetically built for style over space.

It was finished in gold.

As the rain pelted down, the landscape blurred the grey-green hills thick with a woolly tide of sheep. I was wedged into the cramped back seat beside the Camerons' sleeping children as we drove south to Dunedin for the school holidays.

A couple of hours into a drowsy silence, Mr Cameron's hand crept slowly from the gap between the door and the driver's seat. It hovered, then reached further, lower, then closer. My stomach tightened as he brushed my leg. Lightly at first, then more deliberately with strokes that were not a mistake.

I fixed my stare out the window, willing myself to be invisible and terrified of meeting his eyes, which were now upon me in the rear-vision mirror.

In the front seat, his wife gazed steadily out her side window, totally oblivious to his shenanigans. Surely, I thought, she would notice that both his hands were no longer on the wheel?

Mr Cameron was twenty years older than me, already a senior executive on the way to the very top. I was fifteen, still fumbling with how to fasten my first bra and sitting on sanitary napkins so big they felt like bike seats.

On Saturday night the brutality of the biggest provincial rugby match that season would grind Otago households to a halt. We roared with approval as fists flew and jerseys ripped at the collar. As soon as our team scored, we stamped our feet and clapped as hard as we could, partly in an attempt to keep the blood flowing as we sat in the bleachers. The crowd demanded nothing less from their muddy players, their skin split and seeping with blood as they played on through the sleet.

There is no mercy, because in New Zealand, rugby union is nothing short of gladiatorial. The most honourable of them giving their all to score a few points.

Sport is a game of rules, whistles and boundaries. Those rules dissolved later that evening at a family-hosted party in the basement, where players, friends and relatives gathered. Away from the fans, alcohol flowed, and voices rose easily above the music, loud with familiarity and jest.

I stood tucked into one corner, and as the babysitter on duty, I slipped upstairs every so often to check on the children. I wasn't sure at what point the lemonade I had been sipping made me feel disoriented. The floor had started to sway as I turned to climb the stairs to the lounge, where I would lie down for a while. The room had started to spin by the time I had the sofa in sight.

'Are you okay?' a nineteen-year-old rugby player asked as a courtesy seconds before he climbed on top of me and pinned me there. The air left my lungs under his weight, and I couldn't breathe.

The dizziness I'd tried to escape was now thick and suffocating. His hands steadied my head to stop it turning away from his.

I'm not sure how long he had been grinding rhythmically through our clothes, just that his movements were slow, deliberate and growing with certainty, almost as if he was waiting for my resistance to dissolve.

The large frame of Mrs Cameron's brother blocked the hallway behind him. He shouted with such fury, it cut the air. Without warning, the room exploded into action. Then there was the silence.

A two-game suspension would be handed down to their star player. I knew this because everyone was saying it could cost the team the championship. Even the newspaper covered the story, without mentioning what actually happened.

Not once, then or ever, did anyone ask if my fifteen-year-old self was okay, or why I was in the bathroom so long that morning as I scrubbed away the sin from my skin.

SECOND BASE

By sixth form, the girls in my year finally invited me to join them on the sidelines of the First XV. The boys on that team were the most coveted in town, partly because they attended one of the top boys' boarding schools in the country.

The most lithe and handsome played on the wing. But the girls weren't talking about his speed or his ball-handling skills; no one cared about that. It was his green eyes and olive skin that kept half the girls in my year at Villa distracted, because rumour had it he looked even better when he took his shirt off at the end of the game. For most girls, that was all that mattered.

Gossip suggested he was a foreigner, but exactly what that meant, no one really knew.

It was on that lazy Saturday afternoon his eyes found mine. By the following weekend, at a friend's gathering, William bypassed every girl trying to catch his eye. Instead, he took a seat next to me. He tried to be discreet, but his thigh pressed hard against mine.

Later, away from curious eyes, we kissed. He told me he wanted to see me again and asked for my number.

His attention that night came at a cost.

By the time I arrived at school on Monday morning, the girls were openly gossiping about him. I overheard one saying that he was hers, and that 'he wasn't interested in virgins'.

Anonymous notes, folded into quarters, began appearing under my wooden pencil case in the slant of my desk. *Stay away*, one warned. I wasn't quite sure what it meant. In two weeks my University Entrance exams would be over, and I would move back to my parents' place up north to find a job.

It didn't matter what the girls said. My new crush continued to call. He asked to meet up over the holidays. I thought it meant that he was serious about me. Instead, he was simply flying up from Christchurch to the North Island to compete at a provincial sports close to my parents' home.

I'd waited nervously all day to see him before we slipped away to an empty paddock. Tussock brushed our legs as we searched for a spot tall enough to hide us. Cicadas droned through the pauses between kisses and the quiet afterwards, leaving me wide-eyed. That whole summer had now narrowed to one patch of dry grass.

That afternoon he cradled me in his arms, sun-warmed shoulders and olive skin pressed close, his dark chest hair soft against my body. His green eyes, the ones everyone talked about, were suddenly playful and searching, as if he were memorising me. He kissed me again, slow and certain, and his hand slipped beneath my top with a gentleness that made me gasp. After his fingers had found the hem of my seersucker sundress, and lifted it just enough to find what a teenage boy of eighteen was looking for, a girl of sixteen was secretly thrilled.

I was sure of it: the most sought-after boy at school loved me, and only me. But like Rangi, it was over before it had begun. That afternoon would be the last I ever saw of his adoring green eyes and long dark lashes.

THE LION'S DEN

AFTER UNIVERSITY ENTRANCE, and my short-lived fantasy, everything shifted. I had graduated from high school at sixteen, and already I was out of step with those my own age. My life was no longer about schoolboy crushes; I had to focus on survival. I was staring down a future with no map and very few options. Opportunities for girls like me were scarce.

A bank job was the best I could expect in a small town. The very thought of working as a teller sounded like a death sentence. I lived with the quiet fear that someone would discover I couldn't do my times tables and I was still counting on my fingers. For years I prayed no one would notice the glaring gap in my education.

My first job had been hotly contested among almost one hundred candidates. Auckland opened its doors quickly as I snagged a role as a business house travel receptionist, in the centre of the city. There, I'd work with twin models and a team who had travelled the globe. I was impressed to hear they had even flown all the way to London. The other side of the world was where the real glamour lay; that much I knew to be true.

The twins stood six feet tall, maybe more. With their feathered blonde hair, tanned limbs and international style, they looked straight out of the glossy magazines, the ones I'd seen at the local newsagent and that Mum would never buy.

Their beauty, along with their patent stilettos and expensive French perfume, acted as a currency. It also acted as a trap. They had been hired to dazzle and disarm. To me they were living proof that the women in *Valley of the Dolls* existed.

The twins' polished appearance couldn't have been more at odds with my own. I was just out of school and I hadn't yet built the armour I would need to face the world they lived in.

In Auckland, I was back living with the Camerons again. My parents had suggested I rent one of their spare rooms.

Downstairs, I shared a living space with their nephew. In fact, I never knew where he went, or what he did. I only knew he was at home when Cold Chisel's *East* album blasted at full volume from down the hallway.

When I wasn't at my travel job, waitressing, or working in the boutique across the street, I escaped to the beach.

That evening had begun like countless others. After dinner I tucked the children into bed, read them a story and returned to my room to change into my bathing suit for a soak under the stars.

Mrs Cameron had left that morning to attend her grandfather's funeral and wouldn't be back for a few days. I was alone in the steaming hot tub when her husband appeared at the back door of the garden.

'Would you mind if I join?'

Not waiting for an answer, he unwrapped the towel around his waist and climbed in.

The water swirled and slapped against the fibreglass shell and sometimes up into our faces. It was a night not unlike many we had had before. Usually Mrs Cameron and the children would join if it wasn't a school night.

Nothing initially seemed out of place as we talked about the children and my new job. The sharp tang of chlorine hung in the air. Every so often I would shift my position in the tub. I would sometimes have to stand to lift my face up enough to breathe something healthier than the chemicals we were inhaling.

Then, without warning, through the steam and soft crackle of bubbles, he leaned over. Uninvited, he started to kiss me.

Nooooooooooooo.

I jumped up, scrambled out of the tub, and fled to my bedroom. I was horrified, I was scared, and I was confused. I was also dripping, shaking, and gasping for breath.

My place in their home suddenly felt unsafe. I didn't have the means to afford my own apartment. I was earning seventy dollars a week. I couldn't tell my parents. They'd be so upset. I would have to work it out alone. Maybe it was no big deal and I misread the situation.

Switching off the lights, I hid trembling beneath my covers. My racing thoughts told me it hadn't been an innocent kiss. That night I was terrified Mr Cameron would fling my door open, and try to come into my bedroom. I placed my suitcase against the door in the absence of a lock.

That night, he didn't.

By morning, I was still spiralling.

All I knew was that after I had attended to the children, I was expected to make him coffee.

I practised what I would say to him. I couldn't clearly articulate how I really felt. He was the boss, after all. I was his babysitter. I had no rights.

I walked to his bedroom door. I hesitated before knocking loudly.

'Come in.'

My hand was still on the doorknob. I waited a little longer.

'Come in,' he said again, this time a little louder. I had heard him the first time.

'I brought you a coffee,' I spoke through a closed door. Mustering all my courage, I prised the door open over the carpet. It was just enough to show him the mug first, as the rest of me stayed behind.

'You can come in, I won't hurt you. Why don't you just put it here.' He pointed to the bedside table next to him. I could see Mr Cameron's bare chest as he lay there upright in bed against the pillows.

I set the mug down, but before I could step away, his arm swiftly hooked around mine. He pulled me into the space where his wife would normally have lain.

'Just a cuddle under the covers' was how he framed it.

I managed to slip from his grasp so quickly, I stumbled. Back on my feet, I ran to the door and closed it firmly behind me. My heart raced and my breathing began to labour, as it does when something scares you.

I had witnessed a sudden and irreversible shift, from trust to betrayal. It was only the beginning.

Burt Reynolds was the most naked man I'd ever seen. That was, until later that night. After the children were asleep, Mr Cameron came to my room to finally get what was never his to take.

The only thing that stopped him from his frenzied thrill was his son's cries. Ever closer I could hear his tiny voice starting to shrill as he made his way towards my room. The man who had forced himself on top of me, and ripped down my panties to penetrate me, would suddenly panic, and slide off the bed like a coward, and hide beneath my bed.

His four-year-old son was now outside my door, screaming hysterically for his father. I quickly pulled my nightgown down, put my underwear back on and went to my door.

Scooping him up in my arms and consoling him, I carried him back upstairs. All the while his outstretched arm still reached for the man who was nowhere to be seen. Miraculously, he would appear at the doorway of his son's room, feigning innocence and concern only minutes later.

It was only then that I brushed past him and ran downstairs to the bathroom. It was there I could lock the door. My insides felt strangely swollen as my legs shook. Under scalding water and through my tears I scrubbed his contamination from my skin.

It took me a long time to go to sleep that night. I asked myself over and over what I had done to deserve this. Why I hadn't screamed. Why I hadn't stopped him.

Abusers rarely hide in the shadows.

Mine sat at the dinner table, paid the mortgage, smiled warmly as he looked into his wife's eyes and touched her on the arm. He would tell her how delicious dinner was. He would read books to his children as they climbed into his bed on lazy weekends. He would kick a ball in the backyard with the frightened little boy who that night he abandoned. He would be the perfect chief executive officer. He would be everything to everyone.

Except me.

He had taken my innocence. Nothing in my world would ever be the same again.

Mr Cameron's attention towards me then became a leash no one noticed. More than twice my age and clever in ways I hadn't yet learnt. He closed in on me as if I were a natural extension of his fantasies, and there for the taking.

Between cups of coffee, the offers to drive me to work and casual conversations when no one else was home, it always circled back to his desire for me. At every opportunity, he would feverishly reach under my dress, or unbutton my blouse to explore more when I took to wearing trousers.

At home, it was always quick. Usually in the bathroom with the shower running.

I longed for the messiness of boys more my own age, the ones that other girls had. The clumsy ones who didn't know what to do next, even if they pretended otherwise.

Instead I would go to work then return home, and wait for his cue.

As life became more curated and controlled under his roof, my light started to dim. I became more cautious with what I said. I was careful where my eyes landed, avoiding direct eye contact especially in case he took that as a clue for something more.

There were no threats. Only expectations.

While my world started to fold, his kept turning. Nothing appeared to change on the outside. People waved at him from across the street, and then politely asked after his wife and kids. They invited him to barbeques and dinners. His friend down the road organised trips on his boat in the harbour. On one occasion we went to the Bay of Islands the day their wives flew out to Hong Kong to go on a shopping trip. I was naturally invited. There was no end to the lies. These men were Teflon. They hid behind their success, and money took care of the rest.

I had disappeared inside someone else's story. Someone charming, married and predatory.

Six more months passed. By then, he was obsessed. Lunchtimes were taken up at hotel lounges, park picnics, sometimes a good restaurant. It happened openly, without secrecy. No one mentioned the age gap and no one intervened.

Wipers rhythmically swept the windscreen as Mrs Cameron waited in her grey Datsun 120Y, the engine humming to keep the car's heater up high. I had darted across the wet asphalt, rain falling like needles on my face. The chill of another wet New Zealand winter cut through me. My soaked low-top sneakers, the ones I always wore after I finished rehearsals, squeaked as I ran towards the passenger door of her car.

Underneath my hoodie and raincoat, I was still in my neon leotard and Mum's hand-knitted woollen leg warmers. The ones that sagged at the knees and fell down once too often. I cradled my bag closer to keep me warm.

Something had shifted in Mrs Cameron's usually warm and outgoing personality. That evening she was not smiling. She simply glared, her lips had thinned as they pressed tightly together.

Instead of driving off, as she usually would, she reached over and turned down the dial of the radio until it clicked to off. Exhaling in one low, slow breath, she then unbuckled her seatbelt, shifting slightly in her seat to get a better view of me.

'How was dance class this evening?'

'Good.' We'd been preparing for our end of year recital, with stylised disco moves that crossed over into aerobics. It was very much like the *Solid Gold* dancers from the trendy '80s American pop show.

With her back now against the window, she folded her arms. The wipers still swept the rain off the windscreen, back and forth they went, like a ticking clock in the momentary silence.

'Are you sleeping with my husband?' Mrs Cameron spurted out. She had broken into a rage.

Her line of questioning couldn't have come soon enough. Being cast as the villain and home-wrecker was almost a blessing in disguise.

I had been waiting for someone to rescue me.

ADELAIDE, ASTROLOGY

AND EIGHTIES ALLURE

MOST FAMILIES WERE WAKING TO the scent of roast lamb still lingering in the kitchen, or helping themselves to a spoonful of leftover pavlova from the fridge. It was Boxing Day in New Zealand.

At seventeen, I yearned to be in a place where there would be no questions, no hiding, and no more whispers behind closed doors.

While Jupiter slipped out of Capricorn and powered into Sagittarius for the first time in twelve years, I zipped my suitcase shut and headed for the airport. The timing was perfect. Something was pulling me towards a world that felt bright, bold, and impossibly vast.

Australia was beckoning.

As the wheels left the tarmac, I watched Auckland slip away: the soft, green paddocks that held so many memories, then the coastline as New Zealand steadily shrank beneath the wing.

I popped on my headphones and pressed play on my blue Sony cassette player. Spandau Ballet's *True* came to life. As my head pressed back into the seat, I let the plane carry me into the unknown.

I had wanted to go to London. It's usually where people went if you decided to leave New Zealand to travel further afield. That meant I should book British Airways; they'd know the way, although from Auckland, the flight would land in South Australia first. I thought in order to get to London I'd have to fly one stop at a time.

Uncle Barry was waiting at Arrivals, not only looking very tanned but wearing his white leather slip-on loafers. He had unbuttoned his flowing, floral print shirt just enough to reveal an expensive long gold chain. He looked exactly like Spanish crooner Julio Iglesias.

His lime green Mini, one I would soon buy for the princely sum of five hundred dollars, shot out of Adelaide airport like a bullet as we headed straight to Rundle Mall. Uncle Barry was driving me to Sportsgirl for a wardrobe update. My peach eyelet blouse, the one with the scalloped hem and puffed sleeves that I had sewn myself, was apparently not going to cut it in the Australian fashion stakes.

If I couldn't change my past, then at least Uncle Barry could change my future.

I'd barely had time to showcase my latest fashion finds when the skies darkened a few weeks later.

South Australian authorities were urging everyone to stay indoors as thick ash began falling across the city. The air was heavy with dread as smoke from local bushfires began to choke our lungs.

Ash Wednesday, one of the deadliest in south-eastern Australia's history, felt nothing short of apocalyptic. I was convinced Hades had split open the sky and sent the fires of Hell to meet me in the most brutal and unforgiving way, as a punishment for my sins.

Adelaide eventually recovered from its terrible losses. With unshakable resilience, the city reinvented itself as an epicentre of cultural hedonism. It now matched an internal rebellion that had been growing inside me.

The decadence was euphoric. I danced the nights away in patent heels, taffeta and lace as Grace Jones's, 'Pull Up to the

Bumper' blared from the speakers. I found a new freedom that came from staying out all night until dawn at Uncle Barry's favourite nightclubs.

Sometimes I laughed and danced so much I thought I might die a beautiful death under the spinning disco balls that cast their light out in time to the most popular Studio 54 anthems.

Within two weeks I had landed my first Australian job in publishing, as a personal assistant to the editor. My first task, he told me, was to lose my thick Kiwi accent and adopt a more educated Australian one. It wasn't easy.

On weekends, my new friends and I would drive up the Adelaide Hills into Hahndorf, a picturesque German village tucked just beyond the doglegs and the gum tree line, where we'd buy artisan jam and cheese, sit on pub benches with tall beers and eat pretzels. Sometimes we would go sailing and finish with a skinny dip at one of the beaches before heading back to the city.

I fell in love with everything that Australia represented that summer, like the surfers with their sun-bleached hair and laid-back hellos. They'd stride by, sometimes pausing to cast more than a glance in my direction as I lay legally topless in the dunes.

Sex in the early '80s was casual and often careless. Relationships weren't about love; they were about the *moment*. I had no intention of surrendering myself to a man. At least not like I had before.

It wasn't unusual to drive hundreds of kilometres into the middle of nowhere for an infamous Bachelor and Spinster blowout on a remote country station, fuelled by booze and bonfires. By midnight the paddocks were a blur of headlights, dust and laughter, and after the adrenaline finally wore off and the beer had become too much, the boys would roll out their swags beneath the Southern Cross and settle in for the night. A half-deflated blow-up mattress was a makeshift bed for one lucky girl still in her dust-smudged ball gown.

At five foot five tall, I was too short to be a proper model like the ones who graced magazine covers or runway shows. That said, every so often my South Australian agency would call me for a commercial or catalogue job.

I was about to head out to a concert by Duran Duran, who were appearing as a support act for a major international artist, when my model agency called. I had been offered a ticket that evening in return for taking two thirteen-year-olds to the show.

The agency had a last-minute request, they said it would help my modelling career.

Yes, I was available.

'Eleven o'clock? This evening? Are you sure?' It was a strange time to model and I was too naïve to know better.

'Yes. You will be representing us. Just ask for David. He has requested to see you at his hotel.'

I had little idea of his star power at the time.

Security waited outside his top-floor presidential suite. I arrived alone, in my black taffeta strapless dress from Sportsgirl, the one I wore clubbing so its flecks of gold would catch the lights and make it appear better than it was.

After-hours glamour, I was learning, didn't always come with instructions. That evening, I announced in all my teenage innocence, 'I'm here to see David.'

Inside, a small handful of people, his band, and a couple of other girls I would never speak to, were lounging about in quiet conversation.

'Be nice.' That was all they told me.

David Bowie sat with me for a long while, magnetic and eloquent. He asked if I'd seen his show. I hadn't. This man was more a philosopher than a rock star, with conversation drifting from art to politics to the origin of slang.

He told me I was the spit of someone, which is very confusing when you try to take words literally. Although, for the first time I felt truly seen and heard by an older man without expectation. David Bowie's beautiful timbre stirred something in me. His voice was strangely familiar as much as quietly captivating. It was as though we had met before, somewhere beyond this life. Even now, part of me wonders if that moment had been written long before it arrived. Although nothing happened, Adelaide was where I first saw the outline of the person I would one day become and the extraordinary calibre of those people who would help shape my life.

Eventually I moved into a beautifully restored bluestone mansion on Lefevre Terrace, with three housemates, two St Bernards and a ghost. There had been rumours of a murder–suicide in the front room where we liked to light the fire. I'd always look up at the ceiling when I entered that room. The bullet holes were still apparent even though they had just been painted over in white.

I'd even seen a ghost in the house. So had the dogs. They would start to bark moments before the shadow of a fully grown man passed by the frosted glass kitchen door from the direction of my bedroom. We used to laugh it off as we lit more candles and devoured Linda Goodman's *Love Signs*. It felt safer to consult the stars than to confront the dead.

That's when astrology quietly and permanently slipped into my life.

I now had an identity. I was a girl with a Cancer Sun and a Taurus Moon who dreamed that somewhere out there I would find a perfect match.

Ten minutes' walk from our haunted mansion in North Adelaide, Channel Nine had opened its doors to me. I began by answering telephones and greeting guests at the front desk. Because I was a quick typist and trained in shorthand, I was occasionally pulled into technical production. It was my first real step into television.

Through the canteen, next to the reception, was the boys' club. It was also known as the newsroom and sports department. I heard that's where the real action happened.

With my outward, happy-go-lucky nature, it didn't take long before I found myself in the company of their journalists, who loved a chat and a laugh. I had a fast smile and could throw out a one-liner as quick as any. My rise in popularity didn't go unnoticed, there or at the front desk.

Waiting for his on-air interview, a guest lingered longer at the sign-in book in front of me than most; long enough for the silence of the empty reception to sharpen the weight of what he was about to say. He introduced himself as a publisher, but not the type I had worked with before.

'How would you like to pose for *Playboy*? You'd make a great Aussie centrefold.' His American accent obvious.

I laughed politely, nervously.

'No, I'm not interested. I'm Catholic, but thank you for asking.' I wasn't sure what being Catholic had to do with getting naked, but at least he knew I was a good girl and had values.

I shouldn't have been shocked, because *Playboy* magazine was a big part of the Australian landscape at the time. Newsagents sold them without any plastic wrapping, so anyone could flick through. Schoolboys I knew sold them in the playgrounds, a used one could go for five dollars. Even in the nineties.

I also knew the magazine because at the time *Star 80* was playing in the cinemas about murdered *Playboy* model Dorothy Stratten. It was perhaps the reason the publisher was at the station.

He was a good-looking European man, unusually established for twenty-one. He had his own apartment, a waterbed, and a V8 sedan with beige leather seats. Everything about him suggested money, independence, and a life already in motion.

It was during our relationship that my moods started to swing wildly between extremes. The Serb suggested I see a psychiatrist, a friend of his. Eventually, our fallout was messy and unsettling. I knew I'd had a narrow escape. He had once pulled a rifle to my head during a heated argument. Later he apologised. I knew I couldn't stay with someone so unhinged.

I never divulged to him or anyone else why left New Zealand, and the real reason I left Adelaide in a hurry.

SURRY HILLS IN SYDNEY DURING the early 1980s was gritty, colourful and in the early stages of transformation.

Back then it was still primarily a working-class area that was starting to undergo gentrification. It was known more for its crumbling terraces, industrial warehouses and migrant families than the hip cafés and boutique bars for which it would later become famous.

Sydney wasn't a new beginning so much as a retreat disguised as one. Adelaide had been about discovery, the thrill of first freedom. Sydney would be about survival in the real world.

It was no surprise that Uncle Barry had made this place his own and transformed an unassuming terrace into a designer hideaway. This area was beginning to pulse with gay pride, activism and nightlife. Uncle Barry and Surry Hills would give me a leg up initially, and within a few short weeks I had found a bright, sun-filled Victorian terrace tucked away on a back street just behind the trendiest shopping street in town.

My flatmate, a stockbroker, was rarely home, making our living arrangement ideal. My spacious first-floor room caught the afternoon sun, which I only noticed on Saturdays as I gazed up at the ornate cornices, thinking nothing in particular. A plaster cast focal point to contemplate life was at least a start.

I would have preferred to stare at the enormous violet amethyst from Brazil that sat at the crystal shop on the corner of my street. I knew this particular type of amethyst would repel negative energies and support mental clarity.

My mother knew me better than I had thought, and had given me two books to read: *Don't Fall Off the Mountain* and *You Can Get There From Here.* People often laughed when author and Hollywood ingénue Shirley MacLaine spoke about authenticity, truth and the search for meaning. *Don't be afraid to go out on a limb. It's where all the fruit is,* she would say, undeterred by society's expectations.

I knew her as fearless and eccentric and famous. As fate would have it, she would be making an appearance on *my street.* In the very same space where the amethyst I coveted sat. In Paddington, Australia, she wouldn't find any Hollywood red carpets, or handsome men in tuxedos guiding her by the small of the back. In Paddington, she would find herself teaching those who were interested about her deeper spiritual journey.

Instead of listening to Shirley and marvelling at an actress I knew well who was in my street talking about things I was interested in, I was reeling from an incident with my former boyfriend only a few doors down.

The previous night had unravelled spectacularly and unexpectedly. The Serb had rung to say he was coming to town. It was naïve of me to think it was a coincidence, since I had left Adelaide only weeks before.

He thought we'd pick up where Adelaide left off: dinner at a fine restaurant then hours tangled in sheets. But once we got home, the mood shifted. I wasn't inviting him in for coffee, and he didn't take rejection well. The air cracked, voices raised, a door splintered, fabric tore. His grip was terrifying. By the time it was over and the police arrived, my home had been wrecked. My landlord would terminate my lease, and I would need to file a restraining order.

By morning, the Serb was gone. Shirley, too. The street stood empty as if it, too, needed to exhale. Only the crystals remained, the Brazilian amethyst catching the light like a silent witness, gleaming as if to say to me, *Like you, we're still here.*

The shop was closed when I walked by that morning. I wanted to see if the amethyst was still there because, from a certain angle, it still caught the light and stood in its beauty, ready to receive.

Like the crystals in the window that had formed under crushing pressure, growing slowly, drip by drip, unseen and hidden, I would need to be patient if I wanted to be discovered, to shine and to be of value to another.

Fate was wasting no time. I landed three job offers in a single day. It felt as though the universe was insisting I anchor myself in Sydney and begin all over again.

The halls of the Australian Jockey Club carried an unmistakable prestige. Portraits of important men stared down from their heavy frames, beneath which sat racing guides arranged with ritual precision on antique furniture that had not moved in decades. It was a mausoleum of male authority and dominance.

The carpeted hallways still carried a faint scent of tobacco from days gone as I headed down towards the chairman's office for my interview. Inside, a largely immovable mahogany desk dominated the room. It was less a piece of furniture and more a barricade, the atmosphere already too ominous and musty for my liking as I waited patiently for him to finish more pressing business elsewhere.

I couldn't see myself captive among the suits at the Sydney Stock Exchange either.

Instead, a different kind of frenetic energy beckoned. I was immediately drawn to the world of a global advertising agency.

STRATEGY, SILK AND SOPHISTICATION

TAKING A LEAF FROM THE TWINS in Auckland, it was time to invest in designer power suits, those with enormous shoulder pads and cinched waists, pussy bow blouses and stockings with suspenders worn with the highest of stilettos. A spritz of YSL Opium, or Giorgio Beverly Hills, and the total package became not only a weapon, but my armour. It would be disguised in strategy, silk and sophistication.

Women, at the time, were taking their authority back. Our message was clear: *You can look, but I decide the terms.* And advertising was the perfect platform to step into my new persona.

Moët & Chandon flowed, it was the champagne that signalled that you had made it. Cocaine was freely racked up in the bathrooms of parties at Kings Cross and Darlinghurst nightclubs, those that lit up the floor with the Eurythmics, Bronski Beat and Depeche Mode. Overhead, tiny mirrored squares would throw thousands of roaming flecks across the room, skimming our faces, bodies and smoke machines.

As the sweat gathered at the nape of my neck and slid down my spine, my once immaculate hair clung to my shoulders in loose, damp curls. A sheen settled across my décolletage, catching the strobes as I lifted my arms and let the beat take over, never wanting the nights to end. I rarely left the dance floor and would dance with *everyone*. My unapologetically high Charles Jourdan heels, together with my leather and underwear as outerwear, made it the only place I felt free.

For those hours I slipped out of my own life and into a version of myself I understood completely. A creature of rhythm, light and edge.

It was a place I belonged.

Outside the clubs and around the world, the Golden Age of Australia had begun. Elle Macpherson was putting Australian women on the map in the modelling world, and Crocodile Dundee, Mel Gibson and Nicole Kidman were filling the cinemas.

Instinct told me I needed more than corporate polish to survive Sydney. So I signed up for Zen Do Kai, a karate-Muay Thai hybrid, at the hardest dojo in town. The one that trained nightclub bouncers and had no tolerance for the weak.

Between client pitches and lines of speed and cocaine, a cultural fixture everywhere, I channelled my energy into physical discipline. At the same time, the planet of action and aggression, Mars, was blazing through the constellation of Aries, a warrior sign. It was my cosmic cue. I was now primed for combat, and my body, mind and spirit were ready to answer the call. It would also enable me to step away from party drugs, the ones that I didn't really fancy, even though almost everyone else I knew did.

When I met my first and only husband, I wasn't ready for a commitment. He had arrived at Beauty Point with another girl in tow. He'd leave with us both, but not before three bronzed Aussie flatmates in blinding fluoro speedos climbed over the second-storey balcony rail.

With a shout and a flash of muscles, they hurled themselves into the luxurious pool below. The water detonated upon impact, drenching the crowd. Laughter had now cracked open the night, and in that brief, reckless moment, the night found its rhythm.

Waylaying another man's insistence on driving me home that evening, I pointed to CJ.

'I'm going home with him!' I hadn't asked, because a taxi was always my first option. There was little appeal in being squeezed into the half seat of his luxury sports car.

CJ was, at first, charming, athletic, and always the centre of attention at parties with his quick wit. He was the best-dressed man in the room, if beautiful fabrics and customised cuts appealed.

'My flatmate wants to take you out,' my advertising manager announced.

I was confused. There were three that night. Minus him, that left two, and one was a very good-looking, six-foot-three surfer with a ready smile. Without a doubt, a pin-up boy.

'I'd love that,' I said, already imagining the surfer's tanned arms around me. I also knew Brett was single. It all made sense.

Until Wednesday.

When the doorbell rang, I thought I had mixed the names up.

'CJ?'

If he sensed my initial shock, he wasn't wrong. The man on my doorstep was not the bronzed surfer of my imagination. Instead, I would be climbing back into the Porsche next to a fashion choice I wasn't entirely prepared for. A hot-pink shirt, tailored brown leather trousers and suede winklepickers.

I realised I'd agreed to a date with the wrong man. But there was no denying the wrong man had some style.

That first evening he took me to a dimly lit restaurant where the waiter tossed caesar salads as the opening performance before presenting Russian caviar like a diplomatic offering. CJ was attentive, funny and unexpectedly worldly.

One dinner turned into two. Then came concerts, casino nights spent at the blackjack tables and weekends drifting between vineyard tastings and late boutique-hotel checkouts. Everything was curated to impress. CJ never did anything by halves.

In his white sports car we'd push the speed limit with the latest

New Romantics tracks blaring. It wasn't love. It wasn't fate. It was the '80s, and it felt like stepping into someone else's luxury life. It was fast and glossy, and I was deliciously out of my depth.

Wherever we went, we laughed until tears streamed down our faces, and those around us buckled as they gasped for air after pushing him for another joke, another story, another quip.

CJ had been married before. There had also been another engagement and disengagement.

'He's divorced.' My mother was not happy at all. 'I don't think he's right for you.' What she really meant is that we were a Catholic family. We followed the rules, even if we didn't go to church. Marrying a divorced man was against what we believed.

I brushed aside her repeated warnings.

'I think you're making a mistake.' My unemotional Capricornian mother wasn't giving up. 'I don't like him.'

Her word was always the last word.

The geographical distance between us soon started to calcify into polite, superficial conversations. Had her decades-long marriage taught her that silence was safer than the truth? I would never know. Our relationship never fully recovered.

In 1987, a large princess-cut diamond glinted on my ring finger, beautiful, bedazzling, and of superior quality, unlike the impending marriage. It also drew many an admirer's eye, as did my new gold Rolex, a birthday gift that promised permanence in a world that was already beginning to spin a little too fast for me.

The martial arts classes that I loved and was starting to do well in would soon come to an end. I'd spend less time with my friends from advertising. It seemed a small trade-off for the excitement of being in a relationship.

I'd let go of pieces of myself while he quietly rewrote my script. I didn't audition as his dutiful girlfriend, nor as the polished young hostess or the blonde who smiled on cue. I simply played the role so well that before long I would be his trophy wife.

That year, other scripts were waiting in the wings. One that would demand a different kind of performance. One that would change everything: the plot, the pacing, even the person I knew myself to be.

THE DARK SIDE OF DESIRE

ASTROLOGICALLY, A GENERATIONAL change was upon us. Pluto, famous as a lover of taboo, absolute control and the underworld, had just entered a surgical, relentless Scorpio. It was the Australian winter of 1984.

Their energy soon started to fuel the misinformation and sensationalist reportage around the AIDS pandemic. Advertisements, funded by the government, started to appear on the television every night. Every second break, the black-hooded Grim Reaper appeared, famously bowling over men, women *and* children like skittles in a bowling alley. It left an indelible mark.

Unprotected sex, kissing and even cuts to our skin could now potentially *kill us*. The gay community, almost overnight, was marginalised, and due to the hysteria, almost untouchable. 'Trust no one' became the catch cry.

Do you know who you are really sleeping with? Do you really know this person's history, how many partners they've had, or what diseases they carry?

The government-approved campaign's chilling tagline was *If not stopped, it could kill more Australians than World War II*. It was effectively burned into our psyche before – just as radically – being pulled from the air. It was too late. The psychological damage was done, it was in the back of all our minds.

Uncle Barry said it was performative. The government was fear-mongering. People simply needed to wear condoms and avoid sharing needles and, for a time, blood transfusions, until there was more clarity around the medical profession and science.

Paranoia quickly crept into every love affair anyone even *thought* about having. Beside me at the office, a striking brunette seemed untouched by it all, radiant and oblivious to the chaos as if it had chosen to skip over her.

Unlike me, Kimberley rarely hurried. She sauntered. Everywhere. To production. Then from media to reception. She even sauntered to the car park at the end of the day. This was a woman who was unaware that she left a sea of flabbergasted and befuddled men in her wake. With her gilded cigarette holder poised between her red-painted lips, Kimberley seemed to almost glide, inhaling as elegantly as she did deeply as she went. She always smiled widely and had an air of pause, signalled by exhaling large and deliberate smoke circles in my direction, and always before she spoke.

'Stop smoking,' I said to her. 'You're going to kill me, I swear.'

I'd watch the plume of carcinogens rise before wafting over and settling upon me. Pluto in Scorpio through an ancient lens suggested that soon there would be a death. Hopefully it was not from second-hand Alpine menthol cigarette smoke. Either way, I couldn't be sure if the death was to be literal or symbolic, just that an irreversible transformation was on its way.

CJ AND I HAD DECIDED TO MOVE in together, possibly more for safety than romance. Now, at almost twenty-one, it seemed like the natural next step. It was Mother's Day in Australia, and a few short weeks until my biggest celebration.

The morning itself was nothing special. So routine, in fact, it could have slipped by as other anniversaries seemed to do at that age.

Dressed in my favourite red silk kimono, I was in a quiet kitchen flipping pancakes while the bacon cooked in the pan. As its crispness started curling through the air, I realised life was good.

The phone rang. Dad's voice was serious, and he wasn't an officious man.

'Are you sitting down?'

Given we'd often chat, I couldn't possibly imagine why he would sound like that. Pete told me later it was the hardest call he'd ever had to make, because he didn't want to lose a daughter.

'We've found your mother.' He paused and so did I.

It was the only thing my father could get out without his voice breaking. I didn't dare breathe. I also didn't know what to say.

'We wanted to surprise you for Mother's Day, even though you're not a mother yet.' He laughed to break the tension. 'We've been looking for her because we thought you'd like to meet your real mother.'

Oh. Now I wasn't so sure. My heart was beating so loud and

fast I thought I'd have a heart attack right then and there. I would have died of hope, dread, shock and curiosity. I was flooded with questions all at once.

I didn't want to ask the next natural question, one any adopted child would probably ask, in case it was disrespectful.

'She wants to meet you.' There. He said it, so I wouldn't have to. Everything else that had gone before that day now collapsed into insignificance.

Mum and Dad had been quietly navigating their way through government bureaucracy to find her as soon as they knew the Adult Adoption Information Act was coming into effect, and the records of children who had been given away would be released. Before that, we were prevented from knowing what happened to either party.

What was wild, her parents had lived just streets away from my own in Auckland. For a long time Sharon's mother said she'd peer into prams as the young mothers were out walking, to see if it was her baby.

Dad said he and Mum had already met her parents. She came from a 'lovely family'. It was obvious circumstances had been difficult.

A chill settled into my bones. The next step in my life had just arrived. The choice was mine.

I FLEW TO HOBART THE FOLLOWING weekend. By the time my flight from Sydney landed, my nerves were so shredded that I waited until everyone else had disembarked.

Hobart's air that day was crisp, albeit still scented by jet fuel, as I stepped down onto the tarmac. The metal exit stairs clanged behind me as the wind caught the belt of my coat and it tangled briefly on the rail. A flight attendant quickly stepped in to help me and alleviate my embarrassment. Perhaps the universe was holding me back for a reason.

Inside the arrivals hall a large crowd had gathered. That's what decent country folk do; they show up for their loved ones in a blur of reunions. Some idled more towards the back as they waited for someone familiar to appear. It's what I would do when I was late to the terminal to pick up a friend.

Unsure of what I was looking for, I scanned the sea of un-familiar faces. Then I saw someone who looked like they were waiting for me, waving with one hand raised as if to say, 'Here I am, I see you.'

Our eyes locked momentarily. I looked away, scanning the crowd for anyone who might resemble me more closely. Then I smiled. Yes. It was her. Confident, even worldly, slim and much younger than I had imagined.

'Hello, daughter. I've been waiting for this moment all my life. Come here and let me hug you.'

Daughter. What a strange way to greet someone. She knows my name.

She spoke so softly, like someone too young to know the birth of a child. She held me longer than was comfortable, as I suppose all parents do. I was almost twenty-one and not yet into hugging.

This is awkward.

I looked over her shoulder at the departures board, wondering absurdly whether I should catch an Ansett flight out again.

Don't be a bitch. This is her moment. It's been twenty years, eleven months and four and three quarter hours since she's last laid eyes on me.

As we walked over to the luggage carousel I studied her thirty-six-year-old profile, checking for resemblances. Would anyone pick us out as mother and daughter? I decided they wouldn't. Her nose was longer and more elegant, her brown eyes more almond, her skin more olive and freckled.

But our gold chains and knitted jumpers, purple, green and navy blue, practically matched. She drove a Mini Cooper. I liked Minis.

Questions flickered so quickly they were impossible to catch for long, but something in that moment suggested we had all the time in the world.

Maybe I looked like *him*. Sharon told me his name, and in that moment I noticed her Kiwi vowels were very pronounced – unlike mine, which had softened significantly since I'd left New Zealand.

'You remind me of your father. He had a beautiful smile, and was such a nice person,' she said softly.

She still burns a candle for him. Why? What an arsehole. He never bothered to write to her after taking her virginity so knowingly. She's like me. Forgiving of bad behaviour.

She had waited all her life to meet me, but I had waited all my life to look like *someone*. My disappointment must have shown.

Sharon recognised my bone structure was that of her mother's.

She's touching me again without asking. I wish she wouldn't. She's so familiar and shouldn't be; we just met. She wears Estée Lauder's White Linen, though. I own the same fragrance. Thankfully I packed Giorgio Beverly Hills this time around. It would be weird if we wore the same fragrance.

Apparently, I gesticulated a lot. 'You have his hands, you know,' she said, but then added that I moved them like an Italian when I talked.

Yes, because my hands fill in the gaps when the words won't come. You know how it is. You talk in an animated and excitable way.

I wondered whether her memory had blurred. I had heard that when people get old, they forget. I hoped she'd say much more, but what is there to say when you share a fleeting hook-up with a handsome stranger that you'll never see again? It's hardly like we share our life story before an undeniable physical attraction turns into a quick shag.

Part of me suspected she'd once hoped he'd come looking for her. That he'd find out about me, and that discovery would force the truth out of him: what he felt for her, what he didn't, and everything she'd never been brave enough to ask.

En route, Sharon described her university-allocated Sandy Bay bungalow as simple with a lovely view over the water. I suppose it was just her way of lowering any of my expectations. What it lacked in architectural brilliance, Sharon made up with her taste for elegance and interior design.

I would soon find that everything in her home was white or off-white. From the sofa to the rugs, lampshades, cushions and curtains. In my ethereal white bedroom, a perfectly positioned vase of fresh white flowers and two white, large and very fluffy bath towels sat neatly at the end of my single bed. It was obvious she was a clean freak.

'I live with someone, by the way, but don't expect him to say too much,' Sharon revealed as we pulled into her steep driveway. 'He's a Cambridge professor.'

I hadn't met a professor before, nor did I know anyone from Cambridge or Cambridge University. The word Cambridge sounded like it belonged in the upper echelons of society.

Sharon told me he could also play multiple instruments by ear, which was almost as impressive as the fact that he looked like Bob Dylan.

I did not understand his academic prestige at the time. And I certainly wasn't educated enough at twenty-one to understand the significance of his citations in Roman and Greek political and religious history.

Sharon said she was drawn to deeply intelligent men. Not only had she been attending his classes, but her attraction to the professor would have been impossible to ignore given he also lectured in Latin and Greek.

Sharon and I spent the weekend over candles and endless cups of tea piecing our stories together. We ventured down to see a game of royal tennis in one of the oldest clubs in the world, and watched as an old friend of hers hit a heavy corked ball around the Renaissance-inspired indoor court with his wooden racket. There appeared a distinct fondness between them as I watched her watch him. Sharon introduced me to everyone we spoke to as her daughter. Our age difference raised a few eyebrows but most people were too polite to comment.

I flew out from Hobart with a promise not to leave our next meeting too long, even though I was uncertain of the direction our new relationship should take. It was a lot to take on board in one weekend. Sharon had hinted at coming to my twenty-first birthday and later, my wedding to CJ. I didn't extend her an invitation to either because I knew she would want to be the centre of attention.

After everything my parents had done for me, they deserved to be in the spotlight.

STRICTLY PRIVATE AND CONFIDENTIAL

WHEN THE CHAIRMAN'S PERSONAL secretary resigned, I set my sights on her corner office overlooking the Harbour Bridge. As a highly trained stenographer, I was confident I could manage the role easily, despite it having been filled, until then, by more experienced women.

Convincing the chairman would be a formality.

Around the same time, I was spotted in the lift of our office tower by a friend of Uncle Barry's. I was wearing a dramatic cherry-red coat with exaggerated eighties-style shoulder pads and matching red Christian Dior stilettos. He complimented my style, then suggested I apply for Qantas.

'They're looking for people like you', he said.

Sharing the elevator that day was Sir William McMahon, who had once served as Australia's prime minister.

'I would fly with you,' he joked.

From then on, whenever the lift doors opened and we found ourselves together again, he would ask why I hadn't left yet.

In those few suspended seconds between the doors closing and the ground floor arriving, an unexpected door had opened elsewhere. One that would soon lead to an offer to fly internationally.

I prepared my resignation letter.

'Do you have a moment?' I asked, handing the chairman a typewritten envelope marked *Strictly Private and Confidential*.

He glanced at it for no longer than a moment, then swivelled his chair away from me and leaned back, looking out the window over the Sydney Opera House.

'Do you really want to push trolleys up and down aisles on seventeen-hour flights to Los Angeles or Hong Kong? And serve coffee and tea to drunken football teams, lecherous men, chundering children and rows of smokers?' he said. 'Or would you rather keep using my Jaguar and enjoy harbourside restaurants with quality people and even better conversations?'

He had a point. The way he refused to look at me suggested my timing was inconvenient or perhaps it was his way of ensuring I would stay.

My boss was a charming man and more boyish than most senior executives. He also chased fire trucks, which explained why he often missed the start of board meetings. It was obvious he preferred smoke and sirens to spreadsheets.

He had convinced me to stay.

Before I could step into my new office the following Monday morning, the phone rang. It was Dad.

'Klyn has passed away. Mum found him slumped over the bathtub.'

The initial suggestion was that he had raced to the bathroom to be sick, vomited, and as he leaned over the tub, suffocated.

Over the two autopsies that followed, the first revealed nothing. The second, conducted at a later date, found an elevated level of painkillers in his body.

Then, my father's brother, a practising mortician, questioned how a lethal dose could not appear in the initial report. The discrepancy was noted.

At the Coroner's Court, Klyn's cause of death was recorded as 'unknown'.

For my parents, the uncertainty had been unbearable. Only a

week earlier, their eighteen-year-old son had booked a four-seater plane. He was eager to take them flying, proud to show off the pilot's licence he had just earned. His sights were set on flying, he had plans for the future.

In the end, Dad said it became too much so they chose not to pursue another explanation. Not because they didn't care, but because they had already lost more than they thought they could survive.

Mum and Dad had spent months watching me closely, fearful they might lose me to a woman named Sharon and a family I barely knew. Instead, while they were looking in one direction, something incomprehensible took their own son from them.

The next morning, CJ and I flew to New Zealand.

We stayed in my parents' house and we showered over the same bathtub where Klyn had died. It was their only bathroom.

We slept in single beds in his room. His clothes still hung in the wardrobe, exactly as he'd left them, where the sleeves still held the shape of his arms and the collars remembered his neck. It was also a place the past still breathed.

It had all happened too quickly for alternatives. My parents couldn't dismantle his world in a week, nor would I expect them to. I would have to work through the strangeness of it all as best I could as I breathed the air he'd last breathed in that room and slept where the last day of his future had ended.

Apart from the teacher next door dying when his house burned down when I was around ten years old, I had only brushed against death once before that.

I felt the cold waxy feeling of an elderly nun's nose. It was purely out of thirteen-year-old curiosity, just to see what a dead person felt like. I wasn't the only one to do it. We had been instructed to pay our respects as she lay in the centre of the school chapel. It was a directive that was not meant to be a hands-on experience.

The speed of events left me unable to settle. That morning, before Klyn's funeral, in a quiet moment alone, I reached into a drawer where I had unpacked a few personal items. I took the one thing I knew would settle my racing mind.

Cocaine didn't induce a high the way it did for most.

A New York psychiatrist once described cocaine to me as a rich person's lithium. Years later, when lithium was formally prescribed to me as a mood modulator, he warned me to be careful around pharmacies. People lingered waiting for such prescriptions, while others, usually at night, quietly offered cash for a few mood enhancing pills that were taken to save my life.

My little brother, who had bullied me, tied me to the washing line, punched me in the nose and always insisted I 'wasn't one of them', didn't struggle with mental health. He struggled with debilitating migraines.

Later that morning, from where I sat, it appeared the priest barely moved as he stood behind the pulpit. He opened the Bible to a page marked with a long liturgical ribbon in cream and gold. His voice was steady, reverent. He lowered it just enough to carry the weight of the service.

My mother's grief cut through the silence. They had left the casket open. I wasn't sure why. I studied his stillness, the pallor of his skin, the unfamiliar suit. He looked calmer than I had ever known him.

My mind filled with the moments he wouldn't experience, the laughter at Christmas, the trips we'd never take, the apologies he still owed me.

The priest paused occasionally to turn a page or adjust the ribbon. Each time he lifted his eyes, sometimes towards me, I lowered mine. I tried to practise Christianity but I was certain he could tell I had taken a narcotic because he had the eyes of the Lord.

I knew I wasn't who I should have been but I had decided that morning that it was my fault, I was a curse on my family.

Peace would come later, if at all, for my parents. Trauma leaves an indelible mark. What had happened made no sense.

After the burial, my parents would prepare for a lifestyle change. They sold their Auckland home and set their sights on a motel in Australia, purchased sight unseen. It was meant to be a soft reset.

Between a crooked agent and a failing local economy, it became something else entirely.

It was a doomed investment.

I WASN'T SHARON'S ONLY CHILD. Long before she found me in New Zealand, there had been Zak. Her son, and my half-brother. He had already lived the consequences of her chaos, in full colour.

Where Sharon flitted, Zak was left behind. His childhood had remained scattered across boarding schools in England, New Zealand, Tasmania, and even a Hare Krishna camp in India. Each move was another attempt by Sharon to outrun any mess of her own doing and any responsibilities she resisted. He had endured her instability in a way I would not understand until much later.

My early reunions with her, in contrast, were heady and dramatic. For me, they were a pageant.

I flew to Canada to meet her. Sharon was now married to her Classics professor and living in a grand house near the university where he taught. She had also become a vegetarian, or so he believed. It was during a faculty lunch with several of his PhD students, his plate piled high with roast vegetables, that I found her in the adjoining kitchen, bent over the remains of a roast leg of lamb, literally tearing the meat off the bone with her teeth. Her behaviour was a far cry from her sophistication in the dining room.

Not long after she baked his cardigan in the oven, that marriage ended in divorce.

Sharon was well versed in native American tribal ways. Between the ancient history texts, indigenous authors and tribal lore lay *The Witch's Bible, The Complete Witches' Handbook, The Meaning of*

Witchcraft and *The Spiral Dance: A Rebirth of the Ancient Religion of the Goddess.*

It was common for her to cleanse her home morning and night with sage. I watched her work her sacred eagle's feather left to right in small, quick strokes and then upward in longer, sweeping movements. She smudged every corner of every room, leaving nothing to chance.

Crystals were everywhere: clustered by doorways, balanced on bathroom shelves, lining the kitchen bench, and in the lounge room the larger ones kept her witch books upright. Sharon was shaped by the '60s and early '70s; she was part of the original Age of Aquarius crowd. Folk music, feminism, peace and experimentation. It was her all over.

We drove up north to Hudson Bay to see Elvis Presley's former psychic, a Native American. Silverhand's reservation hadn't been easy to find, and we had to go while we had the chance. Sharon had prepared a gift of pure tobacco wrapped in sky-blue cloth and secured with twine. 'An appropriate offering to any elder or spiritual leader,' she said. We needed to honour their connection to the natural world in exchange for their wisdom.

Silverhand was forty bucks for half an hour. He pointed to the hefty ring on his left ring finger, the centrepiece of which was a white turquoise stone the size of a walnut.

'Elvis gave me this,' he said. It looked Elvis enough.

He sat in silence at first. I wondered if we were already on the clock for our short session. Then he began to chant, his words rolling softly in his native tongue then rising to a rhythmic invocation that pulsed throughout the room.

Silverhand quietly began, as if he had turned into another person. 'A spiritual life is a long, arduous one, full of sorrow and adversity.'

I thought I had paid for a tape cassette recording full of

good news.

'You become pregnant. A boy. October. Your marriage breaks, you find another lover. Your lover will become very rich. Bank on it.'

Well, that sounded more promising. I hadn't yet married, nor had I found a new lover. There were so many questions left unanswered. Was that rich with me? Or rich with someone else?

'You are like a little flicker bird,' he continued. 'You always fly straight into the wall. Why do you not go round?'

And just like that, my reading was over.

On the drive home, Sharon put Cat Stevens on repeat, as she had on the way up. I was convinced she was riding her own 'Peace Train'. Like Bob Dylan, his music had shaped her entire world view of protests, mysticism, and reinvention.

Silverhand's prediction stayed with me. Within eighteen months, in October, just as he'd said, I would discover I was expecting.

Forty years on I reached out to him again, not for nostalgia, but to honour the path he'd pointed me towards, and to ask deeper questions about the spiritual traditions he'd carried all his life. He remembered. He listened. And so did I. Very carefully.

OUT OF THE SHADOWS

To be honest, Silverhand's prediction was the last thing on my mind when I said 'yes'. The chosen date? 31 October, 1987.

My off-the-rack dress from a small boutique in Double Bay was, in hindsight, the true '80s bridal dream, with its Princess Diana–inspired puffy sleeves in gold-tinged lace. I had spent more on a veil: sought-after Belgian lace, delicately edged with hand-stitched flowers. It would shield my face from the niggling uncertainty he would see in my eyes. That was, until the veil was lifted and then it would be too late.

The newly renovated Milton Park in the Southern Highlands, south of Sydney, was an enchanting place for exchanging vows. We had woken to a glorious, warm spring day. By eleven o'clock, CJ and I were officially married beneath the dappled sunlight of a magnificent oak tree.

Among the forty guests, few would have known I had called off both my hen's party and our thousand-dollar-a-head wedding only a week prior as we sipped champagne to live jazz.

I chose not to listen to my mother's advice nor my intuition, as exhaustion and nerves pulsed through me. *I haven't even begun to live my life,* I thought. *What am I doing?*

By noon we were dining on oysters, pheasant, and lobster, before cutting the croquembouche that we had chosen as our wedding cake. By four, my wedding dress was starring on the tennis court in a doubles match as guests had already brought out the spliffs.

Others were caught frolicking in our wedding suite. It was not only Halloween, it was Scorpio season again, and the party was just getting started.

Those who had flown in from around the world were left to enjoy the spoils of an opulent weekend in the country, while we flew out to a relatively undiscovered Bali.

Kuta was nothing more than a long, unhurried sweep of sand, with a few warungs, ramshackle along the main dirt road. We happened upon only a few travellers who had come with battered backpacks. They were the kind more suited to India or East Africa than to a romantic honeymoon destination.

The honeymoon glow soon wore off as I returned to advertising. Ten months later, I was pregnant.

I blamed my overwhelming exhaustion on long days in the office followed by late nights. The smell of coffee in the office now made me want to throw up, but morning sickness was mostly attributed to regular bouts of food poisoning.

My regular social scene was oblivious to my condition. Even though I was 'showing', hosts freely offered lines of cocaine to me at backyard barbeques, pubs, cocktail parties and nightclubs.

I even discovered our kitchen scales were being used for more than baking. Our housemate was running a brisk coke trade out of the dining room, which we never used. Sydney was awash with it. Everyone knew, including the media, that the police were struggling to curb the plentiful supply.

If morning sickness wasn't enough, I was now apprehensive and paranoid.

CJ suggested we move away from the eastern suburbs, and closer to his office. I would soon be trapped in a community of new builds. A long way from my friends and all that I had previously known.

The light taps I felt from within were proof that everything was changing faster than I realised. My stomach wasn't just growing; it was taking over. Then my pregnant breasts joined in, swelling from a neat 34C to a bulging 44D; they looked completely out of sync with my petite frame.

Four-foot-something Chinese grandmothers in a faded floral blouse, and trousers loose enough for comfort, would often stop and set down their baskets full of fresh produce.

I couldn't blame them. Built from years of work, early mornings in the kitchen, and steaming pork buns, they always looked like their small and sturdy frames could do with a rest.

They beamed as they pointed to my belly, curious and delighted. They recognised pregnancy at a glance – the knowing look of women who'd spent a lifetime watching their families grow.

'Happy mother, happy baby! You crave salty food?' Their eyes would twinkle before adding, 'Ahh, must be boy! You carry like boy!'

Our family dentist had also predicted a boy. He had hung a ring from a cotton thread over my stomach before watching to see it swing wide and furious, as the pendulum declared its verdict.

At what point do you start believing in signs? By the second trimester, old wives' tales, ring tests, the shape of my body were all pointing to certainty. I was having a boy. With my birth mother Sharon's auburn hair, and the fire-kissed locks that ran through women on both sides of the family, I was sure I was giving birth to another.

Morning and night, I anointed my belly with Clarins Contour Treatment Oil, smoothing it on in circles, as if in devotion. I hoped he could feel how much he was wanted, cherished and safe. He would never have to worry about being abandoned.

They say sex and Chinese food can trigger labour. I think they're right. My contractions started thick and fast within the hour following.

I was two weeks early.

By breakfast, the crippling cramps were six minutes apart. I started to panic. So much for our palatial harbour room at the Four Seasons Hotel. If I didn't hurry, I was convinced it would become my birthing suite.

My husband called the hospital.

'Not yet, wait, wait. Keep track of the time between contractions. Call us back when they get to two minutes.' The nurses suggested I was likely having Braxton Hicks.

At three minutes apart, I could barely breathe, let alone stand up. I could no longer wait. After all, what would a midwife know? This is *my* baby, and my baby was different from every other child who had ever been born.

'Take me to the goddamn hospital. Now. Or I'm having it here, on the carpet of this hotel,' I screamed. My husband panicked at the very thought of it.

The concierge was waiting at the front entrance as I hobbled out. All wasn't lost, he passed us a beautiful bottle of champagne, to celebrate our baby's early arrival.

The hospital was a twenty-minute drive away; in my husband's Porsche, we made it in twelve.

After reaching St Margaret's Hospital in Darlinghurst, the contractions then stopped. My stubborn little Taurus had decided to take his time.

He had also settled the wrong way down and was now pressing directly against my spine. The spot where I had a pre-existing hairline fracture. I couldn't get comfortable.

I needed a shower. Or a bath. Perhaps I should just walk around like the Hunchback of Notre-Dame? The hospital wanted to discharge me. Annoyingly, my cervix refused to dilate a millimetre further.

'I'm not leaving without a baby,' I argued. 'We need to make him come out *today*.'

I was beginning to drown in waves of exhaustion, teetering on the edge of consciousness. Nothing was easing the crushing pressure of this little beast.

Staff agreed to give me an epidural and prepared an 18-gauge needle. I'm not sure how they managed to insert it into my spine as I writhed about.

'Twenty minutes,' they promised, 'and you'll be able to rest.'

When the obstetrician arrived to break my waters, it looked like he was about to start crocheting. He inserted two fingers into me, and then the hook.

Aaaahhhh.

The warm gush released the pressure, and for a blissful moment, I thought, *That's it.* Unfortunately, Lewis was in no rush. I still had four more hours of labour.

Winter had arrived early, it was a wet Saturday afternoon and now that my waters had broken, I remembered I was so miserable because I also had the flu. I shivered, ached and burned up until the contractions started again.

It was time.

Medical staff gathered for the first sighting of the crown. I lay there, legs wide, for all the world to see. Of course. My wax appointment was booked for next week.

At 8:13 pm, after sixteen hours of labour, I became a mum. I was twenty-three.

The doctor and his nurses swiftly prepared their implements for snipping and stitching up what had been ripped apart in the process. There would be no need for anaesthesia.

Lewis was a sight, to say the least; not quite as rosy as I had imagined my baby to be with his bulging eyes, a head moulded into a long cone-like shape by the brutishness of forceps. Then there were noticeable shades of purple on his blotchy skin, which was still slathered in a protective creamy white coating.

The paediatrician said he was going to be a handsome lad. I begged to differ at that point.

By the time I had woken the next morning, I'd completely forgotten I had given birth. It was Mother's Day in Australia and an Irish nurse was standing beside me with little Lewis in a plastic hospital crib she had wheeled in next to me.

'Are you ready to learn how to feed your wee man? Let's see if we can get him to attach.'

The nurse handled my breasts with brisk efficiency, squeezing and prodding to make sure the colostrum was flowing before forcing his tiny head onto my nipple.

I guess there was no point in being gentle. My belly, still round and bloated, felt sadly empty, and the kicks, twists and somersaults that had kept me awake had been swapped overnight for swollen breasts and two uncooperative nipples.

By day three my body had transformed into a full-scale dairy operation. I now had enough milk to feed the entire hospital.

Motherhood had arrived, whether I was ready or not.

LULLABIES

A BABY WAS EVERYTHING I THOUGHT I wanted. What I didn't know was how quickly life could warp. Instead of spending more time together, I spent more time alone.

The main bedroom, the space we were supposed to share as a married couple, had been arranged as a nursery before my return home from the hospital. Our bedroom soon became a place for a rocking chair to feed my son, a change table, and lullabies.

I was now sleeping in the second bedroom on a pull-out sofa, and CJ was dividing all his time between his mother's place and his office. Our home was a place he briefly visited on his way to somewhere else. He claimed our baby kept him awake at night.

Then there were the insults.

'You're fat.'

'You're not as attractive as you used to be.'

I was incredulous because I was back in my pre-pregnancy clothes before I left the hospital – although naturally, I wasn't *in gym shape*. I had just given birth.

Whatever femininity I had left, I started to strip. I cut my hair short and stopped wearing makeup. All I knew was, layer by layer, I wanted to eliminate the person my husband married.

It turned out his exile wasn't just for rest or business convenience. It gave him the distance he needed to slip back to the area we'd just left and to her. Another lover. One he had taken during my pregnancy.

I had caught him playing around before I married him, and even though the tired lines that all men seem to use started to fall out of his mouth, I forgave him.

A man who cheated once was doing it again.

This time I had been looking for my Amex card when I happened across a handwritten love letter in his briefcase. It was addressed *Dear Heather* and wedged between several pages of business correspondence.

My hands shook as I buckled my weeks-old baby into the car. The evidence, cold and undeniable, sat beside me on the passenger seat of my new BMW 5 Series. The letter was a weight far heavier than the pregnancy I had just carried.

At the end of the street, I hesitated. Should I turn left or right?

I turned left and drove towards the only safe haven I could think of, that of an American girl, Lisa, a former advertising colleague. She was the first person who'd ever let me hold her newborn baby. I went there because I thought she'd understand.

My marriage was over just short of my twenty-fourth birthday.

Online, I filed for decree nisi. Four hundred dollars for a dissolution would be cheap considering the rapidly escalating cost to my mental health.

It would be two years before I would discover the legal system which had been designed by men to keep women in sufferance.

They knew to hide their money, bankrupt their company, and feign poverty.

PIECES OF THE PUZZLE

A VISIT TO CHRISTCHURCH CREATED a perfect opportunity for Lewis and me to visit Sharon's parents and also her youngest sister.

Auntie Dot held the key to many forgotten stories in two large dusty cardboard boxes of Kodachrome pictures. They had accompanied Dot from Auckland to London and then from Liverpool back to Christchurch when her husband took specialist paediatric post.

Sitting cross-legged on her floor, she sifted through the photos, some of which had faded with time. Now and then she paused, holding a picture for a moment longer, as though weighing up whether the past should remain buried or be shared. Certain images drew a soft, private smile on her face; others made her mouth tighten before she placed them into a growing 'discarded' pile.

'What about this one?' Dot handed me a small photo with frilly edges.

Sharon sat perched on a stone wall by the sea with her ankles delicately crossed. Her hands were tucked underneath her thighs. Although the wind had teased her hair to one side, she instinctively knew when the camera would catch her best angle. She appeared fashionable, and as I brought the picture closer, her flirtatious eyes were impossible to ignore.

I wondered if that's what my biological father had seen in her the night I was conceived.

'And this?' Dot paused with amusement as she slid over

another black and white photo.

It was of a soldier, caught mid-stride. He was fleeing from a helicopter wreckage with a machine gun in his hands. It was Sharon's first husband, a special forces operative. He looked unstoppable and unshaken, like a man built to lead, protect and survive.

My favourite picture was taken in the steamy jungle of Papua New Guinea, where my half-brother, Zak, had been born. This time her husband sat astride his Harley-Davidson as Sharon radiated '70s cool in her floral maxi dress and floppy sunhat.

He was a Steve McQueen type, together they looked very Hollywood. Their attraction appeared dazzling.

Expat life can appear far more exotic and intoxicating than it actually is, and I knew that living in an army enclave couldn't have been easy in Port Moresby.

THE GAVEL

It was 23 April, 1992, 9:50 am.

I like to be on time, if not a little early, and that day, the day of my hearing, was no exception. The air inside the waiting room was heavy with recycled emotions and even heavier with the decisions they entailed. No one made eye contact.

The women sat apart from the others. I decided to sit with them while they thumbed through outdated magazines, *Home Beautiful*, *New Idea* and the *Australian Women's Weekly*. They didn't look up.

The second hand on the courtroom's clock would be set to someone else's rhythm as it clicked over to the tenth hour.

On the wall, a list of cases. Our divorce case was third on the list.

'The judge doesn't take long; you should be through around eleven,' the court assistant told me. We'd have to wait until we were called.

After two years and five months of limbo, what was another hour? Two years and five months of learning how to be alone, of untangling myself from the idea that I wasn't enough for the father of my son. Two years and five months of waiting for the signature that would finally sever me from a man who had already moved on.

Around the edges of the wood-panelled room stood the men, some who had waited for him, some who hadn't. Those intimidating types, in navy pinstripes or plain, some with shoes that needed polishing. With cologne and wristwatches that cost more than my divorce, and their black leather portfolios in hand, they chatted among themselves.

Occasionally they would glance over to where I was sitting, although without any acknowledgement.

Then *he* entered. It was ten o'clock.

The court assistant called his name.

His divorce mattered more, as did his money and his influence: all the things society loved the most. Powerful men never had to wait; their lives always took precedence.

It was Alan Bond, media tycoon, Foster's beer mogul, and the man who had bankrolled America's Cup and Australia's victory.

Women like me? I would have to wait. That day, as I watched him march in with his legal team, I promised myself, this would be the last time I would knowingly wait for a man to decide my fate. Regardless of who he was.

Princess Anne no doubt felt the same way as she, coincidentally, headed to the divorce courts on the same day. Like my husband, hers had also strayed and, unfortunately, a child was on the way. Even royalty was not immune to falling for an unfaithful type.

I was standing on the same precipice as a princess. We were closing the door on men who philander. Although, unlike Alan Bond and Her Royal Highness, I had little bargaining power.

The judge, an older man, silver-haired, impeccably dressed in his well-worn black robes, barely spared me a glance. His face, lined from years of passing down decisions that would reshape lives, remained unreadable.

'Looking the way you do,' he remarked, 'and being an intelligent young woman, there is no doubt you will marry again.'

Two things that had in the past worked in my favour were now being used against me. To the judge, I was likely just another woman in a long queue of heartbreak and bureaucracy.

He looked at me, not with any sense of compassion or kindness or even understanding, but with the weary impatience of a man who appeared to have long stopped caring about the fate of women.

With my divorce granted, the judge's hands moved towards the pile of files sitting on his right. He was devoid of emotion when the gavel fell.

'Next case, please.'

IF DIVORCE WASN'T BAD ENOUGH, the bank's phone call sounded like a death sentence.

My ex-husband had dissolved his company and the bank were seizing assets to pay the creditors. On paper, they said, I was still personally and severally liable for his debts.

My home, the one I lived in as part of my settlement, the one with its white picket fence, its clean, modern interiors, the one softened by the smell of jasmine that drifted through the glass louvres, would no longer be mine. It would be seized and sold, as would my car, a red Honda Civic.

In Australia during the '90s, young divorced women like me were still footnotes in society; unprotected, uncompensated and easily discarded.

'Mummy, where is our car going?'

'Just to get fixed,' I told Lewis cheerfully, 'so we can drive to the beach faster.'

My heart and mind thundered with betrayal. The truck driver winched my car onto the back of his tray. My son's little hand clutched mine as together we watched it disappear down the street.

Men always knew how to protect their wealth, how to hide behind accountants and loopholes. I hadn't just lost my home and a car. I'd lost the illusion that justice would protect me.

My days started to bleed into nights, and into a heavy, suffocating emptiness.

What got me through were the women who knew me before the storm, my soul tribe, whose loyalty never wavered. They didn't just show up; they held me up.

The bank agreed to let me keep any profit after the bank loan was paid off. A chance meeting with a man from Macquarie Bank helped me invest it. His sage advice would eventually reap enough in the stock market to help me pay for my son's private education.

I moved into a sunny two-bedroom townhouse in Mosman, just down from a surf shop and walking distance to a beautiful art deco cinema.

Even though we were now renting, it felt like a soft reset, much like the little blue bubble car I purchased with my own money. I was now working in the music industry so I swapped the cassette deck for a state-of-the-art CD player.

I couldn't afford automatic transmission, or an upgrade to air conditioning, so we simply rolled down the windows and drove a little faster. It was the only way to cool down in the heat of summer. My little Mazda 121 flew along the freeway down to the Snowy Mountains and up to the vineyards in the Hunter Valley in one little blue ball of happiness. It never broke down.

Mum came to help me settle in to my new place. She brought two things with her: a copy of Louise Hay's *You Can Heal Your Life*, and something more mystical. It was my first Mythic tarot deck.

After Klyn died, I knew Mum had become spiritually curious. Grief had sent her searching for answers that I suppose medication and counselling couldn't bandaid. She had travelled to India to sit in ashram and followed the teachings of Sai Baba. I suppose how else does any mother survive the loss of a child.

Meditation and tarot soon became my anchors. Chinese medicine, acupuncture, I Ching and rune stones soon followed. Rituals that had steadied Sharon were now beginning to steady me.

It wasn't an escape; it was a reawakening, much like the teachings of Buddha which had found a foothold for many of us in Australia during that time.

Lewis was five when His Holiness, the 14th Dalai Lama, visited Sydney. Without a babysitter, I had no choice but to take him with me to hear him speak about his new book, *The Art of Happiness*. I prayed Lewis wouldn't fuss, fiddle and fidget as most kids tend to do when they don't want to be somewhere.

Afterwards, we waited outside the venue. The crowd began to stir, then suddenly quietened. His Holiness was now moving along slowly past the gathered lines of expectant faces. His saffron and maroon robes swirled gently in the wind as he appeared to float towards us.

'Lewis, wait, look, he's coming,' I whispered. My son was standing in front of me as I shielded him instinctively from the spectators. I expected His Holiness to walk past. Instead, he paused.

The Dalai Lama was now standing right in front of me.

Then, he looked down and placed a gentle hand on Lewis's head. *Oh my God, he is being blessed. This cannot be happening.*

I felt that day it was a message from the universe.

While others were still side-eyeing anything 'New Age', I deepened my work around energy and how to work with it.

Only a few months after the bank repossessed our home, Sharon reached out again. She said she wanted to get to know her grandson, so I offered for her to come and stay with us for a while. I can't recall where she was living at the time, or who with, all I knew was that she was alone.

The several white prescription bottles, each with her typewritten name and dosage on a label, sat untouched, a silent witness, on top of my refrigerator.

Sharon had ignored the doctor's advice to stay on her medication. She had convinced me she no longer needed it.

'I've never felt better in my life,' she declared, almost triumphant.

Two days later she swept through my front door, her hair now dyed a startling, fire-engine red – the colour of an emergency. It was an ominous sign.

That same day, I had stepped out to fetch something from my car, which was parked on the street. Before I reached the passenger door she lunged at me from behind. I was now face first on the grassy strip outside my home.

Sharon had taken a fistful of my hair from the back of my scalp and was yanking it back and forth so violently my vision flashed white. I tried to loosen her grip, but she kept shaking my head until, with a sickening rip, a clump of hair from my scalp finally tore free.

A neighbour had heard my screams and thankfully called an ambulance before trying to separate us. When the paramedics arrived, they inserted a large needle into her upper thigh to subdue her.

The last time I saw Sharon, she was strapped to a stretcher before the ambulance drove her away.

She tried to contact me several times but in my mind there was nothing left to salvage.

Only once had we come close to speaking again. It was in the early hours of the morning when I received a call from Algeria, I had been confused by the international calling code.

I picked it up.

On the other end, a French-speaking operator asking me to accept a reverse charge call from Sharon. I simply hung up and went back to sleep.

It was years later that I found out Sharon, at the time, had been living in Algeria in a cave with the Berbers.

Weekends and the music industry were blurring into one long, low hum. Reality had tightened its grip. Single parenting. Full-time work. Mounting expenses. I'd lost my home and my car, and child maintenance was like the weather forecast. Either unreliable or hard to predict.

After two years, my relationship with a guy I was in love with had ended. We had worked together in the music industry and now, the silence that followed was deafening.

It was the kind that makes you feel watched by your own thoughts. I felt so alone, it was as if the scaffolding that had held everything up in my life had started to dismantle.

And so had my mind. The chronic and acute bipolar disorder I suffered had gone unmedicated and undiagnosed my entire life. The bigger my problem, the worse it behaved.

I played the saddest songs I could find. 'Back for Good' was on the charts and it made the loss of my boyfriend feel more official. The lyrics knew me better than I knew myself. Some nights I just drove around the neighbourhood crying so much I couldn't see out the window properly so would have to slow down right below the speed limit.

Break-up songs filled my nights, one sad song after the other. I had CDs full of them. Eventually I became so exhausted with grief I was able to lie down in the stillness of the night and not move.

Then I struggled to stay asleep. Later I struggled to wake up.

Day after day, the cycle continued as I tried the best I could to be a mother.

There were mornings Lewis would tiptoe into my room because he knew not to make a sound unless I was out of bed.

In the absence of a father in the home, he learnt what children shouldn't have to learn so early. He ironed his school clothes. He put the chicken in the oven for dinner. He vacuumed the floors, fed the cat, and walked to the local shops for basic groceries with coins clenched in his small hand as if he were holding our little two-person household together by force of will.

Some days I didn't have the energy to even sit up or open my eyes. One morning he had to help me to the bathroom. I collapsed in a heap on the shower tiles. Lewis was so mad that day, I remember he twisted the cold tap to full blast before shouting at me. 'Mum, wake up!'

The water hit hard enough to shock breath back into me. It was brutal, and it was love, although I still didn't know then how to separate the two.

As I sat there while the shower ran, he went downstairs and made me a coffee. He'd learnt, in our house, that coffee was my medicine first thing in the morning.

He placed it beside my bed and waited.

'Mum, I need to go to school. You have to hurry,' he shouted.

It had always been my line. Now it was his.

With his uniform on, lunch made, and schoolbag packed, Lewis waited for me to walk him across the main road to the bus stop.

Every morning up until now, I could do it. Except my body was now heavy and uncooperative, as though it was staging its loudest protest yet.

I was barely eating. I lived on air, coffee, and whatever was the minimum to keep me functioning enough to get my son to school, and then to bed.

When the phone rang, I watched it ring until it gave up, as if the person on the other end might hear how ruined I was through the receiver.

Nights couldn't come fast enough. Mornings arrived like punishment.

My first real meltdown had come. There are a lot of blank stretches I don't remember clearly. I recall only fragments. I remember the shame of it the most. And I remember the people who didn't stop calling.

Mary was the one such friend who rallied when I was unable to. We had met when we were both three months pregnant. Our babies arrived two days apart in the same hospital, almost twins in timing and temperament. In the earlier years they were inseparable: birthday parties, kindergarten, sleepovers, endless playdates that made my life as a single mother purposeful.

When my world narrowed, and when heartbreak and overwhelm swallowed my capacity to be that person, Mary didn't ask for me to apologise. She simply kept showing up for *me*. She and her husband invited me to their place as if they knew I didn't need advice; I needed a table, a chair, a laugh and a good feed.

Other times she arrived with a gourmet basket or a small bunch of flowers. Mary never made a spectacle of my state. She understood something I was still learning: some things in life aren't meant to be conquered. They're meant to be endured, one small act at a time.

'You just need a little help to get you through,' she'd say. 'Nothing a decent risotto won't improve,' she'd add, half-joking, because humour was her way of bringing oxygen back into the room.

One night in her kitchen, as she poured a glass of our favourite Oyster Bay white wine, she suggested I needed more than just her weekly risotto.

'Have you ever thought about medication? I think it could

help you.'

'I don't need medication,' I said. 'I'm just going through a rough patch.'

She didn't argue. She only met my eyes.

'What about therapy?'

Mary was right. Something had to shift. I was languishing as a mother. I needed a break before I broke altogether. She suggested Lewis should have time with my parents, or his father, until I could find my footing again.

What I wanted was someone to hold me, bring me a cup of tea, and tell me I wasn't going mad.

But life doesn't always want us to be comfortable. Sometimes it sends lessons: about what is owed and what is taken, about secrets that decay in silence, about the cost of swallowing what you'd rather say, for the sake of keeping the peace.

Life teaches you where your boundaries should have been. It often draws a line in the sand, but always far too late.

The universe knew how to help me.

IF SOULS COULD STRETCH ACROSS LIFETIMES, then I was ready to remember either who I'd been, or who I was trying to become. I devoured books on politicians, Buddhism, biographies, I read the saga *The Pillars of the Earth*, and reread Shirley MacLaine's paperbacks.

I was trying to work out what resilience actually looked like, and whether reinvention was even possible after everything that had already happened.

I knew it couldn't be something familiar. It had to be remote, physically demanding, and a long way outside my comfort zone. Somewhere that would leave me with no option but to keep going.

At a mountaineering shop in Sydney, I must've looked like every woman who shows up on a Saturday afternoon, searching for an adventure.

'I'd like to go climbing. I believe you run expeditions.' I pointed to the brochures on the counter.

'Have you been on one before?' the shop assistant replied.

'No, but I used to hike in the Southern Alps in New Zealand as a girl.' (As if that somehow qualified me.)

He smiled. 'Somewhere local? Or further afield? South America? India?'

'India?' I replied.

'How does the Himalayas sound?'

It sounded pretty good to me, to be fair.

'We've got a trip to Sikkim coming up very soon. It's a province that has only recently opened up to tourists, so you'd be one of the first. You'll need a visa and a permit to enter the national park because it's a restricted area for foreigners and visas are limited.'

My mind spun, except … where on earth was Sikkim? He must have read my mind.

'It borders Bhutan, Tibet and Nepal. You'd be following in the footsteps of Buddha for six weeks. It's an advanced expedition so you need to have a high degree of fitness. I think it will change your world.'

I was all in.

'The grandson of Tenzing Norgay, Sir Edmund Hillary's Sherpa, will be leading the expedition. Why don't you come and meet him next Wednesday at a film night we're hosting?'

I not only signed up, but four days later I had booked my ticket to India.

The six weeks would be challenging and at times, lonely. At the time I didn't know what else it would take to piece myself back together.

This would be my first solo trip to what was then known as a Third World country. I'd travelled before to Asia, the United States and Europe, but I was eager for adventure. I was also keen to brush up against a famous Nepalese climbing family.

It wasn't Everest, but it was certainly close enough.

Landing in Kolkata, I now wondered what I had got myself into. I felt completely out of my depth and I was ill-prepared for the chaos I was already witnessing at the airport. Worse, I would be by myself in the city for the first two days until I headed north to meet the rest of the team.

India's scars aren't superficial. They run deep, especially after two centuries of occupation, upheaval and survival.

It is a country that had been left to claw its way back after independence. Industry had been stripped bare, the economy fractured and fragile. Entire communities had been left to exist on the brink. Then came partition – an arbitrary line that displaced ten million people and tore the country in two.

India's population had now tripled. It looked like Kolkata's infrastructure had been unable to keep pace. Poverty had spilled onto the streets.

But I didn't see a broken country. I saw fire in its belly, and defiance in the eyes of the people. My so-called wreckage seemed embarrassing and insignificant by comparison. If the Indians could rebuild in the most fierce, restless and unshakably resilient way, so could I.

Moving forward, they limped, leaped and laughed, one disorderly day at a time.

If I wanted to survive, I would need to move with them.

My taxi inched through the streets at a snail's pace, weaving between rickshaws, sacred cows and a tide of people crisscrossing the road with a baby – or two – swaddled around their bellies and backs.

There was no air conditioning, and the heat closed in like a second skin. I had to keep my window open just so I could breathe. It was suffocating in more ways than one.

Then it happened. A dark spidery hand reached through my open window. Then another. Two hands soon became three, then four. Faces appeared inches from mine as they called for rupees, water, sweets. Anything.

It was then that I realised that my closest friends would likely never cope.

Kolkata had hit me like a fever. Colourful. Chaotic. Not an atom was spared. It clung to the ghosts of the Raj with chipped paint and stubborn pride.

Even the black bicycles didn't sag under towers of cardboard.

Tuk-tuks buzzed like hornets. Diesel buses belched black soot onto the fruit sellers, the hanging laundry and temple doors. Endless webs of electricity lines sagged dangerously low. Kolkata was held together by a string and prayer; I didn't want to think about what happened once the monsoons arrived.

My blonde hair was an instant attraction. The fine hairs on my arms even more so. Curious fingers reached to touch them without hesitation and marvel at their softness, and how foreign they were to them. It was a sensory assault.

As we weaved through the streets, I couldn't turn my eyes away from the blind sitting on the burms or concrete strips that separated the oncoming traffic. The ghosted whites of their eyes alien as the traffic thundered past only inches away from their dusty feet and shoddy leather sandals.

A child with a severed limb tapped on my window. I'd been warned that some families maimed their little ones to increase the pity, and their profits.

Yet, even in all this, beauty could be seen, as composed women moved poetically and silently through the madness of the honking horns. Undeterred, they carried impossible burdens atop their heads as their fire and marigold saris flashed sparkles of gold against the grime and discarded refuse.

Their searching, unflinching stares stayed with me for a long time after. I felt myself shrink under their gaze by the truth of what I represented to them. 'White, western and privileged.'

I quickly learnt to cover up. I dressed for modesty as much as invisibility. Loose cotton. Long sleeves. A scarf for my hair. But you can only hide so much when your skin announces your heritage. In India, I wouldn't pass unnoticed.

At the Tollygunge Polo Club, or Tolly, as the locals would call it, white-gloved waiters served healthy pours of gin and tonic and English tea in silver pots on silver trays, overlooking the manicured polo field. It was fragrant with Britain's former rule and quiet entitlement.

Electricity went on and off without warning. They said I'd need to shower before the rumoured four o'clock outage, which, on the hour, threw my room into darkness. There were no apologies. This was just how it was.

I had slipped into a beautiful, crumbling dream.

Children no older than eight or nine were digging trenches in the heat, not far from the front of the hotel grounds. Grossly out of shape, old men sat idle nearby, fanning themselves in the discomfort of the humidity, simply watching, unbothered by their cruelty.

India had already begun to rearrange me, and I hadn't even left Kolkata.

At the central bus depot I learnt that not only was I the only foreigner in sight, but that all twelve of the buses, whichever one I chose to board, would leave promptly at 8:30 pm in a convoy to the same destination.

As India's national bus service – relics painted in faded blues, greens and yellows – started their engines, they wheezed and spewed thick black smoke into the air.

The noise was constant: horns blaring, drivers shouting destinations into the crowd, the clatter of metal against metal as mechanics worked under open hoods. The crowds started to surge moments before departure, families huddled by the wheels with their belongings wrapped in bed sheets, as chai wallahs darted between moving buses with last-minute trays of hot tea.

The thick, sour-sweet scent of diesel, sweat, spice and humanity clung to everything, including my fresh clothes. My blonde hair started to frizz, and like my face would soon be covered in dust and diesel residue.

There were no formal ticket counters or help desks; just a half smile from a stranger pointing vaguely *over there*, unbothered by my anxiety.

I exchanged rupees with the driver before I climbed up the stairs with my backpack slung over one shoulder, clutching my ticket in the other. I was given the best seat in the bus, *by the window*. Except there were no windows. They were missing entirely, replaced instead by old metal frames. I'm not sure which shook more, the chassis or me, as my bus, bus number three, lurched forward and the city gradually fell away behind us.

I would travel alone through the night along the Bangladeshi border without bathroom access and a bladder that was quickly learning to be very patient as we headed to Siliguri, where I would stop and refresh before pushing onward, up into the Himalayan foothills.

Our driver, like the others, would hurl our bus at speed around hairpin bends. I daren't look for fear it would be the last I'd see of my life. They seemed to have only one speed regardless of the terrain.

I would endure twelve torturous bumpy hours. Twelve hours of nodding as seemingly every male passenger grilled me about the Australian cricket team and their recent World Cup test series.

The Indian national bus service had run very much to time as a result of speeding around corners. Almost precisely twelve hours later I had arrived at my first stop. A rickshaw would collect me and take me to the home of someone's uncle, notable in the township. There I could shower, which meant standing under a small pipe that was positioned almost beneath the storey above. At least clean water flowed enough for me to wash the smell of my journey away from my skin and underwear. Their wonderful family fed me and gave me a charpai to sleep on for a few short hours. Its low teak frame was without springs, but had been cleverly crafted as a cooling and alignment system that supported a hand-stuffed cotton mattress and tired bodies like mine.

I continued my journey to Darjeeling on a second, slightly more upmarket bus with windows.

By dawn, the hot and sticky plains had given way to the cool mountain air. We continued to climb, hairpin after hairpin, weaving our way higher between the velvet green tea plantations and shanty towns that clung perilously to the hillsides. Prayer flags now flapped gently as monkeys made themselves at home on the roadside walls, staring at nothing in particular.

Darjeeling would be the final outpost before our expedition would journey onward to Mt Kunchenjunga, the world's third highest peak.

Each person would be responsible for carrying their personal items, layers for warmth and wet weather, a change of clothing, and enough water between the camp setups. We slowly climbed towards Dzongri, our acclimatisation point, as our yaks and Sherpas followed us through the rhododendron forests and cavernous valleys. At night it quickly dropped below zero, a hot shower would have to wait until the end of our trip.

Our tents would be iced stiff by morning; however, on the odd occasion we were lucky to have a draughty timber hut and indoor furnace, which needed to be carefully managed for smoke. It was in such a hut late one night, as we lay frozen in our sleeping bags with everything we owned on, we were reminded who was in charge.

A massive avalanche was hurtling down the mountain towards us.

All I could think of was Pompeii. They'd find us stiff and startled, zipped up in reds, blues, fluorescents and everything thermal and woollen.

The morning revealed bright blue sapphire skies, and half a mountainside missing.

Thankfully, I was still alive.

With a magnificent plume on one side and the reminder of

nature's indomitable power on the other, it was time to finally shampoo my dank hair and enjoy a hot coffee whilst it dried in the sub-zero sun.

The pain of lactic acid had long subsided, and as my legs, back and shoulders strengthened my heartache began to fade as we moved through Kabru, Pandim and Thansing. Step by step we covered up to eighteen kilometres a day through the shifting altitudes, to over 16,200 feet and Goecha La peak. It was, according to our Sherpas, the place where the Yeti live.

Our lead Sherpa recounted the time he had heard screeching noises. He'd never forget the Yeti, he told me. Their smell or their massive footprints. They were far too big to be human. Many of the Sherpas I spoke to were also *convinced* the Yeti existed.

The line between the myth and reality was now blurred. There was no way I was walking fifty feet to a toilet tent in the darkness. Alone. I decided to pee as close to our hut as I could that first night.

After an acclimatisation day, we set off for our final leg of Mt Kunchenjunga at 2 am. We would need to summit at latest by 8:30 am, which meant we would have to climb in darkness until the morning sun hit the mountainside.

If the Yeti appeared, I prayed I would die of a heart attack first before a seven-foot hairy creature in the Himalayan wilderness came to take me away.

By the time I finally summited, my team were celebrating with a baked cake. I had also missed the team photo. Altitude sickness had made me clumsy, emotional and out of breath. I stopped frequently with my Sherpa, although without him I never would have been able to make the final shuffle to the top.

It turned out the descent was trickier than the ascent. Eventually the mountain levelled out into a valley and a glittering seam of rose quartz appeared ahead of us. I had to blink. It looked like the Yellow Brick Road. Or at least as I'd seen it in the movies –

shimmering, and almost crystalline, under the Technicolor skies Dorothy had skipped. For a moment, I wondered if the author of *The Wizard of Oz* had known it was here all along.

The Sherpas told me were now walking in the home of the deities. It's why the mountains that surrounded us were built of lapis lazuli, turquoise, rose quartz and onyx. They said it was the centre of the universe where the sun, the moon and the stars revolve.

All I knew was that rose quartz heals the heart and mine had begun to beat to a new rhythm.

SCRIPTED DRAMAS

IT WAS MY FIRST DAY ON THE JOB.

'You're here to make me look good,' the director of drama told me.

After working in the record business, this sounded blunt, even pretentious. It turned out to be invaluable business advice. Make your boss look good, and you become indispensable when you offer to inherit all the tasks they'd rather avoid, or don't have time to do. In my case, I was able to work with those who mattered in the industry, from producers and directors, to actors and writers. They helped me learn the ropes.

We had plenty to take care of, and with a slate of productions in the pipeline we were already shaping award-winning dramas. Those that also appealed internationally.

TV drama wasn't just a job, it was a calling, from the thrill of storytelling through to post-production. Everything felt like it was second nature to me. Beyond the bright lights and rolling cameras, it was more just than a dream job; it was a rare moment when life and passion aligned effortlessly.

As an executive assistant, I was on a roster to cover the phones for all the network directors at lunchtime.

That's when *he* would call.

'Where the fuck is he?' the voice boomed through the phone.

I momentarily panicked.

Every call mattered. A lawsuit, a PR disaster, an advertiser pulling the pin; anything could shift the bottom line, and reputations, in seconds.

We were in the business of communication so we had to know where the corporate lawyer, the head of programming, and the news director were – at all times.

The voice on the end of the line was Kerry Packer, Australia's richest, most powerful man, and Channel Nine's owner. He wanted an answer. Fast. He sometimes called on two separate lines at the same time to see if we were on the ball. Then we'd find him laughing as we picked up, because he knew we'd put him on hold, only to speak to him a second time, on 'the other line'.

'Well done. Now, where the fuck is he?'

He wanted people to pick up the phone. You could send an email *after* you had a conversation; that was the rule. Time was of the essence.

At Christmas Mr Packer would throw enormous parties, one for the kids and another for the adults. Every staff member received a hamper packed with a turkey to roast, all the trimmings and a bottle of wine.

He was a man of towering generosity, and I hope he knew what it meant, especially to the single parents who were scraping by, like me.

It wasn't just the gift. It was the reminder: someone saw you and appreciated you.

He made us feel like family. We were lucky.

It was at Channel Nine that I met Martina, who worked in the international travel department a floor below. She'd organise all the trips for *60 Minutes,* current affairs and also my boss. With her I never had to worry about the itinerary or flight cancellations or delays. If she could get a crew in and out of war zone, I knew she could get my boss to Cannes at the last minute.

'Your tickets are ready whenever you are.' Martina was always chirpy.

'Can you pop up to the third floor?' I'd always ask.

The third floor was generally off-limits. It was reserved for network executives and invited guests only. Everyone knew that if someone was in the glass elevator on their way up there, it was because you were either famous, or going to be hired or fired.

It was a chance for me to check out a pair of Martina's endless selection of designer shoes and to chat about her upcoming nuptials. After which she gifted me a black pair of Giorgio Armani satin ballet flats she'd worn once to her rehearsal dinner. For a long time after, I wore their timeless appeal also on special occasions.

She was everyone's best friend, before she became one of mine.

One of the perks of working on the third floor was exclusive access to the bar immediately next to the CEO's office. Drinks flowed freely, no tab, no limits. On Wednesdays and Fridays, my nights off from parenting, I'd unwind there with a glass of bubbles. It was a wonderful indulgence for a single mum working in a world built on power and privilege.

The television industry, like the tide, doesn't stay still for long. No one teaches you how to brace for the undertow.

SINK OR SWIM

ON SYDNEY'S NORTHERN BEACHES, surf lifesaving isn't just a passing interest; it's a badge of honour. Almost everyone knows someone who wore the red and yellow cap and answered the call when the shark siren sounded. It's an Australian rite of passage, stitched into our culture as naturally as backyard cricket and sausage sizzles.

Many Australian children are raised on the sand and in the sea. Surf lifesaving has always been voluntary. It keeps the beaches safe.

I'd been convinced by a girl who could swim very well that it would be fun to join a club. When the sets rolled in, I was caught, flailing between them. I panicked and almost drowned as she dipped and dived confidently through the waves. I was shaken and breathless. All I knew was I didn't want to watch life from the shore. I also didn't want fear to control me. What sort of example would that set for Lewis?

Secretly I enrolled in swimming lessons and joined a squad at the local Olympic-sized swimming pool. When I could swim fifty laps in the pool, I signed up for the front line of volunteers at Queenscliff as a qualified surf lifesaver. Then I volunteered as a nippers' coach for the kids and following that, a surf rescue boat driver.

What no one realised was just how terrified I was of the ocean when I started. Let's not even talk about the sharks, stingers and rips.

I didn't know how to swim until I was twenty-eight-years old. In fact, I'd never been past my waist out into the ocean before. Partly because my parents couldn't swim and partly because I always had a note to sit out the summer swimming carnival at school. Villa's concrete pool was tucked away out of sight and mind in a quiet corner behind the grotto and its walnut trees. It was as cold as the icy currents flowing up from Antarctica where we'd often spot penguins waddling out of the surf.

The Pacific Ocean doesn't care how you feel, or what you look like – it tests how prepared you are physically and mentally. As a kids' coach, I realised I had a talent for building confidence, and soon my little Queensie squad started to win medals. I was lucky to have help from Tony Abbott, a future Australian prime minister, who had volunteered to help the kids swim out around the buoys on Sundays. When they 'vanished' behind the enormous waves, the kids never panicked because they knew mum or dad was there in the water to help get them through.

There was always a barbequed sausage sandwich and a Coke waiting for the brave. It was the best one-dollar incentive to get all the children back alive.

Respecting Mother Nature is one of the first lessons we should learn in life. I learnt a little later than most but she taught me how to survive.

ONCE I HAD LEARNT THE ROPES OF television drama, I wanted to make the move to film. Landing a job as a producer's associate on a feature film sounded exciting, but after almost a year of pre-production and filming, it bombed at the box office. The industry was tight, and not secure enough for a single mother to keep up with the rent.

With my tail between my legs, I had to return to freelance secretarial work to make ends meet.

My next gig was working with Australia's most formidable media personality; the kind who fielded calls from prime ministers before breakfast and spoke with such political dexterity that few could, or dared to, compete with him. He famously survived on four hours' sleep and expected the rest of us to keep pace.

If anyone asked a question, he needed to be ready to debate it immediately, with what he needed to win right at his fingertips. Politics, business, sport – he knew it all. I had to be ready for the inevitable.

'I'm looking for …'. Quickly followed by, 'Where is it? Come on. Come on. I need it NOW.' He wasn't for those who hesitate or fumble.

It was in his home office that I had met a handsome swimmer fresh from winning medals at the Olympics. I had known his name but not his face. He was about to sit for his driver's licence but in the meantime he would need a lift home.

Before long, one thing led to another, as it often does when experience and confident youth collide; however, all good things come to an end when working for powerful people who have similar interests.

'You should be ashamed of yourself for fraternising with such a young boy. He's, he's, he's … ten years younger than you! Don't bother coming to work for me again,' the voice yelled down the telephone after dinner one evening.

When my job folded, so did my short and sweet romance. I heard that the picture of that 'young boy' remained beside his bed. It was always a space reserved for winners.

As Martina often says, 'It's a jungle out there.'

WITH MY EXPERIENCE IN MEDIA and entertainment in high demand, it didn't take long to land a role promoting the Sydney Olympic Games to over a billion viewers. Australia was stepping onto the global stage in technology and I would help shape the message to stakeholders and over fifty thousand staff. For the first time ever in history, the sight, sound and data of multiple sports were guaranteed to reach their audience without a glitch.

In the lead-up, Sydney was brimming with confidence, and with only three months out, the Olympics was scrambling for those with experience in hospitality programmes.

An offer came through for a director's role to run one for thirty of the world's top CEOs for a firm headquartered in New York. The role involved curating experiences that captured the spirit of Sydney, whilst attending the best events the Games had to offer.

The money was worthwhile, it was something I was very qualified for and best of all, I'd still have enough time to dedicate to my son at the end of the day.

As the executives flew in from around the world before the opening night of the Olympics, I soon discovered that the most memorable nights are the ones that refuse to follow an itinerary.

Instead of heading directly to the Opera House, we'd taken a short detour to the Lord Nelson Brewery to fill in a little time. It didn't take long for the group to trade their performance tickets for another few pints of beer and tabletop charades and pub shenanigans. Later I heard it was their most memorable part of their Sydney experience.

Equally memorable are the parties that the hospitality houses throw. After the first Olympic event finishes, countries would fling open their doors in celebration every night for the rest of the Games.

Word had quickly spread among the athletes that the Dutch host the best party in town – simply flash your medal or your Dutch passport, they'd say. With the Games in full swing, a few of us managed to slip in with the help of a practised Dutch phrase and our accreditation to where the music was thumping and Heineken was flowing.

Later that week, at one of the official cocktail parties, I caught sight of *her*. Just over the shoulder of Prince Albert – yes, of Monaco – stood my all-time athletic hero. The Prince had mentioned, almost in passing, that he'd competed in five Winter Olympics. Who knew? I didn't.

Even with his royal revelation, I couldn't tear my eyes away from Nadia Comăneci, the legendary Romanian gymnast. How strange and wonderful it was to be standing in a room full of royalty, dignitaries and former Olympians, and, outshining them all: Nadia. Poised, iconic, and only three years older than me.

Seeing her in the flesh was as exciting as seeing the Dalai Lama. A brush with greatness is enough to keep anyone focused on their goals.

But she wasn't just a gymnast. To me, and many others, Nadia had become a symbol of grace under pressure. Her Olympic excellence had been achieved under the harshest of conditions. Nadia had been the first person in Olympic history to score *seven* perfect 10s.

Back in 1989 when I was twenty-four, navigating colic with a seven-month-old baby, Nadia had returned to the front pages of world news. She had defected from communist Romania and sought political asylum in the United States. Her timing had been fortuitous, given her close supervision with the State. It was neatly wedged between the fall of the Berlin Wall and the outbreak of the Romanian Revolution.

By Christmas Day, President Nicolae Ceaușescu and his wife would be executed.

Not only was I obsessed with Nadia, but also with the mystique of what lay behind the Iron Curtain, and the former Soviet Union. Even my Russian friends would often remark that I must have had a past life there.

Their mechanical, repetitive methods had shaped Nadia Comăneci into someone fearless. She had become consistent under pressure. Every performance was delivered with the same haunting calmness as the world sat back and watched her every move in awe.

Like many communist athletes at the time, Nadia had a gift for tuning out noise and blocking distractions. Such intensity isn't just emotional; it's tactical. With her no-nonsense resolve and laser-like drive, she achieved what others couldn't.

I had a lot to learn from that kind of energy. In seeing her I was reminded: *Be like Nadia. Dig deeper. Stand taller. Chin up. Be resilient. Be defiant. The world is watching.*

NOT ALL CHAMPIONS WEAR MEDALS

MEANWHILE, AT AUSTRALIA'S hospitality house I found myself seated at a table with the newly crowned Olympic champions of swimming, just as the band of the moment, Savage Garden, appeared on a small stage. Given you couldn't buy tickets, I was definitely flying to the moon and back.

Somewhere between their hit songs and the remainder of the Games, I became a minor celebrity. Not for anything athletic. It was thanks to my uncanny resemblance to the Olympic pole vaulter Tatiana Grigorieva. I became an inside joke.

I was suddenly ushered to the front of queues. People asked for my autograph, and for a brief moment, I had a glimpse of what fame felt like.

Tatiana had just vaulted her way into history as an Olympic silver medallist for Australia. Those 'in the know' only referred to me as if I was her.

'Tatiana, pass the salt', or 'Tatiana, where's your medal?'

I leaned into the joke with the poise of someone who'd earned her place. When the universe hands you a twin and a free pass to the party of the century, you play your cards with the utmost confidence.

Did I mean to capitalise on it? No. Did I enjoy the ride? Absolutely.

At the greatest sporting event in the world, one moment you're swept up in the roar of victory, the next you're sharing stories with strangers next to you. This was especially so on the last day.

The stadium was packed, the air electric, as we waited for the closing ceremony to begin.

It couldn't. Not yet. Not until he had crossed the white horizontal line and the officials standing in front of the stand full of VVIPs.

He had been working full-time in the local hardware store and had trained without the luxuries and the spotlight of major sponsorships. Yet suddenly, here he was about to be met with a hero's welcome.

Out of the shadows and into the Olympic Stadium came Elias Rodriguez of Micronesia, running the final four hundred metres of his marathon. Alongside me, one hundred thousand people rose to their feet in a wave of thunderous applause as we cheered him on.

Elias Rodriguez wasn't just finishing a marathon. He was arriving with exhaustion and a heart and mind full of sheer determination.

He was finishing what he had started.

And with that, no sooner had it begun than the Olympics Games had finished. The biggest show on earth packed up and left town. It had been a magnificent chance to be part of something extraordinary; a reminder that discipline, commitment and perseverance aren't just the domain of athletes, but of anyone brave enough to keep showing up.

For those few shining weeks we were all on the same team, bound by effort, wonder and the quiet joy of belonging to something greater than ourselves.

People like Elias are among us every day. Not all champions wear medals. In fact, most may never know what it's like to stand on a podium. They are the ones who save lives, inspire or live in servitude to others. They show up and do the hard things, quietly, consistently and with belief. The values they live by echo louder than any anthem. They are those that also inspire me with their integrity, perseverance and humility.

Raising a child alone isn't easy.

There was the time my baby nearly lost his finger in the electric window of my car as he waved goodbye to his nana. I hadn't realised his little nine-month-old fingers were on the *outside* of the window as I pushed the button for up. A quick visit to the emergency department and a few stitches later, all ten of his digits were still attached.

I had read books on raising boys and motherhood, but it all seemed so prescriptive. A mother's job is to keep them alive and hopefully hand down some valuable life skills.

So when he was eight, I taught him how to iron his school shirts. I didn't want him thinking housework was only for women.

'A man should know how to iron,' I'd say. 'Maybe you can make money from it one day.'

My clothes would, upon request, be returned beautifully pressed. Little did he know he was learning how to keep his future partner happy with a small favour.

Lewis took pride in his appearance from the moment he could dress himself. He noticed how clothes worked together, how fabric sat against the skin, how a good pair of polished shoes mattered. He noticed these things long before it became his profession, years later, as a New York atelier.

Some people read this attentiveness as a sign of 'being gay'. I saw something else entirely. To me he was a conscientious young man learning how to stand in the world. What mattered was not how he dressed, but how he treated people. Lewis was instinctively kind. He gravitated towards those others overlooked: the sick, the sidelined, the homeless, and even those carrying a visible difference.

Charity should be a habit, so if we saw the man from the Salvation Army, who stood strategically outside the coffee shop, at the top of the street, we would always donate.

'If we can afford a coffee, we can afford to give. One day it will come back tenfold,' I would remind him.

He spent so much time running into the supermarket to get our groceries that he soon took a keen interest in cooking – probably because my basic repertoire of risottos, spinach pies and cheese boards weren't enough to feed a growing boy.

'Don't forget to take the chook out of the freezer when you get home. We're having lemon up the bum tonight,' I'd hastily mouth to him through the window of the bus just before it pulled away and sped down the main road to school.

He'd nod and quickly look away, embarrassed his mother was still giving him orders right up until the last moment.

Roast chicken, stuffed with lemon, garlic and herbs, was easy to prepare and something you could slide into the oven and forget about, comforting to come home to.

Later, he would recall in a flash of panic the instant he heard the gate open, his eyes widening as he leapt from bed and thundered down the stairs two at a time, yanking the chicken from the freezer and straight onto the bench where it should have been thawing.

A frozen chook wasn't worth getting upset about. It just meant we'd have to change plans. There was always a ten-dollar steak at the pub.

I rationed his screen time. He was only allowed to watch the six o'clock news, comedy shows, documentaries and sport. That loosely translated to *Seinfeld*, and *Family Guy*, which soon shaped his sense of humour. We often went to the cinema and, as soon as I could, performances at the Opera House and rock concerts.

'Read a book. You may learn something. Don't you have one for homework?'

What I had missed entirely was his dyslexia. He struggled to write what I dictated to him. Lewis had been masking far more than I had ever realised.

It was during a casual conversation with a hard-edged politician I worked with, one with a very sharp eye for what mattered, that it was suggested I have Lewis assessed. This man was not known for his sentimentality. Despite his reputation as a powerbroker, he had an unshakable belief in education. He offered to cover Lewis's assessment and a year's tutoring. This politician may never have won public favour, but for me he was an unlikely godsend at the most critical time in my son's schooling. Not everyone has the benefit of knowing 'the right people' with no strings attached. For many, I understand an offer like this could arrive cloaked in suspicion and unwanted expectations.

I have always had a thing for manners and speaking correctly. I'm not sure whether it was because of my mother, the church, or a need to be thought of as educated. Swearing was strictly banned.

'People who swear don't know how to speak English,' I'd say. 'When you learn to speak English properly, you can do what you like.'

Then I'd have to keep him busy: cricket, oboe lessons, rugby league and rugby union. Later, it seemed natural to add boxing lessons (with adult fighters), basketball and swimming. As soon as it was legal, I added a parachute jump. Life was one big leap after all.

I was going to toughen my boy up so he could survive anything.

'Run, Lewis, run, hurry up!' I'd scream for fear he'd end up with concussion in a football match.

A kind and elderly gent once said to me on the sidelines of a game, 'He runs like the wind.' He did indeed.

Parenting is hard. Between the highs and the lows of my moods, there were plenty of things in my son's life I was at risk of getting wrong.

'Remember, Mum, that time you almost killed me?' he'd remind me at dinner parties. Guests would be mortified. This was a story they had to hear.

'You're still alive, so it's all good,' I'd laugh before excusing myself from the conversation.

Okay, there may have been a peritonitis incident and a few hours in surgery, and then intensive care. Then meningitis. A 'Two Days from Death' story that resulted in an urgent spinal tap and solitary (medical) confinement in Dubai.

To be fair, I wasn't a doctor and my son wasn't one to complain.

'Go to bed and take a Panadol. You'll be right by the morning.'

I was handy with first aid if he was bitten by a spider, snake, or shark. I also had an impressive collection of herbal teas, an excellent acupuncturist together with a robust knowledge of Chinese medicine.

Then there was the chakra chart on the fridge with what we should eat when we felt ill. It was all colour coded and simple to understand. Who needed a doctor, unless your eye was almost hanging out. (Which also almost happened as my little Superman dived into bed one night and struck the corner of the frame instead. Again, it was nothing a few stitches and a bag of peas didn't fix.)

Private school was the biggest financial leap. I had no idea how I was going to pay for his high school education, the one he had been on the list to attend since birth.

THE FEELING OF FINANCIAL PRESSURE and raising a child alone can be overwhelming. I sometimes felt so out of control, I did the only thing I knew how to do well, which was to fix my immediate environment first. This usually happened at two or three in the morning, after a long night out.

I would eventually tire, but not before I'd slide my mirrored wardrobe door open, only to be visually assaulted by a chorus of ghastly wire hangers – the ones that drycleaners use that leave dents in your clothes. The ones that screech like fingernails on a chalkboard when you're filing through clothes to find that pair of trousers but then they have left a horizontal crease on the knee so now you can't wear them anyway, at least not if you are in a hurry to get out the door.

Those hangers would have to be removed before I slept. I made a mental note to buy matching wooden ones.

Then I'd wonder why I owned so many black dresses and 'not enough' shoes, even though forty or fifty pairs would be jumbled up at the bottom of the closet because I'd just throw them in and quickly shut the door.

'Mum, why are you fixing the blinds in the middle of the night?'

'Oh, sorry, did I wake you?'

'I could hear you playing music and banging the cupboards, so yeah.' Someone was grumpy, and not in the mood for school again.

'I was just tidying up. Oh, and remind me not to buy any more cinnamon or nutmeg next time we go to Woolies. We have enough to last us until the end of our days.'

St Joseph's College would offer what I believed young men needed: structure, tradition and firm male discipline. It was my way of giving him the best shot I could, away from my highs, lows and dubious choices.

The first day of a new school was exciting for us both. It meant we'd both be turning a new page. It carried a two-hundred-year-old history and a healthy dose of prestige. Lewis would start as a day boy so he could still spend nights at home with me.

At Joey's, a statue of the Virgin Mary sat at the top of the main building. It was conveniently above the headmaster's office. She'd been watching over the boys from her lofty height for quite some time.

Lightning had once decapitated the Virgin Mary as it struck her clean through the neck. We heard that her head, as it fell to the ground, narrowly missed a boy standing beneath her. He must have had the shock of his life. We laughed as we wondered if it was God's way of saying that any boy who ignored their mother would risk the full force of her wrath from above.

On school nights, once Lewis was in bed, I'd fire up my IBM computer, the one the size of a washing machine. The internet had opened up a whole new world for those of us stuck at home alone as it was rolled out into homes.

Everything I needed to know, but was too afraid to ask, would now be at my fingertips. Astrology programmes. Dating sites. Personality profiles and university courses I'd start with a bang, then never finish.

Online, however, I was a diagnosis waiting to happen.

According to tick-and-flick assessments, I seemed to exhibit 'out of the box' behaviour. I was definitely 'on the spectrum'. Another online site suggested I had a mood disorder. I should immediately seek help. A third hinted at 'bipolar tendencies'.

That's how I found myself enrolled in a pilot programme at a major research hospital. Two professors, a team of psychologists, an MRI and a series of tests, mood charts and talks.

Systems preferred categories, particularly if they aligned with government initiatives and funding. Labels led to trials, which led to data, which led to medical breakthroughs.

I didn't want to be a medical statistic, but I became one. I don't know how, but I was again oscillating between depression and a brain fog. It was so dense I could barely function at work. According to doctors, the drugs would eventually do their work and stabilise me. It was trial and error with pharmacology, unfortunately.

How did it start? I think it began with a midnight questionnaire.

Tick here if you struggle to sleep.

Tick here if you feel 'up' or 'down'.

Tick here if people say you're too much.

If you go looking for what's wrong with you, the world will happily hand you a name for it. Otherwise there is always Ctrl+Alt+Delete.

MAGIC AND MAYHEM IN NEW YORK

NOT EVERYONE WOULD GIVE UP A first-class ticket to travel economy with a friend across the globe, but Martina isn't everyone.

Effortlessly effervescent, she always knows exactly where to go and makes everything seem fabulous. Martina knows what we need before we know we need it. She is a travel designer par excellence.

'What are you doing for Christmas?' she asked, already halfway to convincing me. 'Let's go see Susu in New York. My treat! You'll love her; everyone loves her.' Martina's excitability said it all.

If ever there was a woman who embodied the fierce ambition that the city was built on, it was Susu. She *was* New York, even though she had grown up in a leafy enclave in Westchester County – the one that started as a Quaker settlement and ended up best known as the place where Bill and Hillary Clinton lived.

Her long, straight and glossy dark hair was blow-dried in a way that suggested it was permanently like that. She was the type of girl who wore pearl studs long before she could afford the huge diamond versions she now owned. In her autumnal quilted vest and riding boots, Susu looked like she was better suited to walking a perfectly groomed pooch around Central Park than running a multi-million-dollar company. She wouldn't tell you who she knew, or how she knew them, although we all knew she knew everyone. She would only tell you who she wouldn't talk to. She also quietly paid the bills for those she loved at the best tables in town.

As a Taurus, she had mastered measured decisions. She was

the sort of woman who purchased Chanel jackets without blinking and a house in the Hamptons because it made more sense than renting a place for another season.

I'd never met anyone with a fridge full of Verve and nothing else. Her cashmere sweaters lived in the microwave, the chunkier ones in the dishwasher. That's what happens when space costs more than sense.

Like many New Yorkers, Susu could be formidable. Martina had convinced me that spending a couple of weeks during festive season in Susu's one-bedroom Upper East Side apartment was a great idea. All we needed was a bed and a shower.

It was game on.

'I'll pick you up from your mum and dad's, we'll fly out of Brisbane direct to LA with a two-hour layover, and another five to New York.' Martina didn't waste time.

What's thirty hours to an Aussie? It would basically be brunch with a touch of turbulence over the Pacific.

Mum was in the kitchen, with the scones already in the oven, when she spied through the blinds the unmissable arrival of a Rolls-Royce in their cul-de-sac.

It glided to a halt outside my parents' townhouse like it had taken a wrong turn from the Queen's palace.

Mum panicked. The cream hadn't been whipped. The scones weren't ready and the table wasn't set.

'Peter! Peter! Kirsty! Martina's here!' Mum called up the stairs, her voice jumping a few octaves higher.

Martina was already at the screen door.

'Where does my dad park the roller?' She pointed across the road to a visitor's spot. 'Is that spot legal?'

Even Dad had come racing down the stairs with the energy of a man meeting royalty.

Mum was still trying to plate scones when Martina swept in

with her endless laughter and hugs for everyone. Her ever-quirky British father wasn't far behind, quickly finding common ground with easy banter and a shared sense of amusement.

Martina was about to find out that the most memorable stories aren't in first class.

'63D and 63E, that's us!' She'd never been this far back before. So far back, it was the relatively private back row. As if it were a makeshift sky lounge, our seats were perfectly positioned, right next to the galley for easy champagne access.

'I need the aisle. You're small, you take the middle. The armrest lifts up. We'll be fine.' Martina was cheerfully making the best of an unfamiliar situation. I swear she's the world's happiest person.

I can be mistaken. Martina couldn't push the call button fast enough.

Her eyes had widened in horror.

'Oh my God, oh my God, oh my God, I cannot deal with this,' she hissed, waving her credit card in the air like a distress signal. 'I'm upgrading. Whatever it costs, just get me out of here!'

Across the aisle, a young boy's stomach had suddenly surrendered. The cabin air was now filled with the sour stench of half-digested airline food. Martina started to gag as she fanned her face in disbelief. I pulled the blanket over my nose and fixed my mortification instead on the passenger immediately next to me.

The flight attendants appeared faster than normal. As one leaned in to hear Martina's pleas, her eyebrows furrowed in concentration upon seeing a black credit card, another offered consolation, knowing there was no escaping the situation on each side of the aisle.

'I'm so sorry, ladies. There is not one spare seat on the flight I can offer you. Today's flight is completely overbooked.' She paused. 'But … would you accept a complimentary bottle of champagne instead?'

Problem solved. We still had 29 hours to go. This could work.

We'd already made a decent dent in the cheeky bottle of Bollinger we'd picked up duty-free and carried on board.

With movies queued and the worst of the chaos behind us, we sank into our seats with the kind of relief only an endless supply of bubbles can bring. Beside us: a honeymooning couple on their maiden voyage to New York.

Somewhere over the Pacific Ocean, we became their unofficial in-flight travel agents. By the time we touched down for a short layover in Los Angeles, they weren't ready to let us go.

'Can we sit next to you on the next flight too?' they asked, sweet and hopeful.

'Of course,' we said. 'Who else is going to warn you about Times Square?'

Just before we disembarked, Martina turned to them, all heart and impulse. 'Don't take a cab, we've got a friend picking us up. She can drive you!'

At JFK, still slightly tipsy and riding the high of new-friendship energy, we found Susu waiting at Arrivals. She was not only blindsided, but far from amused to find two smiling strangers trailing behind us like ducklings with their luggage.

'What. The. Fucking. *Fuck?*' she muttered through gritted teeth. Her face said it all: rush hour. Friday night. Dinner reservations. Two glowing honeymooners. And us.

Nevertheless, we dropped our starry-eyed friends at their hotel with our heartfelt goodbyes, fully aware we'd never see them again. Then it was straight to Midtown, where the steaks were medium-rare and the martinis dirty. Smith & Wollensky felt like the only proper way to say: Welcome to New York.

By morning, the snow was falling. It was New Year's Eve. We had purposely packed light.

'Don't forget your passports!' Susu shouted from the other room.

'They give extra discounts for tourists and Saks and Bloomingdale's have the best off-the-rack cocktail dresses in the city!'

First we hit Bergdorf's, Norma Kamali, and a few of those hush-hush fashion insider spots. Our real mission would be to find a bargain or two. We gathered armfuls of everything on sale like women possessed. A silk dress or two, a Belstaff black leather jacket, fragrance, more jeans, white T-shirts, heels and sneakers, lipsticks, earrings, a sports watch and even a wig (because why not?). It was fast. It was fierce. It was fabulous.

At the end of the trading day they practically had to close the doors on us. With bags in hand, we dodged the sleet before entering into a fierce cab war with two businessmen on Fifth Avenue. It was ladies with bags before gentlemen with little care and even fewer manners.

With a tangle of bags, we finally made it home. Did I really need the champagne-gold silk chemise-styled evening dress? No. But there it was. I thought it looked amazing. I would find an occasion to wear it.

Naturally, it was time for bubbles.

Martina and Susu's friend Cressida would join us fresh off a flight from London. Her childhood home was closer to a castle than a house, and her family tree included more than one titled relative. They were all cut from different cloth, yet we were all the same. We were there to have fun.

That night, it was impossible not to notice how quickly Americans turned their heads at the sound of a crisp British accent. Any hint of aristocracy sets New York alight and Cressida was perfectly aware of it.

At our party destination, we arrived to find a long queue as doormen scanned everyone's credentials. We could have been there for almost an hour at the rate they were going.

'I didn't come to New York today to wait at the end of the line,' our friend purred, as she held up her credit card, pointing to her title with a smile.

There would be a catch. There always was.

'We all need to kiss a stranger before we leave tonight. That's the deal for getting you in from the cold, no exceptions.' Cressida quickly led by example at the bar with a wink and a smile.

As we danced and talked to anyone who'd listen, the hours quickly blurred until almost closing. We needed to make a move if we wanted to avoid another fight for the first cab home. Susu had already stepped into the middle of the road, arms and legs outstretched. Cars started to brake, horns blared, and somehow she found an empty yellow taxi. We piled in, with sore feet, wild hair and the usual missing bits and pieces of a good night out.

'Who did you kiss?' our aristocratic friend asked.

'No one,' I said, as I tried to clamber my way into the cab.

I didn't expect such a collective gasp. 'Sorry, but you can't get in the car. Go back in there. Now!' they all yelled. The taxi would have to wait.

Martina told me to just find the hottest guy nearest the door. Anyone who was lurking in a dark corner would do.

'Don't overthink it. You have five minutes. Go. Go. Go.'

Sure enough, just inside the entrance, perched against the bar, there he was. His dark tousled hair fell just right, his jawline sharp enough to cut through any hesitation he may have had as I approached him. He was the same boring guy I had spoken to earlier.

I had noticed his perfect white American teeth and his smile that hinted at a late night, and a silent promise of more. Now I wondered if his kiss would be as good as he looked in the dark.

It wasn't. It was probably why he was standing there by himself on New Year's Eve.

I know I am not the only woman to realise that questionable late-night decisions belong firmly in the past. With the girls waiting I was back out the door in world record time.

'Okay, done, let's go!' We laughed all the way back home that night.

It was an early winter Wednesday in Sydney in 2001. I'd seen a recruitment ad for the Army Reserve Commando Unit. Naturally I had thought I should try something new. Spending one weekend a month running around the bush in camouflage like GI Jane certainly had its appeal.

That's where I met Tom. Tall, self-assured and physically imposing. He didn't need to raise his voice to be heard because he was in command.

I'm not sure how information night turned into coffee. It might have been under the guise of helping with my paper submission to the regiment. That then led to lunch, then a fancy dinner in town, and finally, the next strategic step. Dinner at his place suggested he was ready for combat between the sheets.

At that time, like Sharon, I had been a sucker for a military uniform: the order, the certainty, the fantasy that someone could take control of my life before it spiralled out of control.

Tom's typical army bungalow wasn't quite the post-war brick and weatherboard practicality I could see myself in. All the houses in his cul-de-sac were for the transitory nature of their occupants. Each had a low clipped hedge, a neatly mown lawn, and a front porch just big enough for a couple of folding chairs, the ones that fade in the relentless Sydney sun after being left out too long.

He greeted me warmly at the door and led me towards the kitchen, where dinner was still in progress. He poured a glass of wine from an open bottle and handed it to me with a smile before turning back to the stove. I drifted into the lounge, close enough to watch him move through the ritual of cooking, our conversation flowing easily across the space between us.

Everything inside Tom's government-issued home was as clean and sensible as the outside, as you'd expect from military personnel. As I casually scanned the room, my eyes were drawn to a framed photo sitting in a prominent position next to the television.

'Is this your sister? The lady with you in the photo?' I yelled out to him in the kitchen.

'No, it's my wife,' he answered casually as he poked his head around the corner and smiled.

I hadn't signed up for secrets. What the fuck was this guy up to?

'We're unhappy. The situation isn't easy.' Of course. It never is. Women who discover their little lullaby of lies know that it is only a prelude to more well-worn excuses.

I left before dessert as any girl worth her salt would.

The problem is, there is a particular charm to people like him. They're trained to be invisible, to slip behind enemy lines without a trace, to study every detail and wait for exactly the right moment to act.

For men like him, picking up women must feel like child's play. It would be less of a conquest, and more of an inevitability.

Tom stood at six foot three. He had the kind of athletic frame that turned heads without trying because he just looked so incredibly fit in jeans and a fitted T-shirt. You could see his body had been shaped by years of military precision and outdoor grit rather than any vanity-fuelled gym routine. He was a man's man. His dark auburn hair framed a face that one may describe as kind with a ready smile. His warm brown eyes had a way of softening a room. In social settings he laughed easily and often. Naturally, people fell for his ease, his attentiveness, his affability. For me, Tom appeared more genuine than most men I'd met in professional environments.

When I had a free morning he'd ask me to join him for a workout at the gym on the commando base. There was something magnetic in his restraint and discipline; soon it was apparent there was an undeniable sexual tension between us.

Deep down, I saw him as a kind of saviour, a man who could shield me from the unwanted, from those whose attention I never sought. Tom made sure they stayed away. The men who lingered too long, who muttered something suggestive in passing, learnt quickly not to do it twice.

Six weeks after we met, he followed through on what he'd said he would do: he left his wife and moved into a single waterfront room at the naval barracks. Before long I began introducing him to my friends. They liked him. It was hard not to be impressed by an Australian SAS operative. They were known as the best of the best.

Tom was trained to vanish into a crowd or strike without hesitation. A sniper, a trauma medic, a tactician. That winter, I fell in love.

It was late one spring evening when I watched the black smoke furl through a gap in the building and furiously up and out over the New York skyline. I had turned on the television to watch the news.

At first, I thought I was watching the end of a late-night rerun of *The Towering Inferno* as the first plane sliced through. Then the red ticker burned across the bottom of the screen. BREAKING NEWS: WORLD AT WAR.

This wasn't a movie, it was 9/11.

With the World Trade Towers on fire, I, like many others, was glued to the screen in disbelief, as I watched the skyscrapers' unfathomable, near-freefall collapse. From the safety of my Australian home I sat frozen in rising fear. I'd watch everything unfold from the other side of the globe: late-night news flashes, repeat video footage and anchors lost for words mid-sentence.

By midday, the world was mirroring America's shock. Grief started to turn into suspicion, and soon after, into terrorism concerns. Bound to the Commonwealth, Australia quickly pledged its loyalty to America before the fires were even out. Military orders quickly came down the line. And while the world watched repeats of what would change the course of history yet again, the man I now loved was already preparing to secure our country. Tom had been called up to become an integral part of Australia's new counter-terrorism force.

Shortly after, we moved in together, but our plans gave way to security briefings, rapid deployments and whispered code words in the middle of the night. Having a real-life James Bond living under my roof might have sounded thrilling, but the reality was far more complex. He wasn't Lewis's father, nor was he responsible for him. The dynamic between Tom and Lewis never quite clicked. Tom made an effort; Lewis didn't.

But with Lewis now in a private boarding school, I was bearing the brunt of his expenses, which weren't cheap. Tom had suggested his military wage was enough to cover the rent, but not much more. He encouraged me to work harder, as my sales commission wasn't capped and I was the majority breadwinner.

I couldn't see the financial manipulation at the time, because he was contributing in other ways. Not that teaching my son how to clean-shave military style and polish his school shoes until they gleamed equalled our grocery spend or monthly utility bills.

Then there was the afternoon he took my son to the Killing House. A rare opportunity for Lewis to experience a special forces soldier doing what he purportedly did best. Tom apparently moved with unnerving calm through the purpose-built facility designed to simulate real-life hostage takeout scenarios.

Lewis trailed behind, shifting with caution through its dim-lit interior, watching for life-sized dummy targets that would suddenly spring from the walls. It forced a split-second decision on whether to shoot the enemy or hold fire.

Together Tom and Lewis tested their precision and reflexes in a close-quarter combat situation. Tom would show him how to effectively 'neutralise' the dummy insurgents. From his holster, he could pull a handgun which he had loaded with only five bullets. Lewis carried a far more lethal weapon, a military issue AK-47.

When they got home from their day out, it sounded both strangely comforting and utterly terrifying to hear about Tom's prowess. I knew his job required control and cool detachment, but that day marked a small turning point. Whatever image Lewis had held of Tom was quietly dismantled that afternoon. It was replaced with something far more sobering and impressive: his demonstrated military authority.

Weekends together would soon turn into survival courses as we abseiled down cliffs above a raging ocean, tethered by ropes tied to a nearby tree. Three-day treks through national parks and any other activities that kept our adrenaline pumping were Tom's idea of relaxation. He loved a calculated risk. I later realised his control was disguised as care when I witnessed his temper behind the wheel in a terrifying drive through Sydney's harbour tunnel one afternoon.

He was teaching me to become acutely aware of every situation, even if I didn't know what to expect.

'Go outside at 21:00 hours. Look northwest, just past the tower with the blue, green, and yellow lights.'

A Black Hawk, at exactly the designated time, past the lights, would skim deftly above the city skyline as the rest of the rooftops lay in darkness. Suddenly it was overhead, it was so low its sound reverberated throughout my entire body with its ominous *thump-thump-thump*. Tom's training drills felt like war had already arrived on my doorstep.

I watched as the shadowy figures rappelled down one by one, swiftly, silently and with precision. As quickly as it had happened, everything quickly vanished into the night.

Tom understood the mechanics of stealth and how to bend time and silence to his will. He carried two passports, each with a different name. And in the not-too-distant future, he would change his name again.

Intuitively I knew he was hiding something. The signs were there. I just couldn't put my finger on exactly what. I put it down to elite operations that were there to keep us safe.

Later we would discover Tom had been selected by a panel to join the regiment from thousands of applicants to the SAS. On that panel sat Sharon's first husband. As a founding member of the Australian Special Forces unit, they would speak about what defined the mindset of a covert operator.

Survival ran in their blood. Those in the SAS are never built to blend in. What he didn't know was, like Sharon, who had lived in the jungle of Papua New Guinea when she was wild, radiant and entirely herself, I was also an outlier by design. It was obvious we like men with a taste for danger and no room for vulnerability.

Within three years our relationship had started to fracture. Tom said I needed help, because I was 'the problem'. We tried couples therapy but what should have been a path to understanding and commitment soon unravelled a once dedicated relationship. I continued therapy alone.

I had started to spiral into a dangerous depression. Treatment, without real expertise, can cut deeper than the wound itself. As a couple, a sniper and a woman with bipolar, our therapist realised she was out of her depth. She suggested I seek a second opinion with a view to a more intensive programme.

The psychiatrist agreed. He supported an urgent placement into a rehabilitation facility. Then the Marist Brothers discreetly stepped in, and offered to board my son, at no extra cost, for the rest of the school term.

'A six-week stay would be good for us,' Tom encouraged. 'You need to take responsibility for yourself and acknowledge the ways you challenge others.'

What he meant was South Pacific would be necessary if we were going to have any sort of future together.

EXPECT A MIRACLE

IT **WAS THE MOST PERFECT DAY THAT** Saturday when we drove alongside the coast, the road hugging the surf of a Northern Beaches paradise in Sydney.

My window was down because I wanted to feel the warmth of the sun on my skin and the salty breeze as it whipped through my hair and across my face. I felt good. So much so, I didn't have a reason to go there anymore.

Ronan Keating's 'Life is a Rollercoaster' was turned up inside the car, although its infectious, sing-along optimism was strangely at odds with the truth of Tom's eyes, hidden behind his designer sunglasses as he tapped the steering wheel in rhythm with the music.

As we pulled into the car park of South Pacific Hospital, I suddenly became overwhelmed. I didn't want to go. I didn't *need* to go. I became anxious. *He's trying to get rid of me,* I thought.

Without ceremony he flicked the boot open, lifted out my luggage and with it, firmly held my hand as he walked me up the front steps of the facility. My feet started to stumble beneath me. Tom held his grip. I pulled back. He pulled me forward. I was unable to tear myself away from his powerful grip as he unceremoniously dragged me inside, almost backwards.

I looked upwards, as if the heavens would save me. I was grasping for a miracle. For me, it felt like this was the end.

Then, as if the universe had overheard my quiet desperation, a wooden sign above the door caught my eye. It was one patients would usually see after they had completed their journey here and started to head back out into the world.

Expect a Miracle.

Standing there to greet me was Lisa. I was stunned. She was the woman who had comforted me when I fled my marital home, clutching proof of my husband's betrayal. What was *she* doing here in a place like this?

Online, when I'd been more excited about the prospect of a 'rest', I'd requested a private room. For the price, I was expecting an oceanfront suite, floor-to-ceiling windows, a wraparound balcony, crisp white linen, plush towels and designer toiletries.

Instead, I was shown a far more basic room at the top of the stairs. It wasn't exactly the Four Seasons.

A staff member arrived shortly after with my luggage, which she asked me to unzip.

I hesitated.

'I'm quite private.' Like those moments at the airport security when they ask you if this is your bag, and you shrink at the thought of people rifling through your things.

'Would you mind sitting back? I'll unpack for you,' she replied, in a measured tone that suggested this was a non-negotiable.

She went through my belongings, placing each item into a different pile. My apprehension started to grow. What was she looking for? I was hardly sneaking in illegal drugs or a bottle of grog for some after-hours downtime.

'Sorry, but we can't let you have this, or this … or this. We'll keep it for you until you check out.'

Perfume, magazines, music: all confiscated. How was I supposed to get through the next six weeks without the very things that made my life at least bearable?

I had closely followed their packing list, adding some things

I thought they had missed. Things you'd normally pack for more than a night or two away.

Everything addictive was off limits. Which included a bottle of Chanel fragrance. Little did I know some patients would attempt to *drink* it.

Here there would be no fluffy robes, no poolside cocktails, no cable television and no en suite bathroom.

Those who checked into South Pacific were there for one reason: to recover from their diagnosed psychologically disruptive patterning.

I was assigned a roommate, a young mother battling against raging alcoholism. She was blonde, beautiful, thirty-something, and shaking violently. Her body twisted and jerked in protest, resisting the grip of both the nurse and withdrawal. A sheen of sweat coated her trembling skin; she was caught somewhere between a feverish heat and bone-chilling shivers.

The contrast was not only jarring, it was concerning: poised one moment, collapsed and hollow-eyed the next. In another life, she might have been my friend, someone who would come with me to the races, someone I'd laugh with over champagne as we placed a flutter on the horses.

Unable to register the fact I was sitting just three feet away, her eyes flicked restlessly around the room, wide with panic.

Then the nausea appeared to hit. She'd gasp for air before clutching the edge of her bed, her knuckles whitening, as she tried to anchor herself. When her moans grew louder the nurses would arrive, ready for her resistance just before they drove an injection into her gluteal muscle, below her hip. It calmed the chaos for a while.

Nights were the worst, with her endless twists and turns, low cries for help and the sound of her desperation thickening. I saw so much of my struggle in her. The battle to hold on to what we knew, even through searing pain and suffering.

This was supposed to be my sanctuary; something medical insurance and I paid handsomely for. It rattled me to have someone like this in my room.

After they thought my depression had stabilised, they moved me into a bigger, brighter room. One with more women. Among the laughter and chatter and occasional storm of drama, I heard some had been admitted multiple times, moving from one addiction to another. Personalities collided, before they comforted and then clung to one another. It was messy and it was alive.

Despite our differences, a quiet camaraderie soon formed. Between group therapy sessions and whispered late-night confessions, I saw that I was no longer alone in my struggle. We were all trying to piece ourselves together, one day at a time. I came to understand that everyone carries their own psychological storm; some are just better at hiding it.

I also felt ashamed. Not just of who I'd become, but of how the world would perceive me because I ended up in a rehab. *She has mental health issues.* That phrase alone can do insurmountable damage to someone who is struggling with life.

Mental health was something that few talked about, even at the turn of the twenty-first century. Confessing my darkest moments to complete strangers, those with clipboards under flickering fluorescent lights, would be far more mortifying than cathartic. I'd always been secretive about the parts of myself I was still trying to understand. Like many with depression, we protect what feels raw, a web far too complex for another to understand.

Rehab didn't feel like care at the time. It felt like forced containment.

I knew where the real danger lay. It wasn't with me.

Nevertheless, I was expected to wear my 'diagnosis label' like a name tag. It would briefly sum up the mess within me.

I was labelled a love and sex addict with depression, which I had to add to *Today I'm feeling lonely and abandoned,* or *Today I'm feeling happy, excited and curious.* I would need to repeat it multiple times a day at every group meeting. It was a strange badge of honour to wear.

I thought the adjectives we all chose always sounded a bit basic. To be fair, this wasn't the place to flex your vocabulary. No one was going to give you a gold star for emotional eloquence.

Group hugs were a thing. Initially, I recoiled at the idea. I couldn't stand the thought of being touched by people I didn't know, so I remained seated at the end of each morning session as I watched strangers rush from one embrace to the next.

In the end, those hugs became what I cherished most. They were a quiet reminder that I was seen, supported and loved. It taught me we shouldn't be afraid to ask for hugs, in fact we should give them out readily. We all need eight a day to feel worthwhile.

As patients, we would gather for our designated group sessions. More intensive personalised therapy with psychologists and psychiatrists followed.

In the afternoons, we would be inspired by a guest speaker; those who had come out the other side, alive and more introspective about life. Alcoholics, depressives, drug addicts, gamblers, workaholics and those with eating disorders.

Instead of the confiscated glossy fashion magazines I thought I couldn't do without, I was encouraged instead to purchase self-help literature from reception. Books on co-dependency, trauma, recovery and emotional healing.

I only bought one: Melody Beattie's *The Language of Letting Go.* The daily meditation guide centred on healthy detachment, self-care and emotional boundaries. It would become my handbook for many years to come. I've bought it several times over, as I would always try to pass it on to those in need.

My favourite part of our rehab day was our after-lunch walk along the beach. We could swim at the pool directly across the road, or head along the sand as the surf lapped our toes. It was designed as a download; time to spend quietly reflecting while we walked or watched the sea.

To run along the beach or swim in the ocean was strictly off limits. Soon the swimming pool was added to the list of what not to do. I heard it was because my former roomie swam sixty laps or more of freestyle with such force and urgency that it was deemed too addictive. And addictions were a bandaid for what was at the heart of any problem.

Naturally, once I was at the beach and as soon as I was out of the sight of our carers, I ran. My feet sank into the sand as I chased the surf, rolling and crashing onto the shore. On occasion the sky cracked open with a fierce electrical storm, so I took it as an excuse to run even faster and further. I'd also take a sneaky dip when the rain and wind was at its most furious, because how would they know? It felt exhilarating to be soaked to the bone.

On Sunday afternoons we could receive visitors. We needed to place their names on a list. I tried to ask Tom to come, but the clinicians told me that he wouldn't be one of them. He never picked up my calls anyway.

I wish I'd told Mum and Dad how much it meant to me that they had driven all the way down from Queensland. It was a twelve-hour trip each way. They only sat with me for two. I could see the sadness and concern in their eyes. I was embarrassed I had let them down, especially after Klyn had died. I can't imagine what they felt. At the time I wasn't talking to my older brother. He was in Singapore and things had frayed between us, especially after I fell terribly ill on his wedding night in Malaysia. Instead of spending a romantic evening with his wife, Shaun had to rush me to emergency with an acute kidney infection.

Mum and Dad probably questioned where they'd gone wrong. I was always the one child they had to watch. None of this was their fault. I was trying to tape over a lifetime of missteps. Thankfully, they didn't see most of the self-imposed chaos that then led to some very poor decisions.

Lewis visited every Sunday for six weeks. While most kids his age were hanging out with their friends or families, he was taking two buses across the city from school on the other side of town. It was typical of him to show up exactly on time and just sit with me.

It was on one of these afternoons I saw him looking around the room where we sat. His eyes scanning the framed twelve-step programme on the wall.

'Mum, are you an alcoholic?'

It was a fair question, Lewis was clearly curious. I hardly drank. I told him no, I wasn't an alcoholic, I was just wired a little differently from other mums. The programme was one we all followed in South Pacific.

He nodded in agreement. 'You're definitely more *activated*, Mum.'

Then we laughed. His humour has always been my saving grace.

What I feared most was that whatever was 'wrong' with me, may be in my blood.

The thing about hitting rock bottom is no one tells you the time it takes to get back up. The point of intervention is only halfway to the healing that really needs to happen.

I would leave rehab still feeling hollow although I had a robust plan in place to support me: twice-weekly psychiatry sessions with a professor. A daily dose of lithium. Some Xanax to sleep, and a return to weekly psychotherapy.

It worked on paper. It sounded manageable. What I had was just the scaffolding, because what no one prepares you for, what no one *can* prepare you for, is the part where you have to go home and live your life again.

What if home is no longer a safe place? Or even the same place?

A SNIPER'S SNARE

The day I walked out of South Pacific, I didn't walk into comfort or celebration, I only walked into silence. Tom had left a key under the mat. That was his version of support. I let myself in and dropped my bag. All I could do as I stared at an empty apartment was take a breath.

Baby steps, I told myself. *You know what to do. Start at the beginning.*

I didn't know healing was supposed to feel this empty. Side-by-side support matters in the days and weeks after you leave rehab.

I would have to try to fit back into his life and fall back on his routine, because that's what you do when you think the other has their life in order.

What I noticed the most was my sensitivity to almost everything. Pedestrian signals sounded more like fire alarms. The endless noise of the traffic, especially the buses and trucks as they moved along, was insufferable. I noticed the nuance in people's voices more and wondered what they really meant. Even the clanging of crockery and cutlery being unpacked from the dishwasher or taken out from the cupboard was jarring to my ears. It felt almost impossible to live in peace.

At first, nothing was easy. When Tom finally returned from wherever he had been, he started to wrap his suggestions in concern. *Don't wear that, why don't you wear this? You look better in this. Don't tell that joke, it's too suggestive. Don't draw attention to yourself.*

Don't speak to this person without speaking to me first, there is a protocol to follow.

He said it was for my benefit, he only wanted to help me. Little did I know, he was patiently setting his snare.

I knew Tom's outwardly charming persona could flip the other way. He never shouted or slammed doors.

If he wanted to be heard, he would simply keep talking over me, a little louder each time, raise one hand in front of me as if to keep me at a distance and repeat, 'I haven't finished what I want to say.'

If I paid enough attention, I could see his jaw tightening until it set like concrete. His nostrils would slightly flare and his eyes would fix upon me with absolute intent, as if he were boring a hole right through me.

For a moment he would become motionless, as though regaining control. Every inch of him had been rewired for precision, control, survival. He didn't just look like he belonged in combat, he was trained for it.

A licensed killer.

A crisis negotiator.

A battlefield medic.

My jockey-sized frame was more instinctively honed. By contrast, my life hadn't been shaped by strategy; it had been shaped by strong women, motherhood, clinicians and medication.

SHAKEN, NOT STIRRED

I ALWAYS LOOKED FORWARD TO SATURDAY date nights, when Lewis was either with his father or at boarding school. It meant I could stay out later, play, and sleep in on Sundays.

To Tom's credit, if he was in Sydney, he always made an effort to do something nice – book a dinner, go to a party or head away for the weekend. I hadn't long been out of South Pacific and I was looking forward to a romantic evening together.

Seated side by side in a lovely restaurant overlooking the Opera House, our evening had started out well. That was until we sat down.

Our conversation quickly started to snag. Tom had turned. He was now cool, officious, ready to contradict. His gaze didn't drift away from mine. It remained fixed and deliberate.

Halfway through the entrée, as the band had settled nicely into their rhythm, I hadn't noticed his grip tighten around his glass. As if to take a sip, he lifted it, then he poured his entire cocktail over the top of my head.

Cold syrup ran through my freshly blown-out hair, down my cheeks, over my chin, then splashed over my décolletage and into my lap. For a second I couldn't breathe. The band stopped. People gasped. Even the waiter froze, main courses in hand.

Almost casually, Tom then stood up without saying a word. He turned and walked out of the restaurant, as if he was heading to the bathroom. I watched as he turned right and walked out of the front doors of the hotel. He didn't stop to pay the bill. He simply collected my car from the valet and drove home.

No one stopped him. No one ever did.

Our failing romance had now been played out in front of an audience, by candlelight, in a well-known upscale space. Foolishly, I believed Tom steadied the chaos around me. That evening I realised that nothing could have been further from the truth. Our chemistry, once electric, had now become an illusion.

In my evening bag was my favourite red lipstick, a bottle of fragrance, a small mirror, and a door key. I had no money and had no way to get home.

All I could do was use a napkin to clean myself as best I could in the ladies' room before leaving with an apology for the disturbance. I would fix up our bill the following day.

Feeling shaken, I walked alone through the Rocks to Argyle Street, climbing the sandstone steps to the Harbour Bridge pedestrian path. The wind hit as I reached the open span and a light rain began – pinpricks on my skin, nothing compared to the ache inside. I kept going. This time there would be no photos as I looked back over the twinkling of city lights. What sat with me was the slow, sickening feeling that the relationship was over.

By the time I reached Tom's apartment I was cold, wet and trembling. I opened the door, and slipped off my evening shoes. A lamp had been left on next to where he slept, oblivious.

Out of frustration, I swung my evening purse at his head.

'How could you? How could you? How could you do that to a woman?' My words tumbled out, hot, jagged, furious.

There was only a moment of silence, a heartbeat, before the room suddenly exploded into motion. Tom moved fast, too fast, his reaction came naturally. He was on his feet.

The bed sheets twisted, and the bedside lamp crashed to the floor. His voice filled the space; what was he saying? He closed in on me, almost against me. He was far too near. His rage had gathered momentum as he appeared to overpower the room. He'd had enough.

My body froze, my mind raced. It screamed at me to stay still, stay quiet, stay alive.

I backed into the kitchen, my hands reached behind me, to stabilise me and reach for anything that could help protect me. The room quickly warped, and felt thick with threat. I was aware that Tom would carefully choose his words to provoke a reaction, pulling me into his version of the truth so he could apportion the blame. His voice was dangerously low.

My hand tightened around the paring knife I was holding as he moved in even closer. Tom was used to calculated intimidation tactics.

We collided.

Then everything stopped.

He staggered back.

Blood.

The deepest darkest red. It surged towards me in deliberate pulsing waves, even as he reeled backward. His left hand unconsciously tried to stem the flow from his abdomen but his blood was insistent. Much like the cocktail he had spilled on me only an hour before, it found my dress from several feet away. The blood fell onto the kitchen tiles and splattered across the beige carpet between us.

Oh my God. Oh my God.

Tom's voice was now strangely calm and quietly commanding even though his face had drained completely of colour.

'You've got me.'

How has this happened?

'I'll call an ambulance. Wait.'

Where was my phone?

My body shook; I fumbled as I tried to remember the emergency number.

Is it 911 or 000? What country am I in? Perhaps I should attend to him first. I know first aid; he's a medic, he could talk me through, perhaps I could save him. Is this how people die? Why did he lunge threateningly towards me?

'Forget the ambulance; drive me to the hospital.' Tom was giving me an order in no uncertain words.

I grabbed the car key, which sat in its usual place by the front door. The door shut behind us before I realised I had forgotten to pick up the access pass.

We were now locked out. I couldn't call the elevator to get to the basement parking without it. We couldn't take the fire stairs; we'd be locked out of the building. *Why does security restrict exits in an emergency?*

Frantically I tried knocking on several doors. It was now past midnight. No answer.

A little further down, closer to the elevator, an English guy tentatively peered out. Perhaps he had heard the commotion. I couldn't be sure.

'Please, please, please. We must get to the hospital. Please, we don't have an access pass, it's in the apartment. We need to get to the parking. We're locked out. Hurry.'

I hardly needed to explain. With dishevelled damp hair and covered in blood, we must have looked unspeakable.

I wondered if the neighbour had called the police. It would be the natural thing to do.

One of Sydney's leading trauma hospitals was not far away by car. It would be fifteen minutes to the emergency department, maybe less at this late hour.

We both tried to concentrate, him on his breathing and me on the car lights ahead, where to go, the traffic signals and whether he'd make it.

We didn't speak and I didn't look at him.

I didn't dare breathe.

In the rain, everything had blurred. I couldn't be sure if it was the windscreen or my tears.

Had the incident taken hours, minutes or milliseconds? I couldn't be sure of that either. The cocktail, the Harbour Bridge, the blood, the lamp.

How would I explain that should Tom die, he would have lost his life at the hands of a woman vastly inexperienced in close-quarter combat and killing? I was half his size. It didn't matter that women were killed by their current or former partner every week in Australia, the judicial system would blame *me*.

As we pulled up, the emergency staff were already on hand.

They talked only to him, immediately moving him away from me.

I could hear him calmly say, 'She stabbed me.' He looked me squarely in the eye.

Then he was quickly ushered away and our lives separated forever.

It was strange the emergency department was so quiet on a Saturday night. In the empty reception, I waited in the darkest place I could find on an empty row of blue and white plastic chairs. Overhead, a light needed to be replaced.

I stared blankly at the two receptionists behind a white laminated desk. Before they rose from their seats, they had looked over at me, then nodded. They too moved out of sight.

Did they feel contempt, hostility or revulsion towards me? They gave nothing away. Hospitals have always been indifferent to theatrics.

Sitting alone, everything seemed to sharpen momentarily, then quickly fade into a haze. I looked at plastic coverings on the lights above, judged the expanse between me and the nurses' station, then over to the main entrance doors, and over to the windows where the rain was now lashing.

A feeling of heaviness was upon me. I needed to curl up somewhere. I needed to close my eyes and escape to a place a long way from where I was. Somewhere coffin-like, quiet and dark.

The fabric of my dress was still clinging to my skin. My faded perfume had been replaced by something more sterile, clinical, antiseptic. Our planned romantic evening, which had started with a perfect table, live music, and first-class service, was now anything but.

Two men in light blue shirts cut an imposing presence in the empty foyer. The police patches on their sleeves now appeared more prominent and pronounced. Their thick black belts were weighed down with radios, handcuffs and the quiet presence of a gun at their hips, which swayed with each deliberate swagger towards me. They moved with purposeful strides. Their physicality spoke of their need to be in control.

It was noticeably different from the way special forces operatives *ambled*. They trick you with their friendly, open smile and lethal confidence. I knew how they thought. I was more familiar with them.

I should have stood up, but I didn't. I remained in my seat, a dead weight. Ever since the media and the Royal Commission had exposed their widespread, sordid and corrupt culture, I had lost respect for them. I knew they weren't all tarred with the same brush.

It is what they *potentially* represented. I knew some could be bought.

Standing above me, they blocked out the light from behind the room.

Were they together for their safety? Was I now a risk? Their presence didn't need volume or words. I didn't want them to touch me.

I don't know who spoke to me. It was a short conversation.

I shrank under the weight of their judgement. Anything I said could be used against me. I blinked and tried to swallow then looked down at the floor.

Yes, it was me. I know he told you that. It was an accident. I was frightened; I felt cornered. I thought he would kill me. I wanted to protect myself.

Could I shower?

I wanted to scrub Tom out of my life, until my skin peeled off as if I had a third-degree burn. I wanted every trace of him gone.

A very pregnant blonde resident psychologist walked hurriedly towards me with intention. The police stepped back to a more respectful distance. I knew they could hear, but pretended not to.

She spoke to me briefly, then left.

In an empty corner room at the end of a corridor, not far from emergency, a mattress sat on the floor, almost in the middle of the room. It was stark but otherwise functional, nothing more. The bed had been made up with one pillow, white hospital sheets with the requisite hospital corners. A fresh hospital gown lay on one corner.

A middle-aged police officer that night kept guard outside my door, which he left slightly ajar. Every now and then, he glanced back into the room until I drifted to sleep.

Most of the time, his gaze would be fixed on the wall opposite, as if it were safer to study the paint. Only once when I asked to use the bathroom did he move. He'd rise without a word, walk beside me down the corridor, stop, and point to the accessible toilet door with the instructional blue pictogram. Then he waited outside in silence before walking me back to my room.

I suppose he resented the Saturday night late shift. The money was probably good though. There is nothing to do except think about what you will do later, when it's time to clock off.

Maybe he would take his two estranged kids to the zoo or the local park to kick a ball before driving them back to his ex's place via a drive-through McDonald's. It's what almost all the separated dads I knew did every single time, that is, until the kids got bored and didn't want to go anymore.

My thoughts were still fog-bound when I opened my eyes the next morning. The unremarkable room revealed itself slowly to me. I was lying in a hospital gown. My clothes were gone. I had no memory of how I undressed.

The air carried the sharp, antiseptic scent of disinfectant, a smell I knew well. I had learned to associate it with safety, it was strangely reassuring. Had they medicated me? Most likely. Had I slept for hours or minutes? I couldn't tell.

I searched the room for a clock but found only a white plastic sanitation unit affixed to the wall by the door.

RAIN, RAIN, GO AWAY

The hospital's psychiatric unit sat apart from most of the other buildings on the lot. A room had been allocated for me at the end of a corridor, marked with a number and a lock that seemed to click more deliberately than most.

My room was painted in a soft, pacifying pastel colour, designed to soothe, but not necessarily comfort. It appeared they bought their colour, like their sheets, in bulk.

The reinforced windows were larger and more plentiful than you'd expect. For the next few days I listened to the rain against the glass or watched the wind stir the branches outside, or sometimes both, willing myself back to sleep. It never ceased. One dismal day after another.

I often wondered why hospitals built such unwelcoming solitary spaces for the clinically insane. This wing for the insane was the work of someone with alexithymia. I doubt they'd shown their renderings to anyone of compassion and concern before it was built as a purported place of healing.

Rarely is there anything much to do when you're committed. The highlight of the day is a dose of prescription pills that take your reality away as you then wait for night to fall for the next dose. It was a world away from the now comparative luxury of South Pacific.

Sometimes I could hear footsteps and doors opening and closing, before the voices would fade.

Perfectly starched and pressed hospital-issue pyjamas, of a different colour from before, had been given to me. Probably so they could identify the department in case we decided to make a run for it. Situated in one corner of the common area was a shower, with its one bar of fresh Lux soap in a plastic wrapper. It offered little privacy as everyone saw you go in and out. The architect obviously didn't care and neither did the psych unit.

At very specific times, hospital-prepared meal trays were served in the same common area, although my appetite often failed me. Like in most hospitals, these trays offered little in nutrition, colour and taste. I especially disliked the gravy, placed strategically over the top to hide the taste of the fake mashed potato and overcooked carrots.

I had no interest in speaking to the other patients, so avoided the area as much as possible for the week I was there. I spoke to only two people. One was the brilliant son of a prominent obstetrician, I had recognised his father one afternoon he came in briefly to visit. His mother came at an alternate time, always alone and always stayed much longer. She also appeared far more concerned for his well-being.

A blonde girl in her twenties, with a strong athletic build, was the only other one I spoke to.

'Welcome to the nut house. Are you new?' she laughed. I suppose if you hadn't had a breakdown yet, there was no other way to describe it.

She told me how the police helicopter had picked her up while she was swimming out through the heads of Sydney Harbour late one night. I was secretly impressed. That was a fair effort by anyone's standards to swim that far and not get run over by the Manly Ferry or eaten by a bull shark or worse.

We knew we were just patients on the list and would soon become faceless and forgotten as they rotated us out to make way for the next batch.

Next to the nurses' station, on a nondescript table pushed up against the wall, sat an off-white Panasonic telephone. I stared at it for a long time, because when you have nothing else to look at, architecture and interiors become infinitely more interesting. It was like one you'd find in most corporate offices. It had been designed for utility over aesthetics.

The handset was connected by a coiled cord that was far too twisted, as if it were still tethered to the last call and someone's desperate conversation. I moved closer, focusing on its neatly arranged and labelled buttons with numbers and letters, along with its dedicated keys for redial, flash and volume control.

'You can call anyone you like, anywhere in the world. Would you like to make a call?' The supervising nurse had noticed me staring.

Yes I would.

'**Oh, honey, you can't stay there**; it's not good for you. I'll come and collect you. I'll be there tomorrow by half ten.' Her presence was always reassuring and far more optimistic than most.

Martina would sign me out the next morning with a secret that I would bury from almost everyone, including my own son.

With Lewis still in boarding school, no doubt thinking I was enjoying my time without him, Martina would take me to her beautiful little terrace home in Woollahra.

'I have a beautiful sunny bedroom for you. It's all yours; upstairs on the right, opposite mine. I've just finished renovating it. You'll love it, it's bright and sunny.'

Darling Martina. She understood life. She knew that Tom was no good for my safety, or sanity. This time, as I crossed the Sydney Harbour Bridge, it would be under very different circumstances.

With its tree-lined streets and hidden courtyards, Woollahra whispered of old money and refined taste. It had always had an air of exclusivity, and a slower, more contemplative pace for its residents.

Centennial Park awaited at the end of the street, where mornings were filled with the sound of horse hooves on the bridle paths, joggers' chatter as they wove through the wide avenues with a friend or, after walking their dogs, the regulars who sat underneath the enormous Moreton Bay fig trees with a takeaway coffee in hand.

I hadn't realised how far I had drifted away from the person I used to be. I had once been effortlessly fashionable and stylish. I was now merely existing, in the comfort of black. It had once been my armour, but now the colour had become an emotional crutch.

I was an autumn girl. Black sapped the warmth from my skin and dulled the golden tones in my sun-bleached hair. Black was chic, safe and easy, it seamlessly transitioned from day to night. It now felt heavy, harsh and outdated.

Martina appeared at my door, examining those clothes she had collected for me from home.

'You look like you're going to a funeral.' She was right.

Somewhere along the way I had let my failed relationship dictate my wardrobe. I was now a muted version of myself, drained of the vibrancy I had once carried with ease.

'We need to buy you some colour. We'll stop by the hairdressers for a blow-dry because I'm taking you out this evening for a good meal. You will soon be back to the Kirsty I know'.

Our next task was getting my psychotherapy treatments scheduled.

Tom was pressing charges. He was hellbent on sending me to prison with an eight- to ten-year sentence for reckless grievous bodily harm. Thankfully, I had narrowly missed a vital organ that could have taken his life.

A sharp young lawyer who had once served as a police prosecutor, and had even worked on a murder, had agreed to represent me.

The courts would require statements outlining the emotional, psychological, and physical toll this particular relationship had taken on me in order to understand the charges within the realms of domestic abuse and violence.

Since my discharge from South Pacific, I had been regularly seeing, unbeknownst to me, a forensic psychiatrist. He would dissect the complexities of my past, unpacking the psychological impacts of a partnership between someone trained in warfare and survival tactics and someone with bipolar.

Central to any forensic report is evidence of self-harm and suicidal tendencies. My timeline mapped the peaks and valleys of my mental state and it would ultimately reveal that the greatest danger I had ever posed was only to myself.

Weeks had passed before my court date arrived.

The grandeur of the heritage-listed façade of the District Court loomed above me, its green and gold trim a curious remnant of its former life as a department store. It was a stark contrast to the stillness I felt within and the gravity of what lay before me. The worn stone steps, edged with steel railings, had long absorbed the hurried footfalls of solicitors, defendants and journalists. Each would have ascended, like me, with their own unspoken burden.

The arched glass entrance framed my destination, but before reaching the final step I hesitated for a moment, for a prayer: *God, grant me the serenity to accept the things I cannot change, courage to change the things I can, and wisdom to know the difference. Above all, God give me strength.*

Inside, the air felt stale, thick with the hum of whispered conversations and the distant echo of legal proceedings behind closed doors. I would wait patiently alone on the wooden bench where I was instructed to sit. I hoped no one I knew would see me.

Serendipitously, I had met a retired high court judge socially, a gentleman of quiet authority, calm, and eloquence, at South Pacific. We had struck up an unexpected friendship, and from time to time we'd sit over cups of tea and talk about life. I had reached out to him and explained my predicament.

'The court will closely examine your demeanour, mental state and responses to questioning. You must be prepared,' he had told me. 'You will be under the careful gaze of the sitting judge, the defence lawyer, any instructing solicitors, the crown prosecutor, the investigating officer, the judge's associate and court officers'.

Given the nature of the case, my friend believed journalists would have restrictions placed upon them and would not be in attendance.

'Your forensic psychiatric assessment will likely play a major role in the case outcome. It will influence the judge's decision, including their right to dismiss any charges,' he'd explained.

'Also, you will need to be careful how you present yourself,' the judge added.

I had dressed carefully that morning: even though it was an occasion for black, I wore a simple pink silk shift dress that sat just below the knee. I matched it with lizard-skin shoes. It would have appeared a sharp contrast to that which had led me to the courtroom that day.

Be like Nadia.

So much was out of my hands.

It seemed like an eternity when my seasoned defence lawyer emerged from the chambers. His expression was unreadable, although what was evident in his eyes hinted of something between disbelief and amusement.

He leaned in, his voice low and deliberate.

'In twenty years, I have never had this happen before. The police cannot find your file. They said they've *lost* it. Someone upstairs must be looking over you.'

I blinked, trying to process his words. Was this a catastrophic failure of the system, or had a higher power intervened? I stared at him, searching his face for a clue.

The case, he said, would be put back to the Magistrates' Court, and a new hearing date would need to be set.

'You can go home. I'll be in contact.'

IF YOU INHALED, YOU WOULD SMELL the sweetness of spring. It was the sort of morning that gives you hope and clears your head. Whatever happened next would be the beginning of something else entirely.

I knew legal frameworks were for the most part fortified by men to protect men. Women are, at best, perceived to be unreliable narrators. Our truth and pain are often flattened by cleverly crafted legal arguments, and mine would be weighed and measured against the financial strength and intimidating presence of someone I used to love.

It was no surprise that Tom was convinced he was in a winning position. He had even phoned me to tell me that the only place I was going was prison.

My friend, the judge, told me to bide my time and wait on the will of God. Tom wasn't the court, the judge, or the jury.

The day of my hearing at the Magistrates' Court finally arrived, and so did *he*. Inside, the stage was set.

I had seen Tom arrive earlier at the court with almost a spring in his step. He was quickly surrounded by a bevy of uniformed policemen, their banter light but loaded as they glanced over in my direction.

Tom was playing his cards like a seasoned insider in the boys' club. Maybe they were counting their chickens before they hatched, or relishing the fantasy of a more covert life as a Bond type.

They almost certainly spoke about special forces operations – at least, their focus on Tom suggested as much – because I'd seen it all before.

Let them have their chauvinist moment. It was typical. There was no need for me to stand in their periphery, waiting for Tom to acknowledge my presence.

Instead, I stepped inside and waited on a wooden bench. Soon it would be my turn to be seen.

An eccentric barrister friend, notably brilliant and borderline unhinged, swept past me with his usual cheeky glint, almost unannounced. Noticing me at the last moment, he turned.

'I'll be in the gallery,' he said, grinning like a Cheshire cat. 'Whatever you do, don't look at me, don't even hint that you know me,' he rasped without looking in my direction as he hurried past me and into the courtroom.

Today he would sit in the spectator stand. He made it clear he was only there *for a laugh.*

My defence lawyer was waiting. He was also unmoved by Tom's theatrics and said so. Only facts mattered. He whispered to me that the judge who usually presided over this particular Magistrates' Court had taken unexpected leave for a couple of weeks. In his place would be … *a woman.*

I was lucky to have a representative understand the law in a way few others did: not only was he a defence lawyer, but he had been a lead prosecutor against police corruption.

As we moved into the packed courtroom, I glanced discreetly around. I made sure to avoid eye contact with the barrister, who sat over to my right side and further down. He didn't look up.

I knew that day that a physical comparison in this case would be noted so I had worn ballet flats and a simple below-the-knee fifties swing dress, again in pastel. I swept my hair into a simple chignon and wore only pearl earrings. I knew I would burst into tears as soon as the judge addressed me and asked me to move to the stand, because I was already teetering. I had kept my makeup minimal, so mascara wouldn't stream down my face and turn me into something far less recognisable.

I sat there as a full public gallery listened to car crashes, fines to be paid, and the mundane churn of the legal system. This was just one day in the life of a courtroom, but for me it was something else entirely.

The judge then called Tom to the stand.

He strode through the courtroom with confidence, in a navy suit I'd never seen before. His shoulders squared, as they normally do, and his chin was up. He looked like a man used to being in command, always to be believed and obeyed.

This presence was now noticed, because he had managed to stifle even the faintest murmur. It was as if everyone instinctively understood that this was not just another case. This was a performance that demanded their full attention.

I don't recall what was asked of him or what he said. I remember Tom spoke with the assurance of a man who expected the world to accept only his version of events. Like bullets hitting their mark. There was no hesitation, no self-doubt; just the steady, deliberate cadence of someone who had rehearsed their lines.

His voice had hardened. It filled the courtroom in the same way it had when he had spoken to me behind closed doors. Those times when his patience had thinned before he had unleashed the full force of his anger.

Except for a slight raising of one eyebrow, the judge's face remained unreadable. Had I caught the flicker of something? Was it scepticism, or recognition?

The courtroom started to blur at the edges. Voices had dulled into a whisper-thin hum. The forensic psychiatrist was now speaking. I could see his mouth moving. His words floated and were without volume.

I lowered my eyes. The weight of shame, regret and exhaustion was now bearing down on me, pressing against my ribs, making it impossible to breathe. My body started to betray me. I started to wrack with uncontrollable sobs, the kind that comes from years of being unheard, unseen, dismissed.

But that day I had seen a woman in black, seated apart and above, looking back at me with a knowing. She remained composed and totally in control. She had listened carefully to the prosecution, and no doubt noted the calculated choreography of the prosecution's legal team and their subtle attempts to distort the truth.

I was asked to stand. For a brief moment every eye was on me, until the attention shifted to the judge as she began her address.

'This case is not simply about a single moment,' she began, her voice steady, 'but about a life shaped by hardship, resilience, and survival.'

She let the words sit in the room. I felt them land in my chest.

'The Court recognises the challenges the defendant has carried: long-standing mental health struggles, the weight of single motherhood, and the financial strain that would bend anyone under pressure. Her choices, though imperfect, were guided not by malice, but by a relentless desire to provide, to protect, and to hold her son's world together.'

I stared down at my hands. She had seen more than even I had admitted.

'Desperation can lead people down paths they never thought they'd walk,' she continued. 'It is evident her actions were not reckless, but simply reactive of someone navigating a life threaded with complexity and private pain. The forensic evidence shows the significant role psychological factors played. The emotional and mental abuse she has endured forms the backdrop to her every decision.'

Her voice did not waver as she continued.

'Justice is not merely punishment. It ensures the law does not become another weapon used against those already shaped by circumstances beyond their control.'

I realised it then: she wasn't only referring to my case. She was speaking on behalf of women.

'The past does not define her,' she concluded. 'And the law will not condemn her for fighting to survive. Accordingly, the Court finds that a conviction is not in the interests of justice. The defendant is free to leave.'

The air left my lungs in one long exhale. I didn't leave my seat as the gallery emptied. I waited until after my tears had completely dried. Then I looked for the only friend who'd shown up for me that day.

His seat was already empty.

BLIND DATE

<hr>

AFTER THE COURT CASE, I swore off all tall, charming, sporty types. At the very least, I promised myself a pause.

In my finance job, I worked closely with two boys who became my good mates and unofficial bodyguards. If we went to the neighbourhood pub for a Friday night drink, they made sure I was in a taxi and checked in again with me to make sure I got home safely.

At the Autumn and Spring Racing Carnivals, we'd punt on horses with deadly seriousness. They'd carry my heels when one champagne tipped into three and the soles of my feet couldn't bear the stabbing pain a moment longer. They even tracked down my misplaced handbag after my flood of tears before proudly carrying it home for me.

They showed up for me without expectation or agenda.

They nicknamed me Sybil, after a woman famous for having multiple personalities. According to them, part of my charm was my Sybil-ious nature.

I was with them on the night of Christmas Eve when I spotted a self-assured, fashionable man walking straight towards me. Definitely a looker. I could've let him pass, but didn't, I complimented his style. He paused. Harmless banter soon flicked back and forth between us.

Then his phone lit up. Glancing at the screen, he smirked and handed it to me with a wink. He was hanging for a beer at the bar.

'Talk to Ben. I'll be back. Wanna another one?' pointing to my glass. He was gone before I had a chance to answer.

Ben had the kind of voice that immediately captured my attention. We chatted and before he hung up he asked for my number. Later that night, once I was home and in bed, we spoke for another four hours about everything and anything.

It was during Christmas lunch at a family friend's home, rosé champagne in one hand and a prawn in the other, that he called.

'Meet me at Hamilton Island tomorrow. I'll keep ringing until you say yes.'

He was ballsy. I give him that. With my son at his dad's for the next week, my schedule was clear. His timing was beyond perfect.

Whatever I had promised myself was now out the window.

I checked my frequent flyer points. It looked like a cosmic green light from my end. I checked my travel dates: Qantas showed just one available seat on a direct flight up and only two seats coming back. With some hearty encouragement from around the table, and before dessert was served, I was booked.

There was only one tiny detail. I had no idea what he looked like. The time zone between Sydney and Western Australia was working against us, and the photo he sent, before instant messaging, hadn't arrived. Once I left home I was without the internet.

A blind date to a tropical island with a mysterious man I'd never seen? It was totally reckless, and wildly seductive. And exactly the kind of plot twist my life was craving.

It seems I can never escape my past, no matter where I am. My former neighbour from the time I first lived with my future husband, one we had often had drinks with and whom I hadn't seen in almost fifteen years, was on the same flight.

Like many keen sailors, he kept his yacht in Hamilton Island, and was heading up to the Whitsundays with a new love in tow.

There is no easy way to explain you have just booked a last-minute flight to meet a complete stranger whom you technically met at a pub. Two days ago. On the phone.

As QantasLink touched down at the Hamilton Island Airport, I reminded myself the flight was a turnaround. Should I wait and see who was left standing once the terminal cleared?

I could just as easily fly back to Sydney, and all I'd be out of were frequent flyer points. There'd be no harm done, if I didn't like what I saw. Not knowing what I was walking into made it all the more intoxicating.

As we disembarked, my friend insisted that if anything felt off I was welcome to join him and his companion sailing for a few days. I not only had a blind date, I also now had a sailing option.

As I waited casually by the luggage carousel, I turned to see the spitting image of a young Hugh Jackman casually leaning against the wall, his arms folded across his chest. He was barefoot and only wearing board shorts and a surf tee. Was this him?

I walked towards him, my stare not leaving his. He moved towards me, before starting to laugh.

'You're looking for me, or at least I think you are. I'm Ben.'

Thank you, Lord, and a very Merry Christmas to me.

'Hiiiiiiiiiiiiii.' I stretched it out like I was already floating in champagne and wanted the moment to last a little longer.

'Well, hello … hello, hellooooooo,' he laughed, and leaned in for a generous hug in a chivalrous, instinctive way. I liked that.

Without hesitation he reached down to take my luggage and guided me out of the terminal. Outside, a sea of white golf buggies stretched before us, almost all exactly identical. Except for one. A single black buggy with gold wheels waited by the entrance, parked in a No Stopping zone.

For a moment I felt like I'd stepped into a rom-com scene that had already been perfectly scripted.

'We've got a bit of a drive,' he said as he pointed ahead, across from the landing strip to a very luxurious apartment block in the distance.

In the corridor, we received a cheery hello from one of Australia's most prolific and well-known financiers. One should always pay attention to one's neighbours. They reveal a lot more than you realise.

Just who was this guy in board shorts, with the black golf buggy?

From the instant we met the charge between us was electric, so visceral it felt like the temperature had increased from the moment our eyes locked. We both confessed that our attraction to one another had been undeniable from that first glance. With a whole week ahead of us, it seemed absurd to waste time. So why pretend to play it cool? He liked me and I liked him.

There was no slow burn, nor was there a grand tour of his sprawling island apartment.

He simply carried my luggage into the master bedroom and shut the door behind him. He closed the space between us with the quiet confidence of a man who always got what he wanted. But little did he know, I did too.

There was no need to resist as his mouth found mine and my world fell away. We couldn't even wait until nightfall.

I felt myself pressed back against the door, the cool wall, the bed. He was already naked. Warm, rhythmic, certain. We didn't leave room for shame or doubt. We simply devoured each other, hungry, breathless and greedy.

Later, tangled in soft sheets and still damp from the shower, we lay wrapped around each other, still laughing as if we had known each other far better than we did. We'd barely spoken and yet we already knew: this was far from over. His fingers traced the outline of my hip, then wandered, exploring, learning, teasing. He had just rolled on top of me again when the door flew open without so much as a knock.

'Well, hello you two. Looks like I've got the other room, then.'

In the doorway, his older brother. He was even taller and more good-looking. I hadn't known he would be joining us for the week, complete with several big boxes of homegrown mangoes. Had I hooked up with the wrong brother?

'What a shame you're here with him, when you could have been with me,' his brother teased with a mischievous grin.

I wanted the earth to swallow me. I'd never been caught out so … casually.

'Yeah, yeah. Now close the door. We're busy.' Ben laughed, but our moment had passed. Desire would have to wait.

As Ben's brother began to shut the door, he peeked around. 'Stop fucking and get ready, you guys. We're taking the boat out in thirty. Anyone for a mango daiquiri before we go?'

Outside, the boat crew, head to toe in white, were already running down the jetty. An impressively sleek motor yacht waited as they tore the plastic from its seats and started the engine.

On the stern, in elegant lettering, the boat's name would be a clue to whom I was about to share my week with. The motor yacht's impressive radar domes and antennae suggested Ben was not any ol' Aussie surfer.

We both felt sun-kissed and unburdened as the captain opened up the engines as the boys skurfed before finally dropping the anchor for a lazy afternoon of fishing. Ben's brother and I decided to swim ashore to Whitehaven, arguably one of the world's most pure and beautiful beaches.

Our strokes effortlessly sliced through the clear crystalline waters towards the blindingly-white silica sand and its untouched landscape.

Ben fished as we lay sprawled on the cool sand, where we let the afternoon drift by as we slept and tanned our bodies. The bright light began to fade and the sea took on the tint of its dusk. Soon it would be shark feeding time. I decided it best we head back sooner rather than later.

I could see the yacht around half a kilometre offshore as I swam back alone. By the time I reached the ladder, I was still catching my breath and had trouble climbing up. Ben stretched out his hand to help me back on board before pouring me a glass of wine from the bottle he had opened earlier.

'Your brother wants you to send the tender out to pick him up.'

'That won't be happening. If a little thing like you can make it back, so can he.' There was clearly good-hearted rivalry between two very close brothers as he switched his attention to the food in the fridge. 'Oysters or prawns, or both?'

I was still trying to figure out how two thirty-somethings were casually living like billionaires. I texted Martina to tell her that I had arrived.

I arrived on HI. He has a very nice boat. Still don't know his full name. LOL. K x

Ping.

Hi Honey. Glad to hear ur ok. What's the boat's name? Let me research :) M x

Martina, ever the relentless fossicker, could always be counted on for research.

Ping.

Do u want to know who ur with?

My heart skipped a beat. Were they on the right side of the law?

Ping.

Ur safe ;) Mining $$$. Have fun. C u when ur back. Love M x

For a while our sweet liaison stretched from east coast to west, until it hit the inevitable bump my relationships always seemed to find.

In hindsight, I blame it on a melodrama. Women watch films

like this because it's part of our metabolism. Or mine, at least. It pried open the part of me that wanted to be chosen and held onto, no matter how messy life would become.

I had sobbed uncontrollably through the end of *The Notebook* and all the way home. Instead of calling a girlfriend like any sane person would for comfort and clarity, I rang Ben.

'She's meeeeeeee,' I wailed down the line. I was utterly inconsolable. I'm fairly certain he thought I'd lost my mind. Which, for a moment, I had.

He tried to tell me he'd been researching natural remedies, convinced bipolar diagnosis was more lifestyle related. I didn't need to be so heavily medicated, he said. I drank socially, not carelessly. I had always thrived on conversation, stories and stimulation. We agreed I just needed to slow down and look at my diet and sleep patterns.

What others suggested was chaos, I recognised as a naturally flowing energy. I had a pulse. I wasn't flatlining like so many others. I saw his reading of the situation not as a judgement, but more as a gift. He got me.

Ultimately, it wouldn't be his diagnosis that undid us. It would be *The Notebook*. Ryan Gosling, Rachel McAdams, and that one ill-timed phone call across time zones. Note to self: never ring a lover when destabilised. Let the soundtrack do all the emotional heavy lifting. It's a softer drowning. I sabotaged what Ben and I had. It ended how it began, with one interstate phone call.

THERE IS NOWHERE ON EARTH LIKE ULURU. It is one of my favourite places in the world.

Rising from the heart of Australia's red centre, the world's most famous desert rock doesn't just exist, it hums with an ancient knowing, and with the weight of silent ceremony.

Uluru is also known as the masculine energy centre of the world. An initiatory point for new beginnings.

I'd already immersed myself in the receptive feminine energy of Haleakalā (the heart chakra of the world) on the Hawaiian island of Maui. Central Australia was the yang to Maui's yin.

It was a place of deep listening, encoded with spiritual laws and dreamtime, and as my birthday loomed, the big Red Rock called me back.

'How does Uluru sound, Kirsty?' Martina asked, her eyes gleaming. 'Dinner under a million stars, in the middle of nowhere? You, me, and Susu.'

Oof. I pinched myself. 'You're joking, right?'

She wasn't. Martina had already orchestrated the entire plan. Private helicopter, a flyover of Uluru and Lake Amadeus, then a picnic hike through Kings Canyon. What would normally take three and a half hours by road we could cover in less than an hour in the air. These girls were famous for maximising an experience.

At Kings Canyon, its walls rose around us in shades of ochre and terracotta. It was a tour Martina and Susu happily skipped in favour of a lazy picnic next to where the helicopter had landed. The race car owner turned pilot led me on a strenuous hike past dozens of stunning rock formations, scenic waterfalls and escarpments. Without any other tourists on the track, every step we took felt more like a very special spiritual pilgrimage.

At dawn, I suggested we all walk the ten-kilometre base of Uluru.

The girls weren't overly excited. It was the only way I wanted to really celebrate my fortieth year, so they had to agree. This wasn't a place we had come to climb and conquer, I explained, we had to approach the power of Uluru with quiet intent. The Anangu people asked tourists not to climb the Rock. I knew why we had to listen. For sixty thousand years, not only did the land belong to them, they understood their relationship to it.

Uluru will come to you long before you go to him.

That is why we would take the time to walk, to honour the Dreaming.

The Dreaming is the ancient Aboriginal law that binds land, body, sky and spirit. I knew that a nearby site, Kata Tjuta, represented the mind, and Uluru the heart, only because I had visited the national park together with Lewis when he was a little boy.

Martina's plan to celebrate my birthday in the desert became an initiation ceremony and pilgrimage, especially under the glow of a Capricorn full moon.

Martina would always scoff at what she called my 'woo woo'. She was definitely Capricorn to her core. Yet out there, under that sky, there was no denying everything felt in perfect alignment.

Something shifted for each of us on that trip: Martina would soon step into motherhood, Susu into taking over the family business, and me — well, I would find myself in the Middle East sooner than expected. It was as though Uluru had rearranged the pieces we weren't brave enough to move ourselves.

I blame my girlfriends for one too many mudslide cocktails at the bar. I should also thank Susu and Martina because somehow, my birthday ended in a heated tangle in the back of the young helicopter pilot's 4WD.

DESTINATION DUBAI

A TEMPORARY MARKETING ROLE AT A sports club had ended quietly on Christmas Eve, without fanfare or promise of a renewal. It silently closed the door on the last sense of hope I'd been clinging to. At forty years of age, I certainly didn't think I'd be living pay cheque to pay cheque.

My son had finished his final exams with the marks he needed to pick and choose a university and degree of his choice. We agreed a gap year overseas would give him a well-earned break whilst he decided exactly what he wanted to do. He would leave for England to take up an eighty-quid-a-week role as a teaching assistant at a private school in Surrey.

I had bought Lewis a one-way air ticket, partly because it was all I could afford at the time.

'Mum. I think you've forgotten to book my trip home,' he said, almost in disbelief as he looked at his itinerary.

'We don't have a home, Lewis, so there isn't one,' I answered as I poured a glass of red wine and continued to prepare our Christmas dinner.

'Are you serious? Are you leaving me there?'

'Maybe.' I laughed, nervously. 'I don't know where I'll be in a year. Call me when you finish, and I'll tell you where I am.'

I felt trapped in our rented one-bedroom apartment. It had looked much better in the advertisement. Sleek, modern, full of light, but it felt entirely soulless. It was the best I could find at the time, although I knew the very day I moved in that I wasn't going to stay past the end of the year-long contact, if I could make it that far.

What I did know was that Sydney, as a city, no longer made sense to me. It wasn't a place to be single. All my friends were married or happy in relationships and I rarely got invited out with couples. With Lewis stepping out into the world as an adult, I wasn't sure of my role anymore as his mother. For a time, I felt out on a limb.

A few weeks before the call came in from Dubai, I'd been sitting at Nicky's kitchen counter in Mosman. Helen Reddy's 'I Am Woman' pounded through the speakers. Between us sat a fruit and cheese platter and two glasses of Cloudy Bay white wine.

Nicky was a woman who faced her challenges with a slick of red lipstick and her music turned up more than most. Her arms were always wide open for a big hug. She was the kind of woman who reminded you what quiet strength, a committed wife and a great mother really looked like. Only her ritualistic spritz of an exclusive French fragrance, five minutes before her husband walked through the door, ever came close to whatever else was in the air that day.

'I feel it in my bones. You're meant to end up in Dubai.' Turning to me, she put down her glass.

Her voice was unusually calm and steady. In fact, she'd never sounded more certain. Like most talented hairdressers I knew, Nicky definitely had *a knowing*. She had paused mid-sip as she stared out the window before delivering her prophecy. One that a few months later come true.

Back in May that year I had been selling money in the medical technology space and I had hated every moment I had to sit for hours in mindless traffic.

Five years in finance was enough for me. As I sat in my car, I remember looking up at a billboard stretched over the motorway. *Fly Emirates. Keep discovering.* Before that day, I had never really noticed it. In hindsight it was as though the heavens wanted me to see that exact sign before I got to the office.

Then that morning, a colleague at work had shown me an aerial shot of The World islands and Palm Jumeirah.

'This is your place, it would suit your personality. You should go,' he said. 'I lived there and it's a wild ride.'

He wasn't wrong.

Company layoffs were announced that afternoon as part of an aggressive corporate restructure. My hand couldn't go up fast enough. I volunteered to take a retrenchment package. The universe had been sending me messages that spring day.

I was on a flight to Dubai the following week but had packed for Saudi Arabia: I would arrive head-to-toe in black. I actually had no idea where the United Arab Emirates was. All I knew is that I had landed in the middle of what looked like the world's most glamorous construction site in the middle of summer in a city that was being built on a dream.

I had touched down with only the quiet belief that a job might find me. It initially sounded promising. A role with the team building Trump Tower was initially offered to me. I flew home a month later with the classic refrain ringing in my ears: 'We'll call you.'

Don't they always.

It was an ordinary working day in the Emirates when my phone rang. It was Christmas Day in England and Boxing Day in Australia when the call came from the developer's office. The universe was juggling a lot of things around in my life that year.

'How quickly can you get to Dubai?' With the phone pressed to my ear and the weight of something unexpected rising in my throat, I remembered Shamma's exact words.

'Can you be here in two days?'

I asked her to repeat her question, I wasn't sure if I had heard her properly because of her Arabic accent, even though her English was perfectly clear.

My mind was racing. Who moves to a new country in two days? To the other side of the world?

Me. That's who.

'Can you give me a week?' I replied.

'Perfect,' Shamma said. 'I'll send your business-class ticket and contract over. You will have it within the hour. We can't wait to meet you at the airport on the third of January.'

Everything I owned would fit in half a container. I lived lean, I prioritised health over clutter. Experiences over possessions. I'd witnessed too many people's lives all sitting in a glass cabinet or on the shelves of thrift shops the world over selling for bargain basement prices. Once-cherished wedding rings, family photos, furniture and trinkets sat there anonymously, their sentimental history long forgotten.

Sea freight from Sydney would take six weeks to reach Dubai. With accommodation for the first few weeks sorted, it was one big green light to go.

The freight company packed up my apartment the morning of New Year's Eve. They secured the latch on the back door of the truck as I rang a taxi and headed over to spend my last two nights in Australia with a friend.

And just like that, another chapter in my life came to an end. I was heading to a city on the brink of global rebranding, one I'd be an integral part of with the Dubai government.

The moment I stepped off that fourteen-hour Emirates flight into the heat of the Middle East, strangely, I felt I was home.

Later when I checked the date in *The American Ephemeris*, I immediately understood why moving to the Middle East felt inevitable.

I had arrived under a Cancer full moon, a sign that represents the home, family and emotional inheritance, the very same sign as my Sun, Mercury and Venus. With all this zodiacal energy buried in my twelfth house of karma, I shouldn't have been surprised. For the first time in years, the sky wasn't pulling me apart, it was pulling me back to a place I felt secure.

'Marhaba! As-salāmu 'alaykum. Welcome to Dubai. It's lovely to finally meet you.' Shamma's warmth was as genuine and generous as her perfect smile.

My fully furnished two-bedroom Arabic-inspired apartment would be a short walk from the beach and a thirty-minute drive into the desert down the back roads from Dubai Marina. Outside, wherever you looked, there were cranes, workers by the dozen, trucks, half-finished roads and missing pavements. It wasn't unusual to see a lion or tiger in the back of a Range Rover, staring back at you as we headed for sundowners at Souk Madinat or a simple little beach bar called Barasti.

'A car will pick you up at 6:45 tomorrow morning to bring you to our site office. Our working week is Sunday to Thursday. Did you know you are employee number eleven on our billion-dollar golf project? Alhamdulillah.'

I was now on construction timelines, those designed to beat the rising heat of the day. The reality was, in order to deliver a world-class project on time, my office hours extended regularly to ten- and twelve-hour days.

Outside my window, a baby camel held fort as I sat in a portacabin selling sand and instructing property lawyers, a lifestyle built around two championship golf courses ringed by hundreds of multi-million-dollar villas was breaking ground.

Excitement was already building in the office by the time I arrived. By the end of the month the PGA Tour would be rolling into town at the Emirates Golf Club course, and with it, not only golfer Tiger Woods, but Formula One driver Michael Schumacher and tennis star Roger Federer.

Golf attracted big names and big money. In 2007, it was game on.

GRACE, INTELLIGENCE AND SOLIDARITY

DESPITE WHAT MANY PEOPLE THINK, Emirati women are a vision of composed power with their flowing black customised abayas and impeccably draped shaylas. Their makeup is always immaculate, their skin luminous, every detail intentional, and let's not mention their impossibly perfectly painted nails.

Ayesha, whom I worked with, was one of them. What struck me first wasn't her gemstones, though she wore rubies, emeralds and diamonds the size of small planets as casually as I'd wear something to the office from Swarovski. It was her humour. Her wicked, disarming intelligence flickered in her eyes; the kind that made me blush at times because I'd underestimated what she knew of the world.

It was over cardamom tea that I finally blurted out the questions every Westerner wanted to know.

'Are you actually allowed to work?'

She laughed, almost delightedly. Ayesha was not offended in the least. 'Habibti, why would we not? Why would I waste the chance? My government invested in my education.'

'What about education? Are you allowed to drive? Can you marry who you like?'

'Education?' she laughed softly, lowering her voice as though sharing a secret. 'I have a master's in political science. My father taught me to drive so I could get to university on my own. Then he bought me a Mercedes.' Her lifted brows needed no translation.

'We don't date. We marry. They must win us over first.' It was followed by a conspiratorial wink. This was a woman who knew far more than she let on.

I hesitated. 'Do you ever feel … restricted? I mean, the way the media—'

Her smile deepened again, as they always do in the Emirates when you ask a question. 'The only cage is misunderstanding. You're here with me now, yes? I honour my faith, my father, our family name. That for us is dignity and respect, not limitation. You are with us now. I will show you everything you want to know. His Highness Sheikh Mohammed wants us to compete globally; we must rise up and make him proud.'

It landed with the quiet force of truth.

I'd arrived in the Emirates coloured by Western narratives. I had mistaken discretion for repression. Emirati women weren't hidden. They were formidable: feminine warriors scented in oud so rich and luxurious, it lingered behind them everywhere they walked.

These women lifted women with compliments that felt like blessings. Their solidarity was instinctive, a sisterhood woven together long before Dubai's skyscrapers started to pierce the sky. Their generosity was always so sincere it made my Western politeness look transactional.

The locals didn't only celebrate another's success, they claimed it as a shared victory. I realise now I was being re-educated in the nicest of ways.

'Dress how you want to be treated,' Ayesha suggested. I leaned into their modesty, and more suggestive simplicity. My tastes would eventually evolve to reflect theirs. That of quiet luxury, discreet designer shoes, hidden sexy lingerie, and deliciously scented oils.

Fridays took on a new ritual. As the locals prayed and spent the day with their family, I spent my day poolside before slipping away to beauty salon appointments for blow-dries, facials and manicure top-ups. After a 10 pm dinner with the girls in another new dress, we would head out to dance the rest of the hours away in a swanky nightclub with the other expats and tourists.

On quieter nights, Ayesha and I would slip into the shadow-world of the Emirates, in backrooms lit only by the dim, amber glow of lamps. Those with floors layered with Persian rugs, air thick with frankincense or myrrh and honeyed with trays of baklava and dates. It was here that elderly women wrapped in floral cotton and soft pashminas would beckon us to sit cross-legged next to them on the floor.

With practised movements, they swirled the last of our thick black coffee, before turning the cups upside down onto their saucers. Porcelain kissed porcelain. A long silence would often follow.

They furrowed their brow, as they studied the dark grounds that had soon set into trails and globules. Ayesha translated as our futures were slowly and deliberately deciphered in Arabic. One long pause at a time.

I adored spending an evening in ritual and reverence. On the drives home we would laugh until our jaws ached, teasing out the meanings and maybes. I was still awake well past midnight, high on caffeine and the delectable possibility that our futures were already in motion.

Dubai is a place you very quickly see your real worth as a single blonde woman in a foreign country. There were always so many questions when I was alone, particularly from men who would speak to me in broken English, accompanied by a hopeful smile.

First they would enquire whether I was *Russian? German? Swedish? English?*

I heard it so often, before the inevitable suggestion of something more intimate.

Like a genie in a bottle, my faux husband would suddenly appear.

'Naughty, naughty,' I'd say, wagging a finger in mock reprimand. 'My husband is a pilot for Emirates. He will be very angry with you. Not good, my friend. Not good.' I'd scowl, shake my head and hurry away.

As a single woman, I hadn't always had the luxury of feeling safe. Who would think that at forty, a woman still had things to learn? At least I always knew where I was and how I got there. I knew to clock the landmarks. Bright shopfronts, street signs, the shape of a tree, a roofline. I knew to check the time and project purpose even when I had nowhere to be. I stayed alert, and calculated the distance to the nearest exit. Just in case.

I knew never to be swayed by the charm or advice of a stranger, no matter how handsome, confident or convincing.

Although, never say never.

A DANGEROUS LIAISON

IF YOU HAD TOLD ME IN 2006 THAT BY February I'd be working in the middle of the desert selling homes that didn't yet exist, I would have laughed. In Dubai, reinvention wasn't a fantasy; it was the city's call sign.

It was a short walk from my home to the Emirates Golf Club. With its perfect fairways and manicured greens, it offered a mirage of calm against the chaos of construction and the seasonal sandstorms. Or the *shamals,* as we called them.

It was at the PGA tournament I first noticed him. He was in a sponsorship tent buzzing with elegant and sartorial types who were casually sporting their black designer sunglasses, watches and golf caps.

He sat alone at the bar, looking entirely in control and comfortable with who he was.

At a table nearby, I'd not long sat down with a friend from work for a quick bite to eat.

He wasn't a person who would necessarily turn heads; instead he had a quiet, self-made confidence, the kind that suggested that perhaps first-class travel was no longer a luxury for him.

As a global businessman, airports and boardrooms were time-wasting but necessary for his entrepreneurial investments and acquisitions.

From his tailored clothing and handmade shoes, I could see that everything he wore spoke a language Savile Row tailors understood. It was obvious he liked beautiful things. Beautiful places. Beautiful distractions.

More enticingly, his English accent was smooth and deep. It carried a lived-in quality, far more worldly than even his eloquence suggested. Jonathan was a self-made man, full of quick-fire banter.

He would become my mirror, my magnet, and eventually, my minefield.

'There's my future ex-husband,' I joked to my friend.

'Go say hello. Why not? You're single and have nothing to lose.' She nudged me forward in his direction.

'No. He'll think I'm hitting on him. I'm not that sort of girl,' I whispered back, for fear of someone overhearing our conversation.

'I need pineapple juice … from the bar.'

It was a clever excuse to stand next to him. I had *never* been nervous around men, even in sexually charged situations. Until now.

'Hello. Enjoying the golf?'

I turned to face his question. He was smiling, eyes bright with mischief. It took very little effort on his part. In that moment I forgot all about the pineapple juice.

'I am. And you?' I slowly smiled back, holding his gaze longer than I usually would.

'That's why I'm here! Are you following anyone in particular?'

'Johan, the hot Swede.' I laughed more apprehensively than I usually would. I had only just discovered him playing the course that morning.

He laughed back, a little louder, perhaps because he hadn't expected to hear that. Lifting his tall glass of beer for a long, slow mouthful, his gaze stayed on mine far longer than was acceptable, or polite.

'I'm not surprised. He's a very good-looking man.' He was now meeting me in my candour.

'Do you play golf?' I wanted to continue our conversation for a little longer.

'A little.'

'What's your handicap?' It was the only question I knew to ask at a golf course back then.

'Close to scratch,' he said with a sly grin.

Hmmmm. British public school type. I know his type. Confident. Always something to hide. Those sparkling blue eyes are going to be a problem.

That week, while the world's best golfers were hitting it out for a multi-million-dollar prize pool, we'd randomly cross paths, almost daily. His memory was impressive. He'd always start our conversation with a follow-up question from the last time we'd met.

I hate it when men are so knowingly flirtatious. It's very sexy. This one is intoxicating. Those eyes.

'I'm sorry, but I forgot to ask your name,' I said, feeling sheepish for not asking sooner.

'That's because you didn't tell me yours. I'm Jonathan. How do you do?'

It was the final night, after the tournament had finished, that I spotted him again. The least I could do was wish him a safe flight back to London. I'd pass him my business card in case he may be interested in purchasing something off-plan at our upcoming property launch.

Except someone else reached him first and had locked him into small talk. His eye caught mine and he rose to half-standing, moving slightly in my direction before leaning in close to my ear.

'I'll only be a moment.'

His promise carried the weight of a secret tête-à-tête, even though there was no need for any discretion.

'What are you doing this evening? I'd like you to join me, if you're interested,' he asked more privately.

'Seven-thirty office starts aren't conducive to spontaneous nights on the town,' I weakly offered, half hoping to be convinced otherwise.

He didn't push. I handed him my business card and wished him well on his return journey. But men like him did not give up easily.

RENDEZVOUS AND LIMERENCE

THE CUP OF TEA I'D MADE EARLIER SAT cooling beside my bed. It had become a little less appealing than usual after a weekend of champagne, sport and low scores on the leaderboard.

I had just stepped out of the shower when my mobile phone began to ring. 'Come and meet me.' It was Jonathan again.

'I'm afraid I need to politely decline, I'm about to jump into bed.' I was secretly pleased I'd left my mark.

'Meet me in twenty minutes at the Buddha Bar. I'm going to keep calling until you say yes. I want to see you.'

Another glass of champagne with a charming stranger at a hip bar, or a cup of herbal tea alone in my apartment? I could learn from someone who knew how to juggle their schedule to optimise an opportunity that may never come again.

The taxi ride to the bar was far from glamorous.

My Pakistani driver took off like a rocket. As he weaved through the lanes of traffic, I soon realised road rules in Dubai were, at that time, optional.

This man drove like many others of his profession: hard on the accelerator and a little too violently on the brakes. My stomach lurched every time he swerved or took off rapidly from the lights. My nausea had started to rise.

'Schwaya, schwaya. Please. Slowly, slowly. I'm going to be sick,' I pleaded. It made no difference. He either didn't understand English, or Arabic, or maybe he just didn't care. 'Please. STOP!'

Before his taxi could come to a full halt I flung the door open and threw up onto the side of the road. It was a narrow escape. My driver was relieved I hadn't christened his back seat as he calmly sprayed Febreze Air Effects around the car, on the floor behind him, then in my immediate direction. He then offered me a tissue. I wiped my mouth, and, sitting back, I nodded. We were only moments from the velvet ropes and burly security guards at the doors of the Buddha Bar.

'Okay, yalla, go.'

For a Sunday Session, the dress code was more upmarket than I had imagined.

Inside, the mood was dark, moody, exotic and opulent. It was obviously the place to be, with its hypnotic house beats and beautiful hostesses. I was decidedly underdressed for the occasion in my favourite Texan cowboy boots and colourful Australian sundress.

As I moved further into the room, my eye caught Tiger Woods to the left and a tray of shots to the right. The drinks sat unclaimed, strategically placed beneath sultry lighting which had been designed to make everyone in the room look better than they probably did.

I casually reached for a shot of tequila – and I am not a tequila girl. It quickly tore its way down my throat, burning away the last bitter traces of motion sickness and adrenaline.

A hand now rested on my back, before pulling me closer. It was a moment of déjà vu, intimate and captivating.

'You're my kind of girl.' He too reached instinctively for a shot from the tray and threw it back.

That night we sipped on endless rounds of saketinis and Asian-inspired platters. Conversation flowed all around us as we held hands in the darkness, away from prying eyes. We mingled in and out of each other's sentences, as if we had known each other for much longer, and before we knew it the night had slipped away.

It was now almost three in the morning. In a few short hours

Jonathan would have a flight to catch, and I would be sitting at my desk in the desert.

'I'll give you a lift home,' he schmoozed softly. 'I've a car waiting. You're on my way.'

I knew I wasn't. I didn't correct him. I knew we weren't going to my place.

We swept past the gilded stallions guarding the entrance of his hotel. The grounds were like something out of a fairytale. The valet circle was still humming with cars, limousines and taxis, even at this late hour.

We slipped into the resort's labyrinth of walkways, half-running, half-laughing, the kind of breathless hurry lovers fall into when privacy becomes the next urgent destination. By the time we reached his villa we had lost all sense of time.

His front door opened into a courtyard, where he handed the night concierge five hundred dirhams with a smooth, practised flick. It was too discreet to be casual, too casual to be innocent.

For a fleeting moment I wondered what he was trying to hide by paying someone off, but the thought quickly disappeared as Jonathan's hand guided me up the carved stone staircase to his suite. He already knew the script. There was no doubt he had rehearsed this scene before. He knew exactly where, and how, it would end.

Behind the heavy, hand-carved doors to his room with their geometric inlays, I knowingly stepped over a threshold into something more sacred and illicit.

On my first night in Dubai I had dreamt of this hotel and its opulence. It was where I would have a secret tryst. But in that dream, my lover didn't reveal himself to me. He remained faceless.

Now, with Jonathan's hands through my hair and my dress lifted, my dream had turned to reality. Neither of us knew who was leading who anymore as we moved through several rooms in heated passion. Our limbs tangled, my lips became swollen with his kisses and our skin slicked with sweat. He would whisper things into my neck, and later into the small of my back. Things I didn't need to remember, or shouldn't have believed. I did anyway. On that sultry February night, our hunger for each other never faded.

By dawn, I was stretched out across the bed, in a delirious slumber. I could feel him watching me. It had been a night I would never forget.

When I turned to leave, I glanced back, wanting to etch him into my memory in case I missed something. He, too, had turned, the opposite way, but just in time for me to see him slip a gold band onto his finger. It was a ring that I had never seen before.

Just like he'd probably done a thousand times before.

My heart pounded and I struggled to catch my breath. He proceeded to clip together his designer watch that he had laid out on his bedside table the night before. The one next to the tousled white sheets of *our* California king.

If he noticed the colour drain from my face, as he turned around, he didn't show it.

I left the only way I knew how. Quietly, with shame. Catholic guilt was once again hitting fast and hard. Our chemistry had been undeniable, but stupidly, I'd fallen for his trap.

I took the abra, the slow wooden boat that ferried guests through the waterways of the hotel, floating past palm-fringed restaurants, private majlis rooms and domed rooftops so my mind could rewind to those moments when he had paused before answering a question or two.

Had I overlooked the signs? That which was right in front of me? I remembered him saying he had been in a situation for a long time, but I hadn't pressed him to explain, most men don't bother hiding their indiscretions. They simply say, 'I'm married.'

I then tell them I'm no longer interested.

Not even fifteen minutes had passed. Jonathan was calling. I let it ring. It stopped, then rang again. I picked it up and waited for him to say something.

Already I had imagined him back in London with his wife and the young children he hadn't yet mentioned who would run and jump into his arms, screaming, 'Daddy, Daddy, we've missed you so much!' Then they would sit down for dinner as a family, before he would put them to bed with a tale.

By then Jonathan would have forgotten standing on the balcony as he mouthed, 'I miss you already' as I floated by.

He wanted to see me again. Perhaps we could meet somewhere. Soon our phone calls would stretch from one hour to two, then three to four. It felt different. He listened to me and that made me feel like the most important person in the world.

Jonathan was a striking contrast to the chaos of my turbulent, toxic and soul-destroying relationship with Tom.

I'd quickly fallen into limerence.

Obsessive thoughts, overwhelming longing and a distorted perception were a desperate sign that I craved his reciprocation.

I wouldn't dwell on my situationship long, because the following week I found myself in the emergency room of Jebel Ali Hospital. I had come down with a severe case of food poisoning. I was now in a bed pushed up against a windowless wall with a pink flimsy curtain for privacy. My life was now blurred by morphine, fever chills and the constant hum of medical equipment.

Jonathan called. He was concerned, I could barely hold a conversation. He said it was the morphine when I mentioned I couldn't let go of the thought of the two bright blue body bags, visible through the gap just beyond my door, which had been left ajar. If I stayed, I could be next, I told him.

I kept his songs on repeat. They were the ones we'd listened to under the covers, as we shared his string headphones. He told me the songs he selected were just for me; but I knew later, the lyrics said everything we hadn't.

NO REGRETS AND IRISH GOODBYES

WEEKS TURNED INTO MONTHS WHICH soon sped past. They were punctuated by regular phone calls from Jonathan, but I knew he wasn't coming back – at least not specifically for me.

Tom had taught me what the wrong relationship could do; how it could gnaw at the edges and fracture my sense of self.

I didn't want a repeat of my past.

What I had with Jonathan was going nowhere. I didn't want to wait around for a man who only showed up when it was convenient to him. I wasn't going to be scheduled.

I'd been flown around the world by men without any guarantee of what followed, only the understanding that they wanted me there with them. They made me laugh. They paid attention. And here's what I've learned: when a man is truly interested, it's obvious. There's no mystery to decode because he will tell you everything, sometimes even things you really wish you didn't know. Help is always one phone call away and birthdays are never forgotten. It's not romance. It's clarity.

Six months after Jonathan left town, I started to accept other invitations, including a tryst with a maddeningly sexy, emotionally unavailable Irishman I'd met through work. The kind who was technically single but *spiritually* spoken for. We danced and drank our way through the city's latest nightclubs and house parties, before ending up intertwined beyond his perimeter cameras, electric security gates and swimming pool, in his upstairs bedroom.

He was kind, warm and super decent in that disarming way that we expect from the Irish. In hindsight, he was always behind a half-shut door, no matter how brightly I knocked. What I had was all there was ever going to be. He helped me forget what I was struggling to, or so I thought.

In the quiet moments, Jonathan was never far from my mind. Just like in the Mills & Boon romance novels I used to read at school, I foolishly waited for him to choose me so we could ride off into the sunset. Every cell in my body believed that all love stories still ended that way.

A TWO-MILLION-DOLLAR DILEMMA

WHILST I WAS TRYING TO NAVIGATE my love life that year, Dubai was moving at a velocity nothing in my professional life had prepared me for. The launch of a new residential project went viral. Deposits came in faster than we could count them, with ten per cent down on a single-page reservation order, often handed over in cash still warm from someone's pocket.

We sold more than two hundred homes off-plan in a single weekend.

It was the last day of sales, just after six. I was packing up to leave our pop-up sales centre when a thoroughly ordinary Englishman in beige trousers, loafers and an open-necked shirt walked in. He was the kind you'd expect to find tending his expansive back garden in Sussex, or minding his sister's bookshop in Hackney.

Except he was carrying two million dollars in cash.

'What do you have left? I'd like to put a deposit down on whatever you have.'

Holy cow. Stay calm. This is surely an outlier of a sales moment.

The banks had closed two hours ago. Our CEO had already left for the weekend and he would need to countersign any reservation order issued to the client. He also need to sign as a witness any receipt of funds.

'Would you mind waiting one moment, please?' I needed to make a discreet phone call to someone more senior.

'What do I do?' I asked.

'Take it home,' came the reply, without a hint of hesitation.

'I don't think you understand,' I said, half-laughing. 'I may be in St Barts by the morning, enjoying champagne on my new yacht.'

I certainly wasn't going to sit and count two million dollars in cash, alone, with him sitting patiently nearby. Then have to walk to my car with *two million US dollars* in the back seat. How would I know if it was real or counterfeit? What if I made a mistake and it was short and I needed to start again?

This surely couldn't be the plot twist in my next headline. I'd only just arrived in Dubai.

'Thank you for coming in. I'd love to help, but our finance team has already left for the day,' I said. 'Come back tomorrow and I'll show you the available units, and you can take a master sales and purchase agreement home to review. We're a government organisation, so I have to follow the process. I know it's not ideal, but the villas will still be here in the morning. I'm happy to book you in for an appointment first thing.'

Back in Australia, real estate was tightly regulated. It was a place where I had been code-bound and clear on my ethics.

As tempting as it was to add 'money mule' to the list of questionable chapters in my already unpredictable life, this one was better left unwritten.

THE CYA FILE

THE ONLY APPROVED REAL ESTATE AGENT working on our sales launch who wasn't contracted to the government had shown up at my desk. He asked for a blank sheet of A4 paper. I pointed to the photocopier in the office. Slapping the paper down with a smile, he then casually leaned over and scribbled a dozen or so numbers down the left-hand side of the page.

As I glanced down at all the villas he had supposedly *sold* and was seeking commission for, I blinked in disbelief. At least one of the properties he claimed, I had sold myself.

I wish I got paid like that.

My instincts were already humming. He had been suspiciously friendly with management, and I suspected something was off.

'Could you please provide copies of all the signed reservation agreements, the ones co-signed by both the client and the CEO, and I will make sure you get paid straight away.'

It was the paperwork I knew he didn't have.

His expression darkened. Turning on his heels, he walked away without another word. I knew exactly where he was going. It was straight to the corner office.

With the property market still in its infancy, the lack of regulation and proper systems left gaps wide enough for commercial predators to slip through. Some were already exploiting every loophole they could find.

Tom had at least trained me to think like a special forces operative.

'Pay attention to someone's behaviour, not their words,' he always told me. 'Desperate people do desperate things, so if something doesn't feel right, just note down the conversation, time and date, print it out and file it. You never know when you may need it. CYA. Cover your arse.'

In the agent's haste to get to another office, he had conveniently left his sales sheet behind. I calmly opened the bottom drawer of my desk and flicked through until I found the orange folder.

I casually slipped the sheet into my special CYA file: a carefully curated collection of business emails, notes, numbers and late-night written rants. Those that appeared, to anyone reading them, unhinged and recklessly unprofessional.

The following day, I was asked to completely stop our sales audit. They apparently didn't need to know where the clients were from, what they bought, who paid cash and who was paying by bank finance.

'No need for market feedback, either,' I was told. 'Just prepare the commission for our trusted property agent.'

Something felt off the moment I stepped into HR a week later. The woman behind the desk dressed and spoke like a local, but her lack of courtesy made it clear she wasn't. Ayesha had taught me a lot about her culture, including how to pick an imposter.

I'd come to correct a salary shortfall for a Filipino single mother. Her overtime from the launch weekend, an extra hundred dirhams, hadn't been paid. It was for her son's education.

My employment file sat conspicuously on the HR director's otherwise empty desk.

She was less than thrilled to see me. It was too early in the morning for her to deal with anything.

'Is there something you would like to discuss?' I asked, looking directly at my file before back at her.

Her hand moved to bring the file closer.

I'd be faster. I snatched up *my* file, in an admittedly inflammatory move.

She reached out to snatch it back. I had a firmer grip.

Her seat flung back against the wall as she moved to her feet, her buxom frame towering over me. She was far more intimidating than one would expect from an already physically imposing woman in an abaya. It could have been her overpowering fragrance or her unusually thick layer of makeup that took me aback.

She landed a sharp, calculated punch on my arm. I let go of the file as its contents almost spilled out over the desk. I knew how quickly things could spiral so quickly retreated, heading back to the other side of the office at a faster pace than usual.

'Only your president will save you!' she screamed after me.

Good luck with that. Doesn't she know we don't have a president running Australia? It was clearly discomforting for those immediately outside her office. Their backs had stiffened as their computer screens flickered back to life. They stared at them with exaggerated focus. All at once, keyboards started to clatter. No one dared look up.

My adrenaline had started to surge by the time I reached my desk. I opened the bottom drawer with practised precision. I grabbed my handbag, then reached for the orange folder, which I tucked under my arm as I headed towards the elevators.

'I'll be back,' I said to the receptionist, offering a smile that gave nothing away. It simply looked as if I was heading out to a meeting. It was just before 9:00 am when the lift doors closed. I pushed B2 and left the office for the last time.

Once in my car, I called one of the government's senior executives, an eloquent older gentleman from a country where the rule of law stuck. An educated professional. A man I knew I could trust.

'I think I may have just lost my job, but I have something you might want to take a look at.'

After eighteen months in Dubai, I felt I was now unwittingly involved in espionage.

The next call was to a corporate lawyer, a woman well known for her modesty and razor-sharp mind. Her door was always open. I relied on her in the past to close the loopholes and flag the quiet dangers that required a strategic legal mind.

What was about to be uncovered would normally land any perpetrator in jail if they had operated in any other well-regulated jurisdiction.

I knew the orange file I carried contained allegations that could detonate a career.

Within twenty-four hours I was sitting before a woman who quietly orchestrated the financial affairs of His Highness's entire network of companies.

I was immediately reassigned without any company announcement, and sent to a department in an undisclosed location, far from more familiar corridors. There would be no explanation and no paper trail. I'd been pulled into the government's first internal investigation into financial fraud and corporate corruption.

I was now surrounded by those with sharp mathematical minds and steady ethics. It was only a matter of time before another rabbit would be pulled out of the hat.

WHITE-COLLAR CRIME
AND COSMIC RECEIPTS

NEWS OF MY ARRIVAL BACK IN Sydney had travelled quickly. Invitations to celebrate Christmas had already started to pour in. I was looking forward to a summer break in Australia and catching up with my friends. I had barely walked through the back door at my first party when a woman shouted to me on the back lawn as she stood next to the manicured vines spilling over the wall from the house next door. There, surrounded by others, was a woman you'd expect to find front-row at a charity lunch. Late forties, blonde, dressed perfectly head to toe in tonal creams.

'Oh, you're from Dubai? Do you know…?' she shouted over.

Her gold bangles clinked as she waved me over to join her group and clink glasses. Only then did we introduce ourselves.

'Yes, I am. What a small world.' I was cautious about revealing too much. 'How do you know each other?'

Twelve thousand kilometres away from Dubai, here in front of me in Sydney, was someone who knew the man who had hidden his crimes behind his network and corporate polish.

'He's my cousin,' she shrieked. It was more for the entertainment of those around her. She clearly had a bone to pick with anyone who had been in his vicinity. 'He ripped off his own mother on her deathbed and changed her will! Don't get me started on what he did in Queensland.'

I took a long slow sip as I politely leaned in for more juicy gossip. 'Hmmm, the name rings a bell.'

I didn't offer more.

'He's from the *other* side of the family, but he really wanted to be in ours,' she said with a deep, throaty and knowing laugh. 'You know he's a bully, always has been, right since the day he started at the private school on the North Shore, the one his family couldn't really afford to send him to. We know because we had *all* the money. Did you know he left everything behind, including his house and so-called lavish lifestyle, to move to Dubai? He even left the keys in the car parked in the driveway.' She had barely drawn breath.

I nodded slowly and tried not to smirk. This was a very unexpected revelation. The universe never misses with its cosmic receipts.

Australians don't bother with subtlety. They'll give it to you straight, whether you asked for it or not. Maybe that's why so many keep a bottle of wine chilling in the fridge. It's for those just-in-case days when something could knock you for six.

I lifted my almost empty glass to accept a top-up of champagne. 'Shall I send him your regards if I see him?'

She didn't blink.

'Don't bother.'

With a dirty little secret exchanged and our heads slightly tilted, there was nothing left to say. We clinked glasses and at the same time turned to separate groups in search of lighter conversation.

SYDNEY SECRETS AND
SERENDIPITOUS ENCOUNTERS

THE NEIGHBOURHOODS OF DARLINGHURST, Kings Cross and Potts Point weren't exactly the postcodes people would boast about. At least not when I first moved to Sydney. Most preferred to say they lived nearby in leafy Elizabeth Bay or down the hill in the also pleasant Rushcutters Bay.

As the '80s rolled into '90s, the scene slowly began to shift. Designer apartments emerged, creatives moved in and the rough edges began to soften. It was helped along by enough celebrities to give the area the cultural cachet it needed to feel fashionable.

The Coca-Cola sign glowed like a red electric crown, marking the line between the respectable and the reckless. Kings Cross was a red-light fantasia, where neon signs buzzed above strip clubs, jazz joints, drag revues and back-alley discos that beckoned the unsuspecting (and more often, the suspicious and suspected). Yes, there were gangs, dirty cops and corruption, but there was also freedom, the kind understood by misfits, drug users, artistic types and multi-sexuals.

You could rewrite yourself in the Cross. For someone like me, it was nothing short of exhilarating.

When I returned that Christmas in 2007, it was where Paula lived, in her Harry Seidler-designed townhouse filled with art work and a library of books. It was the kind of place you lived if you were a sophisticated empty nester, or a cosmopolitan city dweller with deep pockets.

Paula first sailed into Sydney at eighteen as a 'ten-pound Pom'. She came to Australia on an assisted government migration scheme that was aimed to reduce the pressure on post-war Britain by exporting those keen to leave.

Paula admitted she had been lured by a travel poster she had seen in the window of her coal mining town in Yorkshire. The one with a girl in a bikini standing next to a palm tree. She carried a suitcase full of hope as she waved behind her family in search of a better life in the sun. It was easy for a woman to build a new life when you're anchored by bravado and laced with wit.

Paula had been married three times. Her third husband, a Cambridge economics professor, called off their wedding after only five months after meeting someone else abroad. Her father had just died, she was in her fifties, and she had already sold the house she personally owned to pay for their future back in England.

It almost destroyed Paula. She told me she thought she'd never recover.

She was skiing black runs in Austria when she met a man who finally understood her. They fell madly in love, and twenty years later they were still hot and steamy. Paula believes in love. More importantly, Paula believes in *herself*. To Martina, Susu and me, she is an icon.

Her advice is simple, and very well tested now she is in her late 70s: keep things smooth where it counts, and always have your nails done. Men notice nails. Wear fresh, matching underwear, even if no one sees it but you. Don't forget your lipstick – Dior red is a good choice, especially when perfectly applied. Wear expensive fragrance, preferably the one he bought for you. Make it your signature scent. Spritz it on where you want to be kissed. Mist the sheets you will soon be between. Men love a slut in the bedroom.

Give him what he fantasises about. Book that trip to Europe. Learn to ski properly. The men you will want to meet are always at the very top of the mountain. You should slide into après together so people notice the type of woman he is attracted to. Know what to order at the bar straight away, and know how to enjoy yourself. Be that energy that inspires and attracts.

'Darling,' she'd purr, 'pop on the kettle as you quickly reconstruct your hair with Velcro rollers. A man wants to wake up and think, *Thank you, God*, not *Oh my God.*'

After a life of failed relationships, Paula reminded me that I shouldn't mistake breadcrumbs for effort.

'Darling,' she'd say with a wink, handing me a crystal glass of bubbles, 'you need a reset.'

RED VELVET SEDUCTION

I**T TURNED OUT P**AULA AND **I** WERE talking about two very different kinds of reset. Mine involved a change of scene, and Asia, undeniably, can be seductive.

Daniel was one of only two people I knew in Singapore. The other was my brother, who, inconveniently that weekend, was buried in oncology work. It had been years since Daniel and I had last caught up. Our kids had all grown up and moved on.

'What about lunch at one? I know a terrific place down on the water,' he said when I called. 'Then let's hit up the Grand Prix. I've got two VIP passes sitting on my desk.'

It sounded like a plan. Although those in the know say: plan early, plan twice.

 Which is why we never made it to the track. Instead, we lingered over lunch and Daniel ordered a cognac. Then we backed that up with a martini. Then a couple more. The staff politely encouraged us to move along before they set the evening meal service.

I have no idea where we went after the restaurant but I do recall Daniel saying it would be a sin to not visit the infamous Four Floors of Whores.

The sun had well and truly set by the time we caught a cab to Orchard Towers. Daniel knew where to go as we went from floor to floor through the mingling expats and neon-lit labyrinth of bars, pulsing with music. Women from all over Asia scanned the room with practised ease looking for their next unspoken transaction.

The bars were full of unfiltered desire and suggestions, you only had to put your hand in your pocket. We laughed until our faces hurt as we watched twenty-something men fall under the spell of some extremely attractive ladyboys.

'Don't tell anyone I'm here,' Daniel yelled over his shoulder as we slithered our way through the crowd.

'Of course not!' It wasn't every day I got invited to a brothel.

By the time we made it back to the ground floor, it was heaving. The bar was now three deep, and there was not another blonde in sight.

'I'm going to look around the room. You'll be fine for a bit; I'll find you shortly.' Daniel swiftly disappeared into the throng. I quickly lost sight of him as I stood awkwardly at the bar waiting to be served.

'What will it be?' the barman asked.

'Gin and tonic, thanks.' I'd had enough alcohol for one day, but it'd be weird to ask for water in a place like this.

'Make that two.' A handsome blond was now perched beside me.

Luck had just taken its turn.

'Are you alone?' He leaned into my ear so I could hear him above the pulsing beats designed to disguise conversation.

'Well, not exactly. I'm here with a friend. He's gone walkabout.' I waved vaguely towards the crush of bodies on the far side of the room. 'And you? What are *you* doing in a place like this?' Our gin and tonics landed and he dropped notes on the bar and told the guy to keep the change.

'I'm here with friends.' He pointed to the room on our right. 'Come join us. You can't stand here by yourself.'

He was right. What if my friend never returned? How long should a girl wait alone?

'Sure, why not?'

Serpentining our way through the elbow-to-elbow bustle, we arrived at a small roped-off stage. It looked like it had been set up for a panel discussion, not as an area partitioned for VIPs.

I collapsed into an empty red velvet seat beside him as we faced an audience of hookers stretched out before us. It looked like a scene from a decadent man's dream.

'Oh there you are.' Daniel was now standing on the other side of the velvet rope. A wry smile matched his very glazed eyes and slight sway. I beckoned him to climb over the rope.

Pausing, then looking behind him, he paused again before mouthing, 'Do you know who you're sitting with? These guys are *my heroes.*' I had no clue what he meant.

Was he referring to men who frequented places like this so often, they had a VIP section?

My newfound blond stranger was surprisingly sophisticated and entertaining for a random Sunday evening in a brothel. Daniel had meanwhile slid his chair closer to his heroes. Unbeknownst to me, I was sitting next to *Jackass* on our little stage.

Whether I drifted away from Daniel or he quietly vanished, I couldn't tell you.

Later that evening, one thing led to another with my newfound friend. I never did quite catch his name. What I noticed instead was the contrast, his youth against my knowing and the way his steel blue eyes lingered as if he understood the risk and chose it anyway. What had felt tender between us at the venue became undeniably electrifying in his upmarket hotel room.

The next morning, my head floated somewhere between a dream and reality.

'I loved our evening,' he said, voice low and unsure. 'It was amazing. ... You're so cool. It was perfect but I have to go.'

By the time he had finished his shower and appeared back in the room with his towel wrapped low and tight across his hips, his expression had shifted dramatically from last night's mischief to something far heavier.

Then he paused. His eyes welled. And just like that, the magic cracked.

The words tumbled out of him, as they do when a man is fifteen years younger and living with guilt. They were followed by an unexpected flood of tears, which quickly turned to hyperventilation.

Only later would I realise our room was a discreet detour from his penthouse a few floors above and his life as a champion Formula One driver.

As the wheels lifted off the tarmac I sat back in my window seat, pushing my oversized black Chanel sunglasses up on my nose. They that famously shielded my dark circles, and an innocent sin.

I'm sure it wasn't quite the reset Paula had in mind. She would later remind me: 'Not everything has to mean something. Something better is always just around the corner.'

THAT 'SOMETHING BETTER' WAS A JOB with Cirque du Soleil. The Dubai government had just secured the most successful live entertainment brand on the planet, and I had been hired to build the local team that would bring their creative brilliance to life.

The skills I'd relied on to survive would now be the skills I needed to navigate their hefty investment at a very volatile time in global economics.

I understood the rhythm of show business intimately: stage, screen, music, events and, most importantly, the delicate choreography of creative egos. Cirque's logistics and touring requisites had always been executed with military precision, something I could claim to be familiar with, though for different reasons.

In entertainment, the key is never to panic. There is always something that goes wrong. During our setup, what went wrong was the only thing I hadn't prepared a contingency plan for. The real circus was about to begin.

Outside our site perimeter a murder investigation had sent shockwaves through the show. Its impact almost derailed our entire production. The police swooped in, detaining our entire cleaning crew and several of Cirque's overseas production team, including their music director. It was for a crime they didn't commit.

To make matters worse, a sexual harassment claim by one of the female riggers on the setup was filed against a construction worker. Apparently a South Asian man had become a little too excited about a large rope trailing between her legs.

It was nothing the sharp, clear-headed team of women I'd hired couldn't handle.

As if things weren't dramatic enough, a wave of unregistered relatives from Eastern Europe arrived to support Cirque's acrobats, contortionists and aerial artists.

They had disembarked without a travel visa, a place to stay, or any firm return date. Compounding the issue, they had missed the cultural memo around dressing modestly in an Arab country. They innocently waited at customs for help to arrive, in towering white thigh-high boots and miniskirts.

I revelled in trying to manage the divide between several vastly different cultures. It wasn't only fuel for artistic anarchy; it was the perfect storm.

As the project sped towards opening night, someone with a very big ego arrived to supersede me in the production. After all my hard work, I had no intention of being railroaded by a man who thought he knew better.

He tried to tighten the budget; I knew cutting corners would compromise the performance, quality and artistic safety of the show. Our personalities clashed like cymbals. It was only a matter of time before we had a run-in.

'It never rains here! You're wasting money on building something that isn't needed. You've got no idea what you're doing,' he raged over the top of me in front of the entire office.

Nothing was more exhausting than having to defend my competence to a man who was threatened by it. As he stood there, I recognised his type immediately. He was another Tom. I wondered how long he would have lasted on any other production.

Traditionally, it only rained in Dubai three days a year. This time, something had told me we needed to prepare for it. If the skies turned against us, it could cost the government millions to replace their technical equipment. The tour would have to be cancelled. Still, it was dismissed as an 'unnecessary spend' by the only man who liked the sound of his own authority more than the weight of his front-of-house responsibility.

For two solid weeks, it didn't just rain; it poured. That 'unnecessary spend' became the only thing standing between us and financial collapse.

Then the Global Financial Crisis hit.

The show was now too deep into the production setup, the performance dates were locked in and tickets had been sold. We were selling out.

Head office continued to slash costs further and payments to suppliers became unreasonably delayed. Critical headcount was next on the chopping block.

'Make do,' they said.

It sharpened my resolve. I worked on a shoestring and a prayer as the entire show sat under the thick shadow of an eclipse season.

We sold out, we filled the seats and Cirque became the most successful show ever to tour at the time. According to my boss it meant I deserved a big pat on the back.

There's a lot to be said for grit and determination. Our team, Cirque's brilliance and Dubai's ambition had made the impossible possible.

BEIRUT

A week in the Levant was exactly the jolt I needed, and the invitation couldn't have landed at a better time. Beirut would feel like oxygen after Cirque had packed up and rolled out of town.

Mariana, one of my dedicated Cirque colleagues, had chosen to wed her Argentinian fiancé in her hometown. Lebanese hospitality is famously a force of nature. The city sweeps you up in its exuberance before you've even dropped your bags. Strangers soon become confidants.

I was on my way to a three-day wedding of food, music, and fun.

The chosen venue was a gorgeous, ancient religious site perched high above the city; its stone walls still carried the pride of centuries past. It was a feast for the senses as Mariana glided past me in Valentino gown, late in the afternoon when the air was still heavy with scent of orange blossoms.

After the Catholic mass and service ended, the drumming erupted, wild and rhythmic, as an all-male troupe beat their way into the reception area. The Argentinians had just ignited the fuse to a long night of fun, which perfectly suited the Lebanese.

We were mesmerised. Grandparents clapped, toddlers stamped, everyone cheered and rose to dance. It wasn't only choreographed; it was contagious.

The wedding, all at once, had exploded into a revelry I had never experienced before.

I'd never seen such elegance. The designer gowns, the jewellery, the unapologetic glamour, every woman looked like she belonged on the cover of a magazine. The men were booted and bespoke suited and gleaming with pride and mischief.

The champagne never stopped flowing that night and the buffet could have collapsed under the weight of choice. It was a generous indulgence.

When only six guests remained, the bride and groom were still too alive to call it a night.

Mariana and her new husband yelled 'See you at the club' from their gleaming Bentley as they rolled down the hill. We, the stragglers, found ourselves hitching a lift back into town in the only ride left. The florist's van.

We perched on top of petals, leaves, pots and ribbons and squeezed in between arrangements. We left a trail of confetti behind us as we scooted away. At a handful of military checkpoints, soldiers shone their torches into our van, then on the driver.

'Where are you going and what are you carrying?' they would ask quickly in Arabic.

'Flowers and … wedding guests. They're still celebrating!' The driver spoke in French, knowing they understood both languages.

I didn't even know where we were heading, as we were wedged in the back. A wild crew of fêtards, still giddy on champagne and the joys of love and marriage.

Beirut was full of people who knew how to celebrate, as if pleasure were a language they'd grown up speaking. It was one of those rare times when everything felt exactly as it should be.

Which was nowhere in particular.

IT'S ALL IN THE STARS

DURING THE GLOBAL FINANCIAL CRISIS, those who had considered themselves indispensable were now ornamental. Dubai had shed its contracts swiftly and mercilessly.

It wasn't surprising that entertainment was deemed expendable, as the GFC quietly exposed the true nature of balance sheets and what had been quietly rotting beneath the surface. Leaders who'd risen through the landscape because of connections, not competence, left with a golden parachute. Most simply walked out with a cardboard box.

It was a shift I'd privately been bracing for ever since the previous eclipse had hinted at an impending roadblock, still I remained sceptical of the astrological interpretation in my chart.

'Come to New York.'

Susu's door was always open. As a CEO of a cut-throat business, and a born and bred New Yorker, she was a woman who had seen recessions and wild swings in the markets already. Before an empire, she had built alliances. While men and the media sold the idea of a 'temporary turbulence', women like her were already mapping new revenue streams and alternatives. Susu had been hardwired for survival in a generational business.

I hadn't planned on necessarily uprooting my entire life, it was meant to be nothing more than a little time away from Dubai. My retrenchment package suggested the choice to return was now mine.

Six months later, after immersing myself in Catalan culture, drifting through art galleries and butchering the Spanish language with an admirable commitment, I landed at JFK.

I was living out of Susu's pied-à-terre on the Upper East Side, which she was now sharing with her boyfriend. In my heart, I knew I was living on borrowed time, surviving on whatever confidence I could manufacture in a city that eats hesitation for breakfast.

New York has never been for the timid.

Somewhere between the pull-out sofa in her study, my self-doubt and endless dreadful coffees, I walked straight into a moment I'd long hoped for; one I never believed would happen.

She was America's beloved astrologer to the stars. Susan Miller had guided me and millions of others through Mercury retrogrades, Saturn returns and Uranus transits through her monthly online forecasts.

Susu told me she lived locally because she had often seen her at a local café. The one that served dreadful coffee. I missed her because I had been going to Starbucks four doors down, partly because of their free Wi-Fi.

I couldn't be sure if that was why Susan Miller was also there that day, sitting calmly alone at a table that faced the street. My mind started to race. Starstruck in Starbucks, I introduced myself before launching into one long, embarrassing spiel.

'Susan?! *The* Susan Miller? Oh my God. I love *Astrology Zone*. I've been following you since '98. I'm from Australia. I can't believe this …'. On and on and on I went.

I wanted to slap myself for gushing. I rarely do it. Okay, I may have once before when I met Jon Bon Jovi in the green room at a concert. As we were taking a photo together, I knocked his tea all over him by accident. It was so embarrassing I wanted the floor to swallow me. Technically, it wasn't a *verbal* gush.

Susan, unlike Jon, was gracious enough to chat longer. So I

mentioned that I was a professional astrologer and we chatted about the stars. But I wasn't *Susan Miller*. She had a degree from NYU in mathematics, had featured in *Vogue*. As any gusher would, I offered to read for her. 'It would be my pleasure, after all.'

We settled on a date for a tarot reading. Anything else would have felt like I was attempting a triple somersault off the end of the beam like Nadia Comăneci.

That said, I finally felt the universe was listening.

From then on, the stars weren't only listening; they were acting in my best interests.

If ever a musical was designed to excite people like me, it would be the wildly controversial love-rock phenomenon *Hair*. Susu bought mid-section tickets at the Hirschfeld for my forty-fifth birthday.

The show's opening notes filled the theatre like a cosmic over-ture. The planets had now shifted into formation; a new era had cracked open and destiny was now clearing its throat for me, one shimmering, psychedelic hymn at a time.

With the show about to end in one ritualistic, communal voice, Susu nudged me, her eyes wide.

'Okay, go. Go now, get up, hurry, this may be the only time you're on Broadway. You're going to be a star. Go. Go. Go.' Susu was so excited she pushed me along the aisle, screaming, 'I want to see you up there! This is your moment.'

I ran up the stairs to the stage to sing my lungs out to 'Aquarius/Let the Sunshine In'. For three glorious minutes I was unabashedly, unprofessionally famous.

With my hands in the air, I was committed to the last song of the night, alongside a cast who were completely starkers. As they clapped and danced their way through to a sold-out theatre, I realised Susu was right.

It would be my one and only night on Broadway.

BOYS, NOT MEN

NEW YORK PULSES HARD AT P.J. CLARKE'S, a known East Side fix-ture where the swagger outnumbers the squeeze of those nearest to the bar.

It's where you find men in sharp city suits and women in sharper heels. It's where you take a break from pitching, chasing deals, or trying to make it. For a while you forget to count the cost of a decision.

P.J. Clarke's was my kind of place.

On Fridays, you're either shedding the weight of what's behind you or leaning into the promise of what's ahead.

It was in the crush of this Midtown bar that a man with perfectly polished shoes asked for my number. We'd had a brief, half muffled conversation under the armpit of a well-known computer mogul that I hadn't heard of.

At five foot eight, he could easily have been overlooked if I hadn't had the computer guy's armpit as a reference.

The next morning, I had forgotten him. He phoned to remind me who he was. I didn't know I had given him my number. I didn't have one with a prefix that mattered in New York, but he did.

'Ah, the trader from Morgan Stanley.' I should have sounded more impressed but didn't.

What I did remember was that he was a little on the short side. I didn't mind short men. They were typically more fun in bed. At least more agile and determined to please with their technique and humour. Short men are also more likely to spend the night because nights with them rarely ended at a more forgivable hour.

Why was this even racing through my mind on a dreary Saturday after breakfast?

This boy from Atlantic City certainly had an assured ease. I remembered his Celtic heritage, a mop of thick black hair, his startling baby-blue eyes and the sweep of long dark lashes that framed them. Ah, Cieran.

He had a conversational range that didn't stretch too far beyond his success on Wall Street. Nevertheless, with a weekend of doing nothing ahead of me, I was happy he called.

Cieran and I arranged to meet at the Met after lunch the following day. It's where people tend to meet before they wander through Central Park. From there we drifted west, over to the Upper West Side, to a bar neither of us really knew. It didn't matter. What mattered was that it had a television, and on it, baseball.

In New York, allegiance to a sport isn't a pastime; it's a weekly act of devotion.

'Unfortunately, I don't follow baseball, Cieran. Although I have been to Yankee Stadium,' I offered meekly. 'Do you like cricket?' I knew he'd have no idea.

'Cricket? Isn't that the thing that goes for a week?'

'Well, almost. Five days. We Aussies love to stretch out a good game with a break for lunch, then tea,' I said with a cheeky grin.

'Five days? Tea breaks?' He shook his head and went back to watching the screen.

He didn't press further. I knew why he was single. He had no banter.

The air was thick with roasted peanuts from street carts and the linden trees were in bloom that late afternoon in Central Park.

Yellow taxis rolled past us in bursts, as joggers and dog walkers darted in and out of the park's entrances. Families with ice creams or baseball mitts in hand headed home, sometimes with a dog in tow.

Cieran then told me he'd never been this far uptown before.

How odd, I thought, that a man who risked money couldn't risk taking a trip to a new neighbourhood. It turned out he hadn't yet travelled overseas, either. I quietly wondered if he had even been to Nashville, Austin or Seattle but there was no sense in spoiling the rest of my day.

By the time we had cut back across Central Park, he had asked if I would like to go on another date. *Rock of Ages* was playing on Broadway.

'I'd love to go, but I've got family in town next week.' It wasn't a lie.

'No problem. Just let me know how many tickets.'

'Would four be a problem?'

Four it was. Centre Orchestra. The kind of seats New York men book if they're hoping to get laid.

Strolling into the theatre that night would be Lewis and his mate from Outback Australia. I turned to catch Cieran's stunned expression before I raised my arm, hoping Lewis would see me.

Cieran's nervous laughter gave him away. He hadn't counted on 'my family' being two eighteen-year-old lads over six foot tall joining us. In one gulp, he downed his drink, leaving only the ice and seconds to gather himself before extending his arm in a handshake.

'Cieran. Welcome to New York. I'm glad you could join us.'

'G'day mate. How ya goin'? Thanks for having us. Whadda ya drinking? Can I get ya another one?'

Lewis had bunged on the accent and sounded more Australian than usual. If the age of my date surprised him, he didn't let it show.

Cieran's eyes darted between Lewis, his mate, me and the exit. He was like a man cornered. It was obvious that whatever he imagined happening later in the evening was off. I pretended not to notice, just as I pretended not to be perturbed by the endless trays of tequila shots that kept arriving at our seats throughout the show.

During the evening, Cieran made a couple of discreet attempts to hold my hand on and off, releasing it quickly as I whooped and clapped my hands to another classic rock anthem. By the time 'Don't Stop Believin'' started to close the show, I was on my feet until I danced all the way down the aisle and out of the theatre.

Lewis was beginning to understand exactly how his generation had been conceived. With a lot of teased hair, tight leather and late-night trysts in the back seats of a car.

As he and his mate peeled away, they left us to drift downtown to yet another bar. One he didn't need, but I went anyway even though the night had run its course. After a drink in a place where I lost my favourite pashmina, we called a cab. On Second Avenue, where he asked the driver to pull over, he opened the door and almost fell out onto the sidewalk before it had stopped. There was little point in trying to sound concerned.

I shut the door and watched him attempt to weave his way among the oncoming traffic, and as soon as he was halfway across, I turned and asked the taxi driver to turn up the music. We needed to continue uptown to 92nd Street.

And that was the last I saw of Cieran. Bless him.

THE GAME

FREE FOR LUNCH? I WANT YOU TO MEET SOMEONE TODAY. A text from Susu. There was no context, just the implied promise of either a job or a man who could complicate my life. With Susu, it could go either way.

We'd meet in a Midtown restaurant, one of those beneath the scaffolding you'd have to walk under. It was a New York enclave that beckoned men who close deals long before their second bottle of red arrives.

You know the place: dark wooden chairs, starched white linen tablecloths, and an Italian menu that included perfectly charred steak, the one waiters always recommend. Susu had claimed the most coveted table in the middle of the room, among a herd of businessmen.

Outside, drizzle slicked the pavement and flattened the atmosphere, as it had for the past few days.

Susu saw me before I reached her table. So had Louis, whose gaze never left mine as he pulled out my chair. Men can be so obvious without saying a word. He had a contagious, easy smile and playful, warm chocolate eyes which crinkled when he was amused.

Reaching for the bottle on the table, he then poured me a glass of Château Latour. I was immediately attracted to his presumption and confidence.

Susu made an excuse to leave. She had another meeting. I knew her day started at two in the morning. I also knew she was finished for the day and was hurrying home for love.

Louis and I lingered. So long, the staff began turning the tables for dinner. He appeared to know the restaurateur well. I watched them exchange discreet nods that suggested favours, history or both.

We ordered one for the road, as a thick roll of notes slipped from his pocket, landing almost at my feet. I looked away, pretending not to notice. He bent down, scooped it up and quietly placed it back into his jacket without hesitation or explanation. His composure remained unbroken.

In the wake of the financial crisis, appearances counted for everything. Cash in hand said far more than a top tier Amex card. It appeared Louis played a different game.

Our late lunch led to aperitifs at the Peninsula, then to everything on the menu at Nobu. That led to me giving him my number so we could see each other again.

Although modest, this very sexy, suave businessman appeared to have a lot of connections. He was so comfortable with his world that I was curious to be part of it.

Louis always walked on the wrong side of the pavement as we walked the streets of New York. It bothered me. I'm a sucker for old-fashioned etiquette.

'You should be protecting me from the horse carriages that splash their street sludge onto me,' I said, stretching out my arm as a suggestion to swap sides.

'Ahhh. But this is *my* town. Someone could jump out and grab you from the doorway.' He pulled me nearer. 'Women always walk on the outside.'

I was worth far more than I thought. Our dates had become even more exciting.

'Are you in the mafia?' It was a fair question. I'd read *The Godfather* and seen *The Sopranos*.

'No, but I was brought up by the mob.'

Well that was an unexpectedly honest answer. I liked a man who could handle any crisis. What was the possibility of me being in a mafia takeout on Fifth and Fifty-Seventh Street?

A late lunch at an Italian restaurant soon turned into champagne in the presidential suite of a members-only club overlooking Central Park. Which weirdly turned into laps in the swimming pool the next morning.

PARALLELED

Europe was always the place to be in summer. The booking
I'd made was to Italy, although I'd apparently changed the dates
two or three times. Nothing would be a problem, as long as it was
on Susu's credit card.

I could not remember ever booking two tickets to Europe, because I had never unknowingly used another person's credit card
before. Certainly not without their permission.

Susu clearly did remember, it was the reason the lock was
changed. I didn't know what I had done until many years later
when she told me. I was mortified. I had zero recollection. I was
so wrapped up in a romantic fantasy. Was I thinking it would save
me from a looming uncertain fate? I couldn't be sure of that either.

Breakdowns not only take their time, they seem to creep up on
you. Some would say it was because I had skipped my medication,
accelerating the fall; I'd add that some rapid and reckless life choices didn't help.

On paper, I sounded interesting, but New York's intensity had
quickly turned from promise to pressure as I tried to wrestle with
chaos and control, freedom and order.

To stabilise my mental health, I'd need clean and conscious daily habits, exercise and a network of trusted friends. Plus a place of
my own and a job. My bank account had run dry and Tiger Woods
was suddenly all over the news.

Things weren't looking great for either of us.

I knew that Jonathan knew him better than most. It was he who introduced me to Tiger in Dubai. The phone calls and accusations came thick and fast from those who knew I had worked in golf. I hadn't realised how much it would start to affect me by association.

'You know these men are all the same.'

'You can't trust anyone who travels a lot.'

'You know you're not the only one. There's one in every port.'

It didn't matter whether it was true or not. What mattered was how quickly I believed them. Every careless comment, every joke made at my expense slid under my skin and stayed there.

I never expected the words people threw at me, or the ones journalists printed, to seep so insidiously and incessantly into my mind. But they did.

Men had been getting away with their indiscretions for years and now they were scrambling to write their way out of their own moral failures. I recognised their tactics instantly. I wasn't blind. I'd worked in media and entertainment. I'd also worked for powerful men. It didn't matter who had to bleed. Their reputation had always been protected.

On the newsstands, on television, and everywhere in between, Tiger had become a spectacle. One man's private failings suddenly eclipsed his brilliance, and media coverage grew so voyeuristic it also exposed those who were cheating on their partners. The unfaithful had become quick to point a knowing finger at others.

Looking back at that time, the signs of my own undoing were everywhere. Men who wanted me only in private. Relationships that lived in the shadows. Promises that required my silence.

Each time I played their game, I had agreed to fade a little more.

SECTIONED

IN **B**ELLEVUE, **DYING WAS TAKING A** little longer than I had expected. Unlike in the movies, there was no soundtrack, no dramatic fade to white and no harped ascension and sparkles.

Death also doesn't come with an itinerary. No one ever says, *Expect delays.*

For me, it was like standing in the slowest queue at an airport, passport in hand, waiting to be called for a rubber entry stamp into the country. I was now shuffling between two worlds, disoriented. Hardly the easy exit from life I was hoping for.

'Are you an actress?'

Oh God, I can't die now, I've always wanted to be an actress.

I was looking up at the triage nurse who was looking down on me. Was he Cameron Tucker from *Modern Family*? It certainly looked like him. Maybe he had taken a break from acting. That's why he thought he recognised me.

I was convinced it was him because of his big, expressive presence, and unapologetically flamboyant style.

I didn't know if I had already crossed over. I felt like I had. They say that when you get to Heaven, you're allowed to do what you always wanted to do. In Heaven I wouldn't need an agent to be an actress, or a drama degree or even a work permit for another country. My classical technique and Shakespearean talent would already be honed for the stage in one grand celestial rewrite.

The room had started to tilt, it blurred before sagging. Even the walls had grown tired of standing upright as my hospital stretcher felt like it was now on a wild rollercoaster ride and sliding steeply down to one side.

In Heaven, my friend told me, they served Krug. This definitely wasn't Heaven. Although who would really know?

Bellevue Hospital was a place you didn't so much arrive at, as get delivered to. This was now a disaster of my own making. It was the kind of place you'd read about in books, or see in film noir. It was a place where the city's most brilliant, sinister and insane are treated with the same professionalism. Presidents had passed through its halls. So had poets, playwrights and performers, and now, far less theatrically, me.

The medical team had worked quickly to stabilise me. The bottle of prescription tablets I'd swallowed had already started to take effect. A heaviness, overwhelming nausea and a foggy disorientation had come upon me. Lithium has a very narrow therapeutic window. I had been classified as a high-risk behavioural patient, which was the reason I was triaged into Bellevue's Comprehensive Psychiatric Emergency Program. I would be held for seventy-two hours, then reassessed.

I knew that the dose that helps was not far from the dose that harms. Although the time release capsules were not immediately reactive enough to end my life, they were enough to destroy my kidneys with their toxicity.

A thick, black liquid, activated charcoal, clung in my throat.

'You need to drink this. Keep going. More. Keep drinking. You have to finish it.' I wouldn't have liked the alternative, apparently.

I caught a uniformed security guard watching from a distance with that blank, seen-it-all stare as the privacy curtain in duck egg blue was wrenched back. It had given me the only dignity in the emergency room chaos of New York's most infamous hospital.

A group of interns now stood at the end of my bed with the

attending doctor, who would use my case as a teaching example.

My lithium levels and kidney markers had been steadily climbing. If my body couldn't flush out the poison in the prescribed time, a machine would have to do it for me. Blood would be taken now every hour. My organs were apparently starting to fail. A clipboard was handed to me with attached consent forms for dialysis so that it could be prepped.

I'm not sure how much time had passed that day, but the bubbly actor, who I thought posed as a triage nurse, was again at my bedside.

'Let me check your levels one more time, just in case.' The IV drip that had been inserted into the most prominent vein of my hand tugged with every move.

He appeared to half skip towards me a short time later while I sat almost upright in my intensive care bed. Although he couldn't take away the reality and annoyance of the fluorescent tubes buzzing overhead, casting their cold pallor across the crimson vinyl chairs, he was beaming.

'I can't believe this,' he said, visibly relieved as he held my hand. 'By the grace of God, your levels have started to drop. You won't be needing dialysis after all. Someone up there must be watching over you.'

I had narrowly avoided not only a chemical triage but a metabolic catastrophe. The universe, for reasons known only to itself, wasn't done with me yet.

BEHIND THE YELLOW LINE

My ATTENDING PSYCHIATRIST WAS too handsome and too well dressed to feel entirely legitimate. He wore mandarin-collared shirts and could have easily given couture model David Gandy a run for his money. Nothing about him belonged to the place he now sat.

I imagined him slipping effortlessly into another life after hours, he looked like someone who loved Sondheim and symphonies and an aperitif. In my mind, he ended his evenings at Dante in the West Village where he lived. It was there he would order a Negroni Bianco as he waited for his husband to join him at his regular table by the window.

Bellevue was well known as 'the deep end of the pool' in the psychiatric ward. Much like you'd expect to find in all the most academically elite medical facilities, my psychiatrist was unflappable.

It was he who would decide whether I was discharged or transferred to another unit.

A wheelchair at half-turn waited in the corner of my ward. The air smelled of old people, antiseptic and stewed vegetables. Patients wandered with their drips, up and down the corridor, some barefoot. Once, upon returning from a bathroom visit, I noticed a man and his hairy, white, saggy bottom. He hadn't bothered to close the back of his gown. A nurse would remind him.

'Mr Markovitz, we can see more than we need to. Please close your gown for the ladies.'

He'd ignore her and continue on his way until she caught up

with him and guided him back to his room, his gown now snatched in for modesty.

I had been transferred to the only available bed. It was in the stroke ward, with a view over the Hudson. A phone sat next to my bed, but nobody called.

A couple of beds over, closer to the door, a very distressed elderly woman repeatedly called out to her husband, and often through the night. The nurses would have to medicate her just so the rest of us could sleep. Sadly, a man who appeared to be her husband only visited once that I knew of. He may have been another relative. Either way he didn't stay long.

The only company many of the patients kept were the machines that beeped constantly in the background. Their life had come down to a whiteboard above their bed listing their condition, their attending doctor, blood pressure and medication schedules. Throughout the day they would all be ticked off in neat black marker strokes.

Bellevue's fluorescent lights never dimmed, even while I lay in a waiting room for the soul. It was more depressing than being depressed.

I was reassured by my psychiatrist's intellectual precision, given that he was surprised to see that after a week I had recovered so quickly.

'You're looking much better but given that you've had a serious medical emergency, I'd like to monitor you for a few days more. I've found you a nice room in another ward, away from here. You can wear your day clothes; it's far more relaxed than where you are now and you will be able to move about,' he reassured me.

I wasn't happy. My bag was packed to leave.

My new room sat at the very top of Bellevue Hospital, as if my madness now required altitude. It was reached via an elevator few would have known about or seen. Even the two law enforcement officers accompanying me needed sign-off and a key to access it.

I didn't know that the twenty-fifth floor of Bellevue Hospital in New York had long been used to house the criminally insane. Later I heard the psychiatric ward for children sat a floor below.

'Turn right.'

Did I have a choice? Two police officers were now positioned either side of me, like bodyguards. Their enormous physiques formed an impenetrable barricade.

Had we turned left, the line between patient and predator would have become distinctly blurred. It was where psychosis could be met with prosecution. Behind those doors, the forensic psychiatric admissions. Those who had been charged with the gravest of crimes: homicide and multiple murders.

We waited behind the enormous double doors on the opposite side as an officer pressed the intercom and waited. The thick black and yellow hazard stripe on the bottom of the door stared back at me as a forewarning. The security camera above served to approve our entry. A sharp buzz cracked through the hallway, and the doors clicked. One officer led the way as the other stood behind me. I was now on the threshold between captivity and whatever waited beyond.

There'd be no escaping. Or popping down to the cafeteria for coffee and a blueberry muffin.

The twenty-fifth floor is monitored by trained psychiatric nurses and hefty, military- or police-trained security guards. A section under twenty-four-hour surveillance. My single room, off to the right and all the way to the end of the main corridor, would barely sit three metres away from those awaiting trial. Only a reinforced glass panel and a permanently locked wooden door would separate me from the left of the building.

I never thought about it much until a few days later, when I came face to face with the other side.

They would have diagnosed him with a fractured mind, but his stare remained locked on mine through the glass as he watched me at the door to my room. He was likely sedated and should have been closely monitored, by one-on-one trained psychiatric nurses and guards. For some reason, at that very moment he was alone. Unblinking, unshaken, unshaven. A middle-aged man of average height who stood frighteningly still.

A wide corridor ran the length of the ward, around eighty metres or so, end to end. It was lined in linoleum and long enough to walk a few laps so you'd feel like you'd at least achieved something. A thick yellow plastic stripe stretched along the floor from outside my room.

My corner suite that my psychiatrist said he had found faced out over Manhattan's skyline. Inside, beside a sealed, barred window, sat a single bed dressed in stiff white hospital sheets, complemented by one pillow too thin to be of any use. Against the wall in the corner was an outdated wardrobe, like you'd see in most dormitories anywhere in the world, and a set of brown laminated drawers, empty, forgettable and unlikely to win design awards.

The ceilings were high and the walls were painted a soft institutional beige. The space, like everything in Bellevue's concrete cube, was intentionally built for function.

The en suite bathroom offered no curtain, no towels and no mirror. Just a white bar of hospital soap, two sheets of recycled brown paper and a stainless steel sink. A matching sheet of steel was affixed to the wall, technically intended as a safe reflection of who we'd become. It was hardly an honest one.

My room sat on the same side as the art room and the TV lounge, where silence and the occasional outdated sitcom blurred together. A communal phone sat somewhere between there and the dining room opposite. Anyone from outside could call, and anyone inside could pick up.

Mental illness, I learnt in Bellevue, can be wildly comical. Whether you spoke to someone who cared was often a lottery. I only knew that to be the case because a Virgo friend of mine, a lawyer from London, would telephone me every day to check on me.

Among the paranoid schizophrenics, the homeless, the bridge-jumpers, the delusional and the lost, together with the archaic parameters I was expected to function within, he at least tried to give me some hope. He certainly gave me a good laugh.

Each afternoon around three or four, the loudspeaker would crackle to life.

'Medication time. Please stand behind the yellow line.'

Naturally, I let my rebellious toes drift over the plastic strip so I could enjoy a tiny moment of freedom from institutional control.

We would wait patiently as Nurse Ratched would wheel her stash of pills down the corridor on her multi-level trolley, systematically stopping at each door.

She always noticed my toes and would ask me to step back further behind the yellow line. For safety reasons.

I didn't always swallow my concoction of tablets. I could ask for something 'extra' if I needed to knock myself out, but there was little point sleeping day and night through it all. How else would I remember this outlier of a moment?

The longer I stayed, the more I began to question whether whatever sanity I had left would survive. I needn't have worried. There was medication for that.

Razors were forbidden on the twenty-fifth. Patients told me the nurses kept a secret stash of them in the supply room, in case a cannula needed to be inserted on someone hairy. They were under lock and key, at the end of the corridor.

'Cleanliness is next to godliness,' Mum used to say. It's a Methodist saying; it's not in the Bible, but she repeated it like Scripture. It was said so often, I thought it was one of the Ten Commandments.

I had therefore developed an obsessive need for cleanliness and hairlessness, so I would plead my case daily and desperately to anyone who listened.

Only the physically intimidating psychiatric nurse who told me he had fought in Afghanistan listened. It appeared he had also been entrusted with the key that unlocked the supply room door.

'You can have this for twenty minutes. A female nurse will accompany you to watch you shower,' he said as he handed me a disposable razor. He was almost apologetic, I could see he was kind by nature, unlike some of the other jaded personnel on the floor.

As I showered and shaved the nurse watched with disturbing intent. She remained a polite hospital distance away in the bathroom, although it was still too close for my personal comfort without a shower curtain for modesty.

She would only leave the room after I'd handed back the razor. Then I would pat myself dry with the recycled industrial paper, slightly pulped and brown, before staring into the stainless steel on the wall. It was Groundhog Day.

Shaving became the most liberating thing I'd do during my time on that floor.

Impossible to ignore was the noise of the meal trays that came clattering down the corridor on their metal trolley. I knew it to be the soundtrack of school canteens and prisons, and now it would forever remain in my mind as the musical score to the twenty-fifth floor of Bellevue Hospital.

The dining room was the Wall Street floor of the psych ward. Loud, urgent and full of sweetener deals. I was one of only a handful of white patients, and likely the only one who owned an oversized pair of black Chanel sunglasses.

The black lads always saved a seat for me in the dining hall. The biggest of them were anything but intimidating. They had the quickest humour and the biggest hearts.

'Look after this one. You can trust her,' they'd say as they introduced me around.

It turned out one of them had been a patient at Bellevue for months. The hospital had become his makeshift home, because he didn't appear to have anywhere else to go.

Their world rarely stretched beyond the streets outside the hospital or New York borough. Australia might as well have been another planet, except there was always a documentary looping on TV, courtesy of a broadcaster with a frozen budget or licensing restrictions.

I was the only real Australian they had ever met, which also meant that I had first-hand access to Skippy the Bush Kangaroo – except I only knew Skippy from the same re-runs they'd grown up with. They were so obsessed with Crocodile Dundee, Steve Irwin and the wildlife of Australia, it's all we ever spoke about during breakfast, lunch and dinner.

In return, they taught me the art of meal-trading: go in fast, go in early, secure the best offerings. If you were good you could score two mains, which I thought many of them needed just to stop their trousers from slipping down.

Bidding started the moment everyone was seated. It was usually led by the same small black guy with his hand in the air. He tried not to stand up too much because he would only be told to sit down again.

'An orange, an orange, an orange, for anything else, looking for beef, beef, or a chicken. Do I hear it once, twice, going, going, gone! Over there to the blonde woman on table six.'

That's how I met Tremaine. Through meal swaps. It turned out he had jumped from the Williamsburg Bridge. You could relive the fall in his energy and his eyes. He'd shattered and ripped apart his body as he hit the water: ribs, femurs, and his internal organs.

The hospital's trauma team had pieced him back together in multiple operations over six months. Steel pins and sutures is how he survived to tell the tale. First came the ICU, then orthopaedics, and eventually a transfer to the twenty-fifth floor as he remained under observation.

Tremaine told me he dreamed of becoming a town planner. He was my favourite on the floor, always softly spoken and very polite. He sounded more educated than I think he was. For a long time after, I wondered if Australia would've given him a different kind of landing.

Then there were Troy and Anthony. They fancied themselves as rappers. Troy would lay down a muffled beat with his mouth, *douff douff douff*, while Anthony freestyled verses about Australia, kangaroos and naturally, yours truly.

It would take me three weeks to earn forty minutes on the roof-top for fresh air, where there was a fenced-in basketball court. For the lucky few, it meant we could stare through wire mesh out over Manhattan and quietly wonder what the world was doing without us. Like everything else, the outside area was carefully monitored.

Rationed were coloured crayons and pieces of paper. We could have three if we felt creative. Sellotape was available at the nurses' station. If I asked them nicely, when they weren't busy, they would tear off six little pieces which I would stick on each of my fingers before returning to my room.

On the wall I'd stick my crayoned reasoning for my breakdown so the doctors could see for themselves that their ridiculous, incessant questions about my sex life and why I tried to kill myself were part of the problem.

MAN DOWN

I NOTICED THAT WHEN PATIENTS are subjected to daily restraint disguised as care, they start to emotionally shut down under isolation and institutional indifference. I was no different. Bellevue's lunatic pavilion hadn't changed as much as you'd imagine over the past one hundred and fifty years. Only now it came with more racial diversity and a plethora of mood stabilisers.

Outbursts weren't tolerated. Not here.

One harrowing night, shortly before lights out and moments after I'd finished another paperback thriller from the cupboard in the art room, the corridor outside my room snapped to life.

'Man down, man down. Car fifty-four. Repeat. Requesting assistance!' A young black man lay face down on the floor, screaming for back-up.

The loudspeaker sprang to life.

'Attention all patients. Do not cross the yellow line. You are to remain in your room with the door closed. Under no circumstances should you leave until you are instructed.'

Of course.

I didn't close my door. I peered out and along the corridor towards the heavily secured nurses' station by the entrance to the floor. I could see two officers, heavy and tactical, straddling the guy on the ground, whose arms had been wrenched behind him.

Crime Scene Investigation was playing out right before my eyes as a very young Caucasian man in a white coat appeared. He was holding a syringe the size of my forearm. A tranquilliser. The kind that erases hours from a person's life.

The patient was then dragged to the empty rubber room next to the nurses' station. Except it wasn't rubber. It was the usual cream-coloured room lined in institutional foam like you'd see on K9 training suits. It was hardly designed for the safety of someone psychotic.

Health and safety hadn't accounted for the room's geometry, as that night the incomer apparently slammed his head into the sharp edge of the only corner that jutted out.

I heard his eye had popped out, although I didn't see the evidence, only the intern who was tasked with popping it back into its socket, and presumably stitching it into place. Or whatever they do to stop it falling onto the floor.

It was a turbulent end to an otherwise quiet evening. I requested two Xanax before shutting my door and going to sleep.

The next morning, on the way to the dining hall, they'd placed our new friend in the room next to mine. There he'd stay for the following few days, comatose and firmly strapped down to the bed as the door stayed open. Then as quickly as he had arrived, he mysteriously disappeared from the floor and I never saw him again.

Troy and Anthony were there waiting for me at the big double doors the day I was finally discharged from the ward. With loose shoulders and flexed knees, their splayed fingers chopped the air before tapping their chest, they rapped a song in my honour.

I regret not asking for the lyrics.

'See you in Australia,' they yelled from the other side of the door as it began to close shut.

I headed to JFK for a thirty-hour flight back home to Lewis, Martina, Paula and Kimi, who would be waiting for me. With tears in my eyes, I knew I was leaving behind a problem much bigger than myself.

At the end of the day, who is really sane?

THE SEVENTH WAVE

SWALLOW THE PILLS. Don't question the pills. Then repeat, return, change or add more pills. Apparently my life depended on it. Until the day they put me in the ground.

The wealthier my doctors and the pharmaceutical companies became, the closer I drifted towards the poverty line. I would need to take more responsibility for my frame of mind. That is if I was to survive the slow, costly grind of endless and experimental blister packs of pills.

Bellevue had discharged me with an invoice large enough to pay for a deposit on a home and a compulsory commitment to ongoing treatment, even though I had left the country.

Scientia Professor Gordon Parker, founder of Australia's Black Dog Institute, was already a towering figure in psychiatry and one of the world's top mood disorder specialists. I now carried a certain clinical currency after my stay in New York so joined his five patient roster.

Martina accompanied me to my first appointment. She filled in the gaps I couldn't quite remember, as I was still heavily medicated. That day, I dressed up and fixed my hair so I wouldn't arrive at the Prince of Wales Hospital looking like the wreck of the Hesperus.

'I'm Gordon. Please,' he said, gesturing to the black leather lounge in his office.

The fact I could call him by his first name told me everything. I could *trust* him.

'So. Bellevue,' he said. 'That must have been … an interesting experience.'

And so our consultations began. Stabilising any suicidal ideations and emotional rollercoasters would come first, with a refreshingly new perspective.

'We will need to monitor your lithium levels with blood tests and adjust the dosage accordingly. But there's something I'd like to add,' he said carefully. 'A new drug. It's something that will smooth the ride.' His hand moved steadily through the air, flattening an invisible line. 'Lamotrigine has seen some terrific results in trials, so I'd like to introduce it slowly and incrementally, and let's see how we go.'

Turning to Martina, he added, 'It will help her get back to who she used to be.'

It would be a slow recalibration, as feeling calm became the new normal.

Recovery for me has never been an Instagrammable fortnight in Bali, nor a neatly packaged week of sound healing, yoga and colonics in Thailand, or ayahuasca in Costa Rica. It has always been something slower and far less seductive. I needed a personal philosophy to live by.

Professor Parker's academic rigour and compassion helped me believe that, like the small handful of patients he treated, I was intelligent and capable of functioning at a high level again.

'Think of yourself like a border collie. You just need the right stimulation and a lot of exercise,' he laughed.

Psychiatry offered structure, a necessary scaffolding, but it was never sufficient on its own. What sustained me were routines. The disciplines absorbed through the eighties and nineties were finally put to the test: yoga, quiet spaces, clean food, fresh air. Every day. I was held by a small, deliberate circle of friends and family who asked almost nothing in return, except that I stay committed to getting better.

EEGs, MRIs, new dietary requirements soon followed as I volunteered for a bipolar pilot programme at Professor Parker's institute.

Martina would give me somewhere safe to sleep before I moved in with Paula at her bungalow by the beach.

It was in this quiet coastal pocket, where salt wind tore through my unbrushed hair and sand scoured my skin almost raw, that I started to get back to me again.

I'd spend my days reading and watching the ocean waves as they gathered themselves before the seventh arrived with force. I'd watch them repeatedly break against the shore then retreat in a swift swish to where the cycle would begin again.

Sometimes I'd watch the surfers, who out of the water always said hello if they passed. I'd watch them battle the barrels unless their boards flipped into the air without them.

I wondered if ever they got tired of being pummelled like I did.

Then it was Kimi's turn. She'd strengthen my body through Iyengar yoga – bending, stretching, restoring – as I learned to slow my breath and move the energy through my chakras.

She knew how difficult it is for the body to cope when someone is forever living in crisis.

As a professional hairdresser, she would also snip, brighten and blow-dry my blonde hair. She'd often say with her dry English wit, 'Good Lord, look at your hair, you can't go out tomorrow looking like that. They'll think they need to prescribe you with more pills. Let me freshen you up.'

When I returned to Dubai, my body was finally strong enough to survive anything and my mind was no longer afraid of the future.

ENDURANCE

I DECIDED TO STOP NEGOTIATING WITH my fears and live life differently. I'd been given a second chance and I was ready to try something new. It would be significant enough to outpace my past and it would demand technical ability.

At forty-eight years old I would learn to ride again. Queen Elizabeth still rode out in her nineties. If she could do it, then I definitely could. At twenty-one, I was full of misplaced bravado when I completed my first forty-kilometre endurance race. I was far more ambitious at the time than skilled, because I had fallen off when I was pregnant with Lewis. Alone and in the middle of the bush I decided perhaps riding wasn't for me after all.

This time, I would refuse to be thrown down and defeated. This was going to be a reclamation.

My new riding instructor, Amanda, was as stocky, broad-shouldered and solid as a paddock post. Her fresh navy polo shirt with the riding school logo on the left breast was stretched across her large bosom. She wore her hair like she wore her shirt, pulled tight. Her bun was fixed with a navy scrunchie and her face appeared flushed from either rosacea, the heat or frustration, or perhaps a combination.

Amanda always stood in the middle of the training ring, an arched shelter of timber and steel, the structure farthest from the office. For the school horses it represented some shade and a little work. For the birds, it was a sanctuary as they flitted and darted between the beams. Mostly they nestled in the quiet corners above us.

I noticed Amanda's outdated running shoes were coated in arena sand. She rolled her feet when standing with her legs apart and she wore her black socks pulled up over her fitted caramel riding pants. Amanda would want her students to see that she knew how to ride. And very well.

We weren't to mount our horses a moment before she told us to. Nor should we walk them in the wrong direction. We had to follow her instructions carefully.

'Get your leg on. Nowwwww!' Amanda shouted. Then there would be a momentary silence as she checked the horse's movements.

'Change your diagonal. Change! You're on the wrong diagonal.'

How was I supposed to know she was trying to get me to balance the horse around corners? Her lessons were quickly becoming far from enjoyable.

'Slow your rising trot. Slow it down. Control your horse.'

I was ill-prepared as a beginner and totally out of my depth. I still had twenty minutes of her lesson left. Her instructions were coming at me thick, fast and foreign.

'Ride your leg into your hand, push your horse from behind.'

I wished it would all end, and soon.

'Collect your horse!' Her voice was now more a shrill than a command. 'Collect your horse, leg on, leg on, and now into canter.'

I knew she wanted to scream, 'Fucking collect your fucking horse!' Amanda was paid to remain professional.

'Right rein! Inside leg on the girth, outside leg slightly behind, heels down. Heels. Down.'

She was unimpressed by my efforts. Her clipped tone had been honed from years of telling people like me what to do. I was trying not to let her see my tears.

As if it couldn't get any worse, a bird suddenly flew in front of my horse before he shied. He took off around the arena at what felt like breakneck speed. It had probably happened hundreds of times before. In the same arena, with the same horse.

What didn't change was my determination. I'd paid for ten lessons, so I would request a less abrasive, more empathetic instructor. If I had to deal with Amanda again I would ask for a refund.

It was ten o'clock the following Saturday when I arrived at the equestrian centre. There she was standing where we always find her. She was still teaching. I decided to wait.

'Okay girls, dismount. Very well done today. You're riding like little superstars.'

Amanda was laying it on thick for the well-heeled parents of twins in matching Burberry outfits and shiny little riding boots.

I couldn't bring myself to even look at her.

The grooms were now leading the twins' ponies straight past me. Amanda followed and swept past me without even so much as a hello and straight across the paddock.

'Kirstyn? Hello? Are you here? Let's go, it's lesson time!' A chirpy little blonde with a fresh horse headed into the arena.

The Suffolk girl from a small rural village was half the size of Amanda. Polite, poised, and posh.

'Helloooooo! I'm Emma. I'll be teaching you today. How much have you ridden?'

That was a loaded question. My limp smile was her sign to check my horse's bridle and the length of my stirrups.

'Okay, hop on,' she said cheerily, 'and walk out on the right rein.'

By the end of the lesson I was ready to canter. I thought of the bird.

'Hop off. I'll show you. This is what I'd like you to do. Not this, or this, but this.' Emma guided the now-alert horse through its paces with effortless precision.

Riding horses is like dating. This one was forgetting what he knew how to do.

'I don't think riding around in circles is for you, to be fair. You'd be better off spending your money on the endurance stable next door. It's more suited to your personality.'

Emma was right, I was looking for freedom.

'All the sheikhs' horses are stabled this area, including the ruler of Dubai. If you ride well and enjoy it, one of the stables may take you on. You can even win money in races after you qualify with an Eighty-One Star.'

Well, that sounded like a plan. She had more trust in me than I had in myself. Before long I'd be riding out of a private stable with her on a lazy Saturday afternoon.

'Let's race back to the stable. Yalla.' Emma was already nudging her horse to pick up speed as we cantered slowly along a long, flat stretch of sand.

The horse had understood the word *yalla*. He knew he needed to drop down a gear before picking up significantly more speed.

No. No. No. Terror rose in my veins. I was now straddling a muscle-bound war machine, every nerve twitched in anticipation of a win.

His nostrils flared and his ears pricked up and forward, my fingers tightened around the reins as my thighs gripped the sides of my horse. I was now astride a five-hundred-kilogram rocket.

Stay balanced. Stay balanced. Don't fall.

My life, the one before Bellevue, flashed before my eyes.

Emma flew ahead with one hand outstretched to the sky and her infectious laughter trailing behind her.

Against all odds, I made it back in one piece and, with the rush of adrenaline, I was now not only flushed, but positively alive.

People say Arab horses are difficult. You simply have to earn the right to be on their back. They have already sized you up before you get on, and only then will they decide whether you are worth their effort.

Perceived power doesn't impress them. Someone willing to get to know them does. It was a dynamic that felt very familiar to me.

You don't ease into endurance racing. You survive it.

Before dawn, before the heat, before the world wakes, that's when we train. Only the horse's breath and the sound of its hooves as gazelles dart across our tracks.

Endurance isn't glamorous; it's gritty. Knowing how to pace a horse over long distances in a single day under the desert sun requires skill and strategy, especially when you're riding a hot-blooded Arab.

A broken stirrup, a bleeding thigh, a dislocated thumb: none of it matters. Don't complain. The horse is doing its best. So must you. If you fall, you get back on and keep going.

Tallo, my training partner, was a formidable South African. I would have to earn her respect one sandy, muscle-aching kilometre at a time if I wanted to ride alongside her.

Our connection existed long before we spoke of ecliptics or solar returns. We enjoyed the silence of dawn, the air cool against our faces, and the energy between us. We'd look to the horizon as the sun lifted on one side, then marvel at the moon, vast and slipping away on the other.

Suspended between them, we'd pick up speed, slipping into a steady canter along the sheikh's private tracks. Tallo and I filled the miles with obscure facts as we paid attention to our horse's fitness and focus.

Over two hours, we'd talk about the race horses in the stables and their individual personalities, boys we half-liked, and birds we noticed dead or alive at the edge of the track. Other days the conversation darkened to exorcism, death and reincarnation. They were inevitable detours when you ride beside a Scorpio.

We spoke of profiles and transiting planets as I taught Tallo how to think as an astrologer. Some days, much to my delight, she gave astrology as much attention as the horses beneath us.

After 'Did you know?' we'd sing, starting with our favourite songs. As our voices lifted into the open air and out into the desert, we believed it would cheer anyone who cared to listen. When the lyrics deserted us, which happened more often than either of us liked to admit, we belted out our national anthems instead, loud and unapologetic.

It was no surprise our horses were keen to get back to the stables, away from our out-of-tune medleys.

Absurdly small and no bigger than a spare bedroom, Starbucks stood alone behind a row of trees and a boom gate at the end of a long, private driveway. It was owned not by a franchisee, but by a sovereign prince. After training, sheikhs' riders were waved through. It was a place we could order a free flat white or something fancier that wasn't too next level.

Riding horses was worth every brutal, bleary-eyed morning.

It was on those mornings in the dunes, past other stables and along the tracks, as camels and towers of giraffes grazed quietly along the high wire fence near the far edge, that I started to find my joy.

A loved and trained horse doesn't lie. They read your nervous system with exquisite and unnerving precision. They give you their best. They keep you going when you want to give up, and they don't flatter or deceive.

Horses make it abundantly clear: if you don't know how to handle them, you'd better be ready to hold on.

EIGHTY-ONE STAR

In Abu Dhabi, the desert horizon glowed a hazy orange as I drove out to the Al Wathba track. That day, I would be the only rider from our race stable competing. It had been four years since I started to compete on hot-blooded race horses. Most riders had taken a season to ride for their country. For me it had been four years of riding without fully qualifying, four years of proving, mostly to myself, that I was not a rider worth choosing for more.

I had failed multiple times over long-distance endurance desert tracks. Luck was not always on my side. Sometimes it was my lack of skill on an unfamiliar horse, sometimes it was because I fell hard and couldn't complete, other times horses I'd ride would be vetted out lame. It wasn't easy getting an endurance horse through. Passing regular vet checks after every 'loop' was critical even though both the horse and I were fit enough to ride comfortably over eighty kilometres in one day.

My grooms would sort out the pre-ride vet, and sort out the necessary paperwork and collect my race number the day before. On race day, I would simply need to show up and weigh in.

This gave me an opportunity to visit a somewhat audacious exhibition, *Napoleon: Revolution to Empire* at the Louvre Abu Dhabi museum. I'd already been to Corsica to visit Napoleon's birthplace, and much later, to Waterloo, to feel his defeat first-hand.

As I stood in front of the highlight, *Crossing the Alps,* a piece that dominated one of the largest of rooms in the Louvre, the small plaque to one side would orient me and frame Napoleon atop his majestic beast.

Napoleon's grey Arab stallion gave the impression he was panicked. No wonder, judging by the way Napoleon appeared to be riding him. Any competent rider would have screamed *Heels down*!

The artist had no doubt pandered to his ego, portraying him as a hero, triumphant on a horse bred for war.

At the time, I did not understand the deeper meaning behind why I gravitated to that particular piece. The following morning I would.

The fifth and final qualifying race had weighed heavily on my mind. I had cost the stable money in race entries. I'd also been unable to ride in the more prestigious races set aside for sheikhs' stables in the Emirates. Our vet Mariana, and the other riders, Tallo, Tanja, Tess, Maitha, Micha and Marlie, had my back over the years. So many times I had been relegated as a water girl. More often I had a place not on a race horse, but in the back seat of a groom's car as an unofficial photographer.

That night as I settled into my hotel room, I imagined how Napoleon's artist would have painted me. My horse would have been calm. It certainly wouldn't be rearing. I would have been astride my favourite grey, a gelding called Ambiance. To those he didn't like, he was a much bigger asshole than Napoleon ever was. His artist would have painted me with a frothing mouth and eyes wide in panic.

I knew I had to think more positively. Manifest, manifest, manifest.

Had my stable sent one of my favourite horses up from Dubai to ride? I had no idea. My grooms from Pakistan and India refused to tell me. With a sideways wobble of their heads they all politely and quietly feigned ignorance.

It was 4:00 am. My phone's alarm pierced the darkness of my

hotel room. I had laid my sports clothes out so I could quickly shower and dress without thinking, as I had done many times before. It would be a thirty-minute drive to the Endurance Village.

I'd eat the banana on the way; it was enough to settle my nerves. By 6:30 I would need to be mounted and ready for the start gate.

As the fog rolled in, thick and ghost-like, my grooms were already quietly preparing for the long day ahead. They had slept in the horse trailer before preparing my horse and all the water, feed, ice and post-race essentials they'd need that day.

By the time I arrived at the village it resembled a hauntingly beautiful painting, with horses, grooms and riders half-shrouded in the mist. Even a photograph I took that morning looked like it was a scene from a bygone era, as if my spiritual ancestors had returned to support me. More than one hundred and fifty horses would ride out within the hour. Some snorted and pranced restlessly about. Others just stood there. They were seasoned, the real athletes; they knew how to conserve their energy.

Waiting would be a steaming carafe or two of Karak. Sweet, milky, spiced with cardamom. It was not only a pre-race ritual, it would be my fuel for the long, sun-spilled hours ahead.

I looked for my horse. None were familiar to me.

'Who am I riding today?' I shouted to the head groom as I neared my team's allocated area.

Majestic stood before me, powerful, imposing and built for speed. Majestic by name, Napoleon by nature. He radiated strength and self-possession. Not only had I never ridden him before, I'd never laid eyes on him until that very moment. There were eight dozen horses in our stable, after all.

This was a sign. The exhibition. Napoleon. *Crossing the Alps*. The artwork. The plaque: *Napoleon on his majestic white stallion*.

I shuddered. I knew something magical was about to happen.

'Majestic is headstrong. He could stop at any moment and refuse to move. Sing to him.' That was the only advice I was given.

I would have to manage him for the next several hours as best I could with what I knew. I already had a track list in my head, as I did for every ride. Anything I could remember. National anthems, 'American Pie', ABBA, the Beatles, and 'Row, Row, Row Your Boat'.

6:20 am. The two painkillers I had taken at the hotel still hadn't kicked in. Damn it. I was hoping to dull the aches and pains of the day ahead as well as the injuries I already sported.

All around me, as horses' flanks began to twitch beneath their satin-smooth coats, their veins pulsed and rose like maps. Majestic started to fidget. Riders began to mount, then trot out as they warmed up their horses for the eighty-kilometre ride ahead.

I slipped my blue bib, number sixty-two, over my head and fastened my helmet before slipping on my favourite non-slip black riding gloves, designed with glow-in-the dark skeletal hands.

I stood on the left of Majestic and placed one foot in the stirrup, then I was up and over. My grooms adjusted my stirrups as I got comfortable on my red Setzi racing saddle.

'Hold him. He's strong,' the head groom warned.

Great. Just what I needed to hear in that moment.

A final check: bridle, girth and stirrups, and again a gesture to suggest that I would need to pull back strongly on the reins.

My eyes widened. The groom's gestures said it all. I was now a bundle of nervous energy, and my horse knew it. Majestic was half a tonne of Arab muscle. I weighed in at little more than a tenth of his weight.

It would be me, him and an army of horses for the next several hours. We'd need to trust one another. I decided I wouldn't fight him; I'd guide him and encourage him, and I'd listen to him. Hopefully he would feel my energy and know I was a woman determined to finish that day.

All around me, a sea of lean silhouettes in lightweight performance clothing from well-known sports brands. They all waited for the signal to trot through the gates and start on the siren.

I was a rarity among the riders, a blonde woman, and, in this race, by far the oldest. The local riders covered their faces, barely recognisable beneath their helmets and behind their mirrored glasses.

I knew their dark eyes gleamed with pride and purpose. They ride for the legacy. That day, some were riding for wealthy private owners, and others, like me, for sheikhs' stables. We were all there to honour our royal rulers and their favourite pastime.

In the distance a row of Toyotas and Nissan Patrols hugged the edge of the track, but beyond that, it simply felt like we were charging into battle. A cavalry of riders and horses, silent and focused, like an army of fearless warriors ready for war. It was like this at the start of every race.

A low rumble cut through the stillness: the Mercedes G-Wagons, in matte black and white with dark tinted windows. They rolled to a stop on a rise overlooking the course to watch the start of the race.

It wasn't uncommon for Dubai's ruler to be present at the start of an endurance race. In Abu Dhabi, it was a different family. As a qualifier this one wouldn't have mattered as much. Perhaps a son or daughter from the royal family was riding. Other times they wanted to check the form of the next new champion mare imported last season from Spain, Uruguay, France or Australia.

I knew this because we often saw the ruling families on the track.

The ruler of Dubai had, in the past, driven by, u-turned and driven back alongside Micha and I during my very first endurance race on a feisty Arab. As an ex-flat race horse, he had been too much for me to handle. I'd spent most of the day in tears as he frequently reared then bolted.

'Is everything okay?' His Royal Highness had been less than six feet away on my right, driving alongside our galloping horses.

'Yes, all good,' Micha had yelled back from my left. It was a mortifying experience to be so close and riding so badly.

In my final qualifier in Abu Dhabi with Majestic, I was determined to do better.

A sharp, guttural sound signalled the start of the race. The equine world exploded into motion. The energy was electric. An army of horses and riders and cars thundered down the track at terrifying speeds.

Majestic surged forward, and his gait spoke of his former power and grace. He wasn't expected to finish. He moved quicker than I had anticipated and was already pulling. He wanted to be near the front.

'Hold your horse,' Eissa yelled. My Emirati stable mate from Dubai was riding for an Abu Dhabi team. He was now alongside me, looking very concerned.

'I'll let him go for a bit, and catch him when he finds his stride,' I yelled back.

There was no way Majestic was intending to settle at twenty-two kilometres per hour when we were already close to thirty-five.

He was on a mission. I think he had forgotten I was even on his back.

The pack started to splinter, as riders began to fan out across the desert track. The leading horses were still kicking up clouds of sand, making it difficult to see through the dust ahead.

The horses' tails streamed behind them like war banners as the Emirati riders pressed on relentless, weaving through the throng. The screams from those less experienced were left behind. The race would be a test of will rather than speed.

In endurance, to finish is to win.

Most of the desert was flat and vast, except for the wave of dunes alongside the track as their shadows haunted the landscape. I didn't dare look too long. I was focused only on where we were headed, the railings, patches of scrub, brittle and defiant like me, which clawed at the earth, then the police and adjudicators who dotted the track, directing oncoming traffic as we thundered through first.

Majestic remained uncomfortably quick and powerful. My heart hammered as I rode on pure adrenaline. His ears were still pricked, his breath steady and his pace rhythmic.

To my right was a young Emirati woman, her horse's pace now matching mine. The energy of a strong female, horse or rider or both, could be hard to beat on their best day.

I was not afraid of competition and neither was my horse that day.

Majestic's ears began to flatten as he picked up his pace, his hooves carving a path through the chaos. Miraculously, we found ourselves out in the lead as the noise of the cars faded into the haze behind us. Those that would stay with their riders, waiting to see who would emerge from this crucible.

Only my grooms were following me, their Toyota ute filled with water and ice. Their smiles said it all.

By late morning the sun was a blazing disc, painting the dunes in hues of a fire's glowing embers. The desert still stretched ahead, infinite and unforgiving.

A falcon circled overhead. That day, the signs were all around. That day, I had my chance to outrun the ghosts of Sharon, the scars of Tom, the weight of every hospital ward and courtroom. Out there, I wasn't broken. I was unbreakable. I was a heroine in my own movie.

After forty kilometres, Majestic and I rode into the vet check.

'You're first, you're first,' my grooms screamed as they poured buckets of water over my horse and quickly removed my saddle. Majestic would have his hydration levels and heart rate checked, before being checked for lameness in front of the vet committee.

I couldn't speak. My mind was on finishing.

We passed the vet checks and rode out, another loop of forty kilometres. This time a sheikh, who was in second place on his mare, was alongside me.

'Let's ride this loop together, I like your horse, very nice.' He smiled as we went through the gates.

We were on the clock again.

The sheikh didn't wait. Off he went, full tilt into the distance, weaving left and right on what looked like a troublesome mare. I heard later they had been vetted out.

Majestic had finally settled. Beside me, a white Nissan Patrol, and hanging out the window, my female support crew.

Our stable vet had joined those who had supported me from day one. They were now soundtrack-ready, as they knew Majestic was known to notoriously stop mid-race.

Majestic settled into cruise control with 'This Is What You Came For'; I thanked Rihanna. I couldn't say the same as AC/DC's 'Thunderstruck' came to life across the desert. Majestic surged ahead at full speed. He was now running close to forty kilometres per hour, all I had to do was stay on. Who knew he liked Aussie classic rock?

Five kilometres out from the village, I heard the girls shout out the window, 'If you pass those boys, you'll be fourth!'

Fourth? It would be my dream to finish fourth.

'Yalla, Majestic, let's go.' I loosened my reins and we powered past just as a teenage boy hurled his empty plastic water bottle at me, 'Shway, shway!'

Slow down? I don't think so.

Majestic and I miraculously thundered into second place that day.

Driving back to Dubai late that afternoon, still covered in sand and dirt and smelling of Majestic's sweat, I called Tallo. At fifty-two years old, I had finally qualified as a professional rider to represent my country, through all the tears, triumphs, falters and falls.

I pressed play on Spotify. The Foo Fighters' 'Times Like These' sprang to life. I increased the volume, put down the windows and sang at the top of my voice all the way back home.

KOALA HUNTING

I'm in Thailand. There's a deal on business class flights to Sydney. I can be with you by breakfast. I'm online. Ready to book. Where are you? I want to see the koalas. A.

That message set a new plan ablaze. With Lewis settled in a committed relationship and working in New York as a fashion director, I returned home in 2018 to spend time with my father.

It was Annie's opportunity to visit a land she had always wanted to see. Wait, was Australia ready for Annie?

First you'd need to imagine a white-wine-swigging, silk-and-leather-clad real estate version of Patsy from *Absolutely Fabulous*. One with decades of Rolling Stones concerts and African adventures under her Isabel Marant belt.

Everyone loved Annie. Everyone *remembered* Annie.

Do it. I'll meet you in Sydney. xx

Ping. My fingers fired back without hesitation.

It wasn't often someone would fly an entire day to see me. A ten-hour flight to Sydney from Asia felt deceptively close.

Annie had been another rock in my life. She was there when my mother Dawn died. We hit the local pub, doubled up on our orders and swapped stories about our mums, her pet gazelle in Yemen, her dad escaping from aged care without his trousers on as he startled unsuspecting locals.

Annie not only had a room for me when I was between homes,

She gently pushed me towards my dream to work as a professional astrologer. 'You have such talent.' It's a shame I doubted my ability to monetise it.

I would often house-sit her designer Swahili bungalow, the one opposite the Arabian Gulf with a riot of tribal artefacts and lazy plantation ceiling fans. I'd feed her street-rescues, Micky, Keith and Marianne, and keep her furry friends company while she jetted off to London, Lamu or the South of France.

I hadn't been back on home soil for over a decade, and Sydney had changed, but I knew my old neighbourhoods hadn't.

Ping.

Let's meet at Balmoral for breakfast. Will send location map. Easy drive from the airport after you land. Kx

It was a name guaranteed to stick in her brain. Except this time there'd be no castle or corgis, just a quiet bay of scattered sailing boats, some smashed avo done properly and a sublime view.

Sydney had been voted one of the best cities in the world to live in, but what now stood out was the soaring cost of everything. And the lurking parking inspectors. A single minute over the time limit, past a pole, or over a line on the road, and it could cost a day's wages.

As Annie and I sipped a well-earned glass of champagne overlooking Balmoral Beach, a dreaded ticket was quietly left tucked under my wiper.

Welcome to Australia. It wasn't the best start but we had friends to see and places to go. We would drive two and a half thousand kilometres through New South Wales, only one state of seven in a very large, dry continent.

Kangaroos wouldn't be hard to find, especially in the Hunter Valley. Australia was in the grip of a drought so severe it had brought them out of the bush and into the backyards of the country towns. Everywhere the world usually imagined they might be, they now were. On the back roads we'd find a lot of them lying a little too still just off to the side.

Annie wanted to see our fatter, furrier friends.

Trading sandstone homes and sparkle for the cooler hush of autumn in the Hunter and a wine tour of local vineyards, we left Sydney at dawn after an evening at the Opera House.

It was that afternoon Annie spotted her first Australian monster. Her shock was palpable as she spied her first hopping native. One could hardly blame her reaction on the vigneron's generous pours earlier in the day.

'Bloody hell,' she whispered, eyes wide, 'look at the size of him.'

Standing over six foot upright, a large kangaroo fossicked through the vegetable garden.

'He's probably eating our dinner,' I said with a laugh, knowing there would be no pansies or nasturtiums left to dress the chef's salad that night.

The next day we drove on to Gunnedah. The koala capital of the world. It was a leisurely three-hour drive via more wineries, roadside antique shops and a ploughman's lunch that ended with Annie holding her glass of Piggs Peake aloft and asking, very seriously, 'What is a oooo-tee? Tim Winton always writes about them in his books.'

'An oooo-tee? Like that one, and that one, and that one.' I pointed to the dusty white Falcon utility parked next to our four wheel drive and those next to it.

Australia had always been a sunburnt dream for the English.

She was learning that the ute came with a dust-covered, dent-kissed badge of honour, a declaration of allegiance to either a building site or the Outback.

Like the car you think you want to buy next, once you've seen one, you suddenly start to see dozens. Just like we did that day en route to Gunnedah, home of many a swaggering bush lad.

From then on, every time one thundered past we'd dissolve into laughter. 'Ooooh! An ooo-tee!'

Forget Bondi. This was what she'd come for.

We pulled into our destination along with the rain. It was a somewhat dreary town made famous by the Victoria's Secret model Miranda Kerr and another billionaire's wife. The town itself didn't scream the glamour it produced by way of a beautiful model, but it had its charms.

According to the internet, we were now in the backyard of one of the largest and healthiest populations of wild koalas in Australia. We pulled up at the visitor centre, had a chat, picked a map and set off on our hunt.

First stop, the golf club. No, they told Annie, they hadn't had a koala at the course for *months*. 'Try this address down the road.' They kindly drew a cross on our map and circled it.

We roared off to Wandobah Road, where Annie was out of the car in a flash and running up the driveway to knock on the door of an unsuspecting lady's home.

Annie's clipped English accent clearly stunned the poor woman standing behind her meshed screen door in her cardigan and floral dress. It was an unusual request for a Tuesday.

'I hope you don't mind, the golf club said you have a koala in your back garden. We're here to have a look.'

No such luck. 'Try the phone booth, two blocks down, back towards the golf course. Or try Booloocooroo Road.' Another cross on the map.

It was still potting down with rain when we finally reached the dead-end road which skirted around a conservation area.

Every hopeful sighting until that moment had been crossed off the list except for this one, where we could find them in their natural habitat, across the gully from where we were now sitting in the car.

'They'll be here, up in the eucalyptus trees. We just need to look. The cheeky little buggers are hard to find,' I said, as if I had any idea what I was talking about. I'd actually never seen one in the wild, and I'd spent a lot of time in the bush.

This was our final stop, the grand finale.

I opened my door, determined to get a better vantage point, and in a classic moment of misplaced confidence I misjudged the distance of the embankment and slid straight down the muddy slope on my butt and completely out of Annie's line of sight.

It wasn't our day.

While the so-called koala capital was apparently raking in millions to protect our beloved eucalyptus dwellers, it appeared that they had packed up and moved away.

All wasn't lost, because at one of the several pubs, Annie learnt how to play the pokies with the mullet cut council boys in their high-viz orange vests, as eighties Australian rock played on the jukebox in the background.

I waited for her winnings perched on a vinyl stool at the corner of the bar. There's a simple pleasure in sitting by the fire in a country pub, chatting to a stranger you'd never normally engage with.

Heading northwest along the Kamilaroi Highway through Breeza and Carroll, we stopped in Narrabri mid morning for a coffee. Outside parked utes sat more mullets, and more high-viz vests with a pie and litre of coke for 'smoko', otherwise known as morning tea in Australia.

We cut short our visit to the several star-gazing satellite dishes recommended to visitors, only because of the snake warning signs. A lesson in radio astronomy would have to wait for another day. These two blondes were heading to Moree.

It was a town a long way from the sea and near nothing else

in particular. Upon our arrival, the local agriculturists emerged in force with their RM boots polished, collars ironed and hopes held very high.

Clearly, we had been oversold as overseas blonde visitors, but we were invited for a roast dinner and bread-and-butter pudding anyway at the PO, a former post office turned pub opposite the police station. It would be the farmer's treat in honour of Annie from London, they said. Even though she lived in Dubai.

The next morning our quest for wildlife continued. Kangaroos were still very much a topic of interest because they were everywhere, in every backyard. We found one unlucky soul, belly-up with his legs tangled in a wire fence, electrocuted several dusty days ago out on a farm towards the opal town of Lightning Ridge.

The drought had settled deeper into the land, its grip clearly visible in every cracked paddock and exhausted tree. In the Outback, even the horizon looks thirsty.

Moree, thankfully, still had water. Hot, bubbling, and determined to be the town's entire personality. Also known as the local thermal baths. It was because of Annie's clipped accent that we were ushered into the VIP section, where we spent an afternoon in steaming bliss.

That was the thing about travelling with Annie. If you leave her alone for five minutes, as I did, you needn't look further than the neighbour's balcony where you'll find her with a gin and tonic in hand, having a right ol' chat about koalas.

Even as we headed back to the coast through back roads jammed with cattle, or along those with nothing at all to Byron Bay, Annie was living the dream.

For the people like us, discerning boho-lux travellers, vegetarian burgers had long since given way to lobster and hand-rolled pasta, oyster bars and the magnificent sight of breaching humpbacks as they migrated north.

Stay too long, like many did, and you'd never leave. In the end though, it was Queensland that had the last laugh. Annie found her missing koalas lounging around at the Currumbin Wildlife Sanctuary by the dozen. It was barely twenty minutes from where I'd first started the entire trip.

Spontaneity and freedom are easy to romanticise from afar. How often do we chase that which has been right in front of us all along?

THE COSMIC CALL

Society was on the brink of enormous change. That much was clear, at least in astrology. I heard people say that I had lost the plot, laughing long and loud behind my back.

It was then that I realised I just needed to trust my own instincts if I were to cut through the madness and survive. I wasn't alone in believing that things were 'written in the stars', but abiding by the very advice I gave for a living had proven difficult, even for me.

After a twelve-year cycle, Jupiter was about to change signs, two days after the new moon in Scorpio. I knew the universe was ready to reveal something very favourable for me in 2018 around my living situation, career and long-distance travel.

On a Friday evening in November, while I was sleeping in Australia, Jupiter quietly moved at full speed into the constellation of Sagittarius.

At the same time, a text message slipped into my inbox and waited silently for me beside my bed. It was almost unsettling in its simplicity.

Edward rarely texted without good reason.

Let me know when you have time to chat.

Edward and I had both worked for the Dubai government in the past, at a time when one exciting project blurred into another. We had stayed in contact but he travelled so much I didn't know if he was in the Caribbean, London or Dubai. I'd soon find out.

At first it was just small talk, then came the clincher.

'Would you be open to planning a global itinerary? We'll be using our private jet and our own custom-built superyacht.'

'Of course.' I laughed, and so did he. The team was back.

Those who had farewelled me in Dubai were about to welcome me back yet again. This time I wouldn't stay long, because London was calling, as was a luxury two-bedroom apartment overlooking the Thames.

I had decided a European base wouldn't only be convenient; it would be strategic because soon I'd be knee-deep in logistics. Cross-checking weather patterns, sea temperatures, landing permits and ports, restaurants, clubs, festivals, UNESCO World Heritage and dive sites. One country after another.

With an unlimited budget, the sky was the limit. Like the captains and first officers I worked with, I also understood that working in ultra-luxury meant a 24/7 focus on precision, discretion and safety.

Together, we were spinning time zones and global currencies like plates. Midnight calls blurred into sunrise briefings, as weather and a change in schedule would upend our plans. Billionaires have their quirks. Our job was to make the impossible possible.

Tracking geopolitics and the shifting sands of diplomacy demanded vigilance when working with those who demanded reputational excellence. I never took world news at face value; it had to be cross-checked against a variety of credible and trusted sources.

As the world began to tighten its grip, I was more than prepared for the patterns that were starting to emerge.

Borders can snap shut without warning, visa privileges can quickly vanish and the strongest passport in the world means nothing if your health betrays you.

ECHOES OF SURVIVAL

I LEFT LONDON TO WORK AS A digital nomad, moving through Portugal and Spain before spending a month in French-speaking Corsica. I arrived on the island armed with Google Translate loaded onto my phone and a handful of French phrases left over from school. I would be sorely tested every time I stepped onto the street.

I was there because not only was Corsica on the yachting schedule, it appealed precisely because it lay beyond the summer frenzy of the Amalfi Coast, which I thought was always too expensive, too crowded, and far too eager to perform for the summer crowds.

From Bastia's bullet-scarred stairwells to the sun-baked squares of Ajaccio and Sartène, or Propriano and Porto-Vecchio, I was aware I was moving through Napoleonic history. His place of birth. And after my ride with Majestic, I was eager to see what else the great general could pull out of his hat for me.

My host manoeuvred her Smart car deftly through Bastia's narrow cobblestone streets until we almost reached our destination. There, I would have no other choice but to haul my indestructible red Samsonite bag the rest of the way to her freshly renovated Airbnb overlooking the old harbour.

As many people discover when they secure a bargain, the reason it was so inexpensive soon becomes clear.

It's not easy climbing a stone stairwell to a top-floor apartment with a suitcase in tow, one bump at a time, when there's no lift. But I was not a woman to be defeated on the slow, graceless pilgrimage upward.

It was a building where intimidation still breathed in its shadows. Its walls remained sadly scarred with bullet holes from the Nazi occupation.

It was in that stairwell in Corsica that I first realised that war doesn't always retreat from the spaces it once tried to claim. Survival, I knew, had little to do with strength and everything to do with timing.

Sometimes the enemy isn't a man with a weapon. It's a moment your nervous system decides you're no longer safe. The one where all you can do is wait for something, anything, to shift.

What I couldn't imagine was the sound of a door splintering under the weight of boots and shouted commands. A mother would barely have time to gather her children or shield her parents before the gunfire began.

Even when the uniforms change, the body doesn't forget. For many women I know, myself included, loud noises, sudden movements, and raised voices can still send the nervous system into alarm.

I've watched how that same dynamic survives in meeting rooms and on the streets, where authority is insinuated rather than stated. Where women learn it is safer to take a step back.

By the time I reached my apartment, five floors up, I wondered whether the occupants had recognised the intensity in the eyes of their perpetrators, the moment when control replaces hesitation and the weapon becomes incidental.

It was a reminder that working in any foreign country requires more than competence. It also demands an unflinching awareness at all times of who holds the power in any situation and how quickly it can be asserted.

I understand why so many women live in fear of travelling alone.

SIXTEEN WHEELS

When it was time to leave Corsica for the next place, I wasn't ready to subject myself to a flight to Belgium. I just needed to get to Florence. It was just over the way. The former Italian island and now French colony didn't make it easy.

In the interests of time and scenery, I decided to head to the port and take the ferry instead.

It felt infinitely more civilised to travel by water, even if it was on an unsightly car ferry. From there I'd take the train to Lucca, one of Tuscany's more peaceful, historic cities, not far from Florence, where I had decided to celebrate my fifty-fourth birthday. Life was taking me where it needed to go, this time with no luggage restrictions and no security lines.

It was on that car ferry that I met the Corsican trucker.

As we sailed out of Bastia with my luggage locked away in a cabin downstairs, I made my way to the comfort of the restaurant lounge, before heading up to the deck to take some photos.

There is a quiet thrill when you stand on the deck of any vessel as the salty wind whips through your hair. It breathes pure freedom.

I had vaguely noticed the trucker hovering in the distance, like a fan about to meet his version of Kylie Minogue. Should I be nervous? People from rural pockets of the world, like Corsica, are always more curious. I was alone, and as a blonde I stood out as a foreigner.

As the trucker sauntered over, the wind whisked his hair up into a side-swept mohawk.

I wasn't in the mood for middle-aged men, pot-bellied men in tight T-shirts and laced-up utility boots, the kind with the composite toe. But he was up for a chat, and there was no reason to be rude to anyone. Corsica had been good to me.

'Comment ça va? Vous êtes suédoise? Où allez-vous?'

His second question was a common one. I glanced over and shook my head slowly, mouthing a quiet no. *I'm not Swedish.* I was often asked if I was. Or German, or Russian.

'Lucca, then to Florence, to meet my … [fictional] husband,' I offered.

Unperturbed, he continued, but this time with more excitement.

'Ah … you are Australian? C'est excellent! Je suis rock musician! INXS … Midnight Oil … Cold Cheeeezel!'

My grin started to mirror his. There's something infectious about a random person name-dropping the gold standard of '90s Australian rock.

'Bon, Bon! Jimmy Barnes? I am Jimmy!' He placed his hand on his heart and lifted his gaze, as if to thank the Lord for his talent.

I wanted to be sceptical. I really did. But bless him, he had heart, and four hours to kill. We chatted on the way back to the lounge downstairs after the wind became impossible.

Wine, beer, coffee?

I was fine, but he insisted.

'What? What? What? Anything you want!'

I opted for water. He brought me wine. It could have been a French thing.

I was beginning to feel a little trapped, although I couldn't help but commend his commitment to music. It wasn't often you'd run into a random stranger on the other side of the world who knew Jimmy Barnes.

'Lucca, oui? I will take you. It's on my way. The honour is mine, Miss Australia, it's only thirty minutes from the port.' He placed his hand on his heart.

I wanted to take the train, but this Corsican trucker appeared single-minded.

It was time to escape, so I thanked him and retreated to my cabin.

The disembarkation call came. We were about to arrive in Livorno, and it was time to drag my bag through the ferry one more time and up to the lounge deck.

Halfway up the stairs, there he was again, standing at the top and grinning as if he'd correctly predicted the exact minute I'd appear. His hand reached for my bag before I had time to blink or think, let alone argue.

'I'll take you! No problem. I have a truck.'

Good Lord. A truck? I had seen enough true crime shows to pause for a moment.

He knew a suspicious amount about Aussie rock. Was he more excited to meet an Australian than go on a killing spree? I couldn't be sure. I had to think on my feet.

What could possibly go wrong? On the eve of my birthday, I had hoped to get to Lucca in one piece.

Here we go, I thought, climbing into the high cabin of the semi with my red Samsonite swallowed behind the front seats of the biggest truck on the ferry. I was now sitting in his industrial beast, one packed tight with refrigerators bound for Paris.

The ignition fired with a deep groan, and the cabin rumbled so much the floor pulsed beneath my feet. The hiss of the air brakes released, and we shuddered before lurching into motion with a chorus of rattles, creaks and low-frequency growls.

The Corsican trucker's sixteen-wheeler started to crawl off the ferry. We'd be the last due to our size, waiting as the procession of much smaller trucks crept up the trembling steel ramp and onto the road.

I wondered how far the train station was.

Would the ferrymen waving us past be the last to see me alive?

'Music?' My new trucker friend was already twiddling with the dials.

Why not? I didn't have a choice.

On a positive note, I wouldn't need to trail my red Samsonite through unfamiliar streets, squinting at signs, mangling foreign phrases on Google Translate as I tried to locate the train station.

Instead, I half-calculated the distance to the ground. In case I had to jump. It would be a moving escape, I decided. A commando roll. Ideally not under his sixteen wheels. I figured that if I landed badly but alive, that would be enough. I could always buy another suitcase and some clothes.

People have survived worse.

'Are you ready?' He was now fiddling with the volume.

With an escape plan, I was.

The opening chords of 'Where the Streets Have No Name' filled the cab, at concert volume.

Bono.

Well, almost. It was the unmistakable soundtrack of U2, except the voice now soaring through the studio-quality cabin speakers wasn't Bono's.

The Corsican truck driver was already mid-sentence, explaining with immense pride that the voice was *his*. He wasn't just driving to Paris; he intended to *perform* his way there.

'Wow! You must be famous,' I laughed.

I was half in disbelief, half in awe that he had taken the time to re-record his voice over Grammy-award-winning tracks. My initial cringe soon melted into admiration. I couldn't carry a tune if my life depended on it, so who was I to judge?

The trucker wasn't just singing; he was inhabiting the music. And somehow … it worked. The audacity. His sincerity. The sheer volume.

So why not join him in a sing-along?

I threw my hands into the air and let the chorus carry us both down the highway. It had been a long time since I'd sung without caution next to a total stranger, a refrigerator truck as our stage.

Somewhere in Tuscany, between the port of Livorno and the outskirts of Lucca, we became a two-person stadium tour, roaring well above the highway hum. We laughed out loud between verses as the truck vibrated beneath us, as if it, too, knew its rhythm in the song.

Then came the encore, his pièce de résistance. Jimmy Barnes and 'Drivin' Wheels'. One of the most-loved Australian rock singers was now being reborn as a Corsican.

The trucker's voice cracked in all the right places as his fists pounded on the wheel with conviction. I pictured him in a Parisian pub, mic in hand and beer in the other, giving it everything he had. He would've brought the house down, whether they knew Aussie rock or not.

That's what defined him. Not his job, not his journey, but the pure, unfiltered joy of claiming rock's most anthemic songs as his own.

I've never seen a happier man. A Corsican trucker with a dream, a voice and a sixteen-wheel truck full of refrigerators.

As we pulled up at the gates of the old city I was alive, slightly stunned and absurdly grateful we had time for one last Jimmy-Trucker duet, this time with INXS.

Happy people make the world a better place. My first and only hitchhiking experience, I decided, would also be my last.

It wasn't lost on me that sometimes our ride through life chooses us. Italy, you never fail to entertain.

CANDLES, COBBLESTONES AND FAITH

Meandering around Lucca's walls, I found a place to linger in the Piazza San Michele. It was here I would celebrate my birthday with one of my favourite dishes, a vongole, and a glass of full-bodied Tuscan wine at an osteria along Via San Giorgio, one that was intimately steeped in Middles Ages architectural charm.

It was a place, I mused, I would be happy as a short-term resident, ambling along the cobbled streets, exploring more eateries and bespoke fashion and handcrafted leather stores.

I now knew that nothing in life was in vain. Everything unfolded as it did for good reason, and often in ways I could never have imagined.

Later, as I parked myself in Florence for some weeks, I timed my days to catch the sun over the Arno at dawn and dusk so I could capture the city's watercolour skies.

I'd leave in search of yet another espresso or gelato, then head back to my desk.

Every day I made a point to leave my apartment and explore something new or go back to something sublimely familiar, like the corner gelato bar.

Up the hill, not far from my front door, I would pass Galileo's last home. For years, he was the only scientist I actually knew because he was talked about so often in our family when I was growing up. He was also the reason we had a telescope on our back porch and the reason my brother studied astrophysics and topped his faculty at university. I doubt I would have developed an interest in the stars growing up in New Zealand without him. Through Galileo, I learned early that what science holds to be true at any given time is not necessarily so.

Some days I'd slip into the hush of the Boboli Gardens, so I could feel as if the whole city had once belonged to me. I'd find retreat in the Uffizi's quieter halls after marvelling at Medici's collections, Leonardo's genius or Botticelli's *Birth of Venus.*

Walking past the grand Medici fort on the Oltrarno hillside, I'd reach my farthest point on a morning walk, the Basilica San Miniato al Monte, standing on one of the city's highest points. I'd linger at the steps as morning prayers came to a close, waiting for a man of the cloth to pass.

'Buongiorno! I know the basilica is closed, I hope you don't mind, could I pop in to say a quick prayer? It's just me, and I shan't be long,' I pleaded.

A young priest had just finished his own morning prayer and agreed to quietly usher me in. He waited by the door, which he left slightly ajar, perhaps to let a sliver of light into the dark gothic space.

Inside the basilica, beneath a mosaic Christ glowing in gold, with the quiet gaze of saints over me, I was excited to see a zodiac wheel etched into the marble floor. It had been used to chart divine time since 1207. Now I knew why I had been inexplicably drawn here.

Symbols don't survive centuries unless they're meant to be found.

This sacred geometry had been waiting for me. I could feel its energy drawing me in. It was proof it wasn't always heresy. It was a language. The Church's language, and reserved only for those in power.

The catechism was clear: those that trusted the stars were heretics. Only God had control over human destiny. It also warned that casting charts to foretell the future, as if it were cast in stone, was forbidden. But there it was, cast in stone right before me. Thanks to the patriarchy, one could have a good guess that we were being gaslit the entire time.

Even Galileo, a Catholic, had been forced by the Inquisition to deny his expanded view of the universe and God's creation, despite his empirical and mathematical models.

It seemed everyone was searching the same sky, through a different lens, for the same answers.

It was, for me, an unmistakable sign that I, too, was in step with divine timing, whether it was right or wrong. Another piece in the puzzle had just found its place. On my way out I thanked the monk and enquired briefly about his family, and what had drawn him to the clergy.

'I had a deep calling to serve others.'

He understood that service to others gives us a place in the world. There's a lot to be said for how we will be remembered.

SICILIAN ADVENTURES

MANY OF MY FRIENDS MOVE THROUGHOUT the world, often on a whim. We always have each other on speed dial, ready to rendezvous at a moment's notice, Annie has always been the most spontaneous amongst them. It should have been no surprise to hear she was itching for a change of pace.

'I'm on the Emirates site. Shall we do Sicily? I'll fly into Catania, let's check out Ortigia, Mt Etna and Taormina. I can be there next week.'

And just like that, Sicily it was. For both work and play.

I would fly from Florence to Rome and onward from there. Like our koala trip, we had decided on a driving holiday, so I booked a brand-new rental for our adventure.

At Fontanarossa airport, Mario, behind the rental car desk, had been expecting me. I handed him my passport and Australian driver's licence. I was there to pick up my Clio Zen.

He went about photocopying my documents and shuffling papers on his desk, moving up to the counter then back down again where I stood waiting, pen poised. His brow furrowed. Perhaps it was unusual for a foreign woman to ask for a stick shift.

'Aaaaaah … I want-a to recommend you … before dere is-a problem … in See-cee-lee.'

No doubt he wanted to upsell me something. Probably an automatic. I was on a budget, so I had also deliberately skipped the extras he was bound to push.

Windscreens, flat tyres, towing – all covered in the protection. I'd already bought my insurance online.

'You weel-a need-a compre'ensive in-soo-rance.' His tone suggested it was more than a non-negotiable. 'Eet doesn-a matter what-a happen to da car, you are-a covered. One-a in every four-a renta car is-a stolen in See-cee-lee. Eet's-a better to be safe, eh?'

One in four cars stolen? Who tells tourists *that*? Were we in more danger than we realised? Sicily did have a reputation, after all.

I signed for the insurance immediately and paid the difference. It would be cheaper than replacing a new car.

Annie and I decided to stay only one night in Catania. We were keen to escape to Ortigia first thing the following morning. I was now hoping our Clio would still be where we left it.

Pulling up to the modest motel Annie had booked was nostalgic. Its architecture was reminiscent of a faded Vegas, untouched since the '80s. There would be no point unpacking. We started instead with a crisp white by the kidney-shaped pool.

'There's a pink café across the road. It looks okay, and there's some outdoor seating. Shall we eat there?'

I peered through the high wrought-iron railings into the failing light. It looked like we'd be one of only two tables. I wasn't in the mood for pink or polite. It was a no from me.

We decided to go for a wander. Further down the road, something more alive beckoned our attention.

'That looks good, what about that one?' I said, standing on the side of the road. 'It's probably a wedding, but let's go anyway and check it out.'

This time we stumbled into something more like a Freemasons' lodge. Tuxedoed men and women shimmered and sashayed through the reception in an overload of sequins and chiffon, the ladies' hair had been lacquered to withstand both the drama and the week ahead.

Small children in small shoes ran around at breakneck speed between the tables. The place reeked of cologne, grilled seafood and cigar smoke and looked like a Scorsese outtake.

It was operatic chaos, and our perfect idea of nothing fancy.

Annie and I watched with amusement as a constant parade of dishes arrived and left, together with plenty of wine, and an espresso or two in between.

From a corner speaker on the wall, music throbbed. It was brassy, and, for our tastes, out of date.

We couldn't be sure if the white waving napkins were celebrating or commiserating a turf war or football victory, so we called it a night close to the stroke of midnight as the crowd became more raucous, for fear of saying the wrong thing to the wrong person.

Clio, Annie and I left Catania early. We had hoped to outrun the inevitable traffic chaos, but Sicilian roads aren't designed for clarity. One needs to carefully interpret the inches between your car and others, then commit with the accelerator. It's important not to glance sideways or check your rear vision mirror.

I remained hunched over the wheel as if I drove this route every day and knew what I was doing. I pressed Clio's pedal to the metal. Rules were mere suggestions and lane markings optional. Don't bother indicating, either. Roundabouts, however, need a little more theatrical negotiation.

In Sicily, hesitation would be seen as weakness. Annie had no option but to place her trust in my driving as the car horn spoke the only Italian we needed: 'Move!', 'Ciao!', 'Grazie', or 'What are you doing, idiota?'

In Castiglione the car insurance came in handy.

'Noooooooooooo! Oh my goddddddddd!' Annie was in full panic mode, gripping the doors as if her life depended on it.

I had Clio wedged on a steep incline. It's unfortunate that Italian streets aren't constructed for today's cars. It leaves navigation open to misinterpretation.

'Don't worry, I've just … slightly misjudged this street,' I said, trying to reassure her. 'Hang on, let me reverse.' We listened to the slow, sickening scrape of metal along a stone wall. Even the tyres squealed in disbelief as they kissed Castiglione's ancient stone gutters.

Normally this would trigger a full-body cringe and the stuttering panic of future repair costs. Not today. God bless Mario's reassurance: 'Eet doesn-a matter what-a happen to da car, you are-a covered.'

That comprehensive rental insurance had now become a very worthwhile investment.

A Vespa soon pulled up behind us, either to observe the carnage or to scoot down the same street. I couldn't be sure. His hands were in the air as he mouthed a less polite version of 'Mamma mia!'

Nothing is a problem unless you decide to make it one. And so began another grand tour.

Castello was perched like a postcard with sweeping views north towards Mt Etna. Being an Aries, Annie hoped it would erupt. She said it half-jokingly. Then the thought stuck. What if it *did* erupt? Would it be one of those slow, Instagrammable lava flows, or a full-throttle detonation that buried us instantly in molten ash?

I pictured us fossilised mid-pose. Annie would still be clutching a glass of wine, and I'd have a phone in hand, trying to Google *Etna's lava how fast?*

I didn't sleep much that night.

We didn't need the random Italian designer outlet mall, but we stopped anyway. Why not, when there they are, in the middle of nowhere?

We were looking instead for the magnificent Roman ruins in Agrigento, then Taormina, and back to Syracuse, by the sea, where we were happiest. In Ortigia, no one cared what day it was. It was a place where couples lounged on the rocks or beneath their striped umbrellas on the patio.

We would love it when children trailed behind their leathery grannies in bright polka dot or gold bikinis, all with ice creams in hand. We gaped at the drop earrings and enormous designer sunnies, slinky speedos and endless applications of tanning oil as we, too, tanned ourselves, but with another bottle of rosé.

If you can sidestep the crowds and avoid the Instagram influencers and their tech necks, Italy tugs at the heart.

Mother Nature, like Annie, kept her own schedule. Annie had been gone for three weeks, and the following day I would have to fly out. I'd already met our yacht in Palermo, visited the UNESCO village of Erice and looped back to Taormina.

There was only last thing to do: a day trip to Mt Etna. It was 'just there', after all. Vast, silent and still unpredictable.

In Taormina, hotel guests would be sipping their aperitivos and recording their Etna moments on their phones, then posting to their social media accounts. Hashtag Sicilian sunset.

Instead, I would walk around the rim of one of her craters, half-wondering if she might blow. Would I be flung skyward with only my limbs, lava, and the flimsy plastic helmet I was handed for protection visible as I launched from the earth?

Only hours earlier I'd been inside Etna, threading my way through her ancient lava tubes, feeling a little like David Attenborough as I posted to Instagram.

'So,' I asked, as casually as one might, 'what happens if Etna decides to explode and the lava flows through here, where we are standing … and incinerates us?'

'Good question!' our volcanologist replied. I'm sure he'd heard it a thousand times. 'Lava never takes the same path twice. It carves a different one every time.'

It wasn't reassuring enough for me. I don't think he understood

I was asking for our escape route.

Out across the sea, Mt Stromboli decided to erupt, with a thunderous roar. We watched as a tower of fire and smoke launched like a missile.

'She's finally released,' our volcanologist whispered. Much like those who win the lottery, he admitted he'd waited his whole life for that moment and with that started to cry.

It was breathtaking to witness, and in the same breath, utterly terrifying. Then I wondered, was anyone there? Like us, on the edge of her crater? Sadly, one person was.

We all stood on Etna in silence, watching Stromboli's drama in the distance. I couldn't help but think of the quiet pressure that builds in all of us. I didn't realise at the time that the world was about to rupture. And like Rangitoto, it would also leave its scar.

THE RUPTURE

AFTER MONTHS OF WORKING AND travelling throughout Europe, I returned to the Gold Coast to visit my father. Four days later, the borders shut – for longer than the reported two weeks.

I had arrived with ten days' worth of summer clothes in my carry-on.

Every time I return to Australia for any length of time, it is for another lesson. Throughout my life, as in astrology, lessons arrive in threes. This one, the second, asked me what I could live without. The final lesson, the one unfolding on these pages, would ask something harder of me again: to set down the emotional weight that I had been carrying and to do so in all honesty.

As one airport after another fell silent, the world was soon swept into isolation, whether we liked it or not. I was lucky to be with my 83-year-old father.

COVID would divide Australia into stand-alone territories. In Queensland masks weren't compulsory. Like most holiday destinations built on tourism, it would face its own challenges.

Lewis spent the pandemic even further away from me. He was now in relative isolation in the Hamptons, away from the New York shutdown where he had been living and working.

I knew then that this was what astrologers had seen coming but couldn't quite articulate. The astrological cycles had been pointing to a global reckoning and a historical realignment for years.

For a time, work carried on as it always had, although now I was trying to find out what countries remained open and COVID-free. Not even a billionaire could buy their way out of a virus. Soon my job, like many others, came to a grinding halt. I would no longer be needed for the 'foreseeable future'.

What was foreseeable was fresh air, fresh food and freedom. I would now spend my mornings walking into an ancient volcanic crater and World Heritage rainforests only twenty minutes inland from home. In the other direction, only ten minutes away, I could walk on near-empty world-class beaches where pods of dolphins and migrating whales could be seen surfacing offshore.

Nature and wildlife had come alive.

Other days I would ride out on stock horses with the local ringers, horsemen whose lives had been shaped by dust, drought and decades on the land. For those on the land, COVID barely registered. In Australia, their hard work and harder seasons had forged generations of farmers. They had been through far worse – droughts, floods, and cyclones.

Then there was Australia's killer wildlife.

I had time now, like many others. A pile of books on ancient history, astrology, philosophy, and psychology, subjects I had experimented with for decades, sat on my bedside table. I went down the rabbit hole with a variety of astrological methodologies, online lessons and podcasts. Reading for several hours every day became one big, happy habit.

During this time, on US Memorial Day, I received a random email in my inbox. Military records were free to search via Ancestry.com. I was curious. I knew my biological father was American. First I would need to cross-reference it with US naval vessels docked in Auckland Harbour at the time of my conception. I used the name Sharon had given me. The trail narrowed quickly. There was only one match: the *USS Archerfish*. Pearl Harbor. There he was.

The Ancestry.com search had also suggested he was far older than twenty-three, the age he had told Sharon. His rank was chief torpedo officer. An archived news clipping suggested genetic similarities; I could see I shared his hairline and his slim physique.

Beside his name read *On eternal patrol.* In naval language, it meant he had already died.

I clicked on the Ancestry link and entered the details I knew. His birth records listed Florida and Hawaii as places of birth and former residence.

I then wrote to those who had served with him on the *Archerfish* list, those that were still alive. There were only a handful left. Two of them responded within the week. It was obvious the men were closing ranks, as they brushed my questions aside.

I now knew from the records that he was far older than he had ever claimed to be.

Then another email. Someone had panicked. One submariner suggested I could be the ship's doctor. His detailed description of the night in question was a little too farcical to be true. I wrote back and told him a young girl doesn't forget her first.

We all did things we regret. We were young, these things are best left in the past, one wrote back.

It was polite, brisk and evasive. It was clear there would be no further information forthcoming.

I had uncovered an invisible line I was not meant to cross. In the military, it appeared enlistment was a lifelong contract that protected the backs of those they served with.

A year later, they too would be on eternal patrol.

OPALS AND AN OUTBACK ODYSSEY

THE NEW SOUTH WALES BORDER WAS closing within the hour, but I wasn't about to let a line on a map decide my fate. Queensland's roads were still open, wide and wild, and the Outback has a way of reminding you what matters. I needed that reminder during a COVID lockdown.

Lightning Ridge, Australia's most famous opal town, was only eleven hours away. It felt practically next door. I didn't have a booking, only a full tank of fuel, a curated playlist for road trips and the kind of bravado that comes from solo adventure.

At the border the army and police were too busy barbequing to bother with my paperwork. They waved me through the concrete barricades designed to stop escapees. They had been placed beside the only army tank I've ever seen in Australia. It felt less like a checkpoint and more like a comedy sketch.

Black opal has always been tied to magic, intuition and the unseen. So after a morning underground with the town's only female black opal miner, and leaving with a small pouch of what she called sorcerer's stone, I headed towards Moree to stay with Sarah.

By the time I reached the town, a neighbour had alerted Sarah that there was a deadly six-foot brown snake on the loose. It was last seen slithering towards the house.

It was nothing a ten-year-old boy with a stock whip couldn't sort out.

'He's probably in the feed room, just go in there and check,' yelled Sarah to her eldest as he cracked his whip a couple of times.

I stood well back just in case I needed to make a run for it. With a snake that size I wanted a head start. If it went for me we'd be hot-footing it into town and hoping I would make it to my birthday alive. We stayed on high alert for the rest of the week, but clearly the snake had better things to do. It was never seen again.

For my birthday we decided to have a bonfire. Once it was stacked and ready, out came the petrol can, just to get it going.

'Okay, everyone, stand well back,' the eldest amongst the group shouted from more than a few metres away before firing a lit arrow straight into the middle of the pyre. On cue, the bonfire exploded with flames so fierce I had to crouch down to hide my face. As it roared into action, I was certain I'd lost my lashes, half my brows and all the hairs on my arms.

We barbequed and shared good red wine as the fire eventually sank into a quiet, golden crackle. The cold started to creep through the gaps in our blankets, chilling our backs, and we decided to call it a night. The house had already disappeared into the dark, save for the faint kitchen light glowing in the distance.

Above us was the Milky Way, and the ancient river of light had already revealed itself the way truth does when there's nowhere left to hide.

In the Outback it's impossible not to feel the thread of its power and reflect on all the stories we have inherited, the mistakes we've repeated and how love eventually softened us even though the wounds took time to heal.

I WAS NEVER THE TYPE TO WANDER into a jewellery store without good reason, unless someone else was buying. A ring, ideally.

My friend had already disappeared into the glittering depths of Bulgari in Pacific Fair on the Gold Coast. She left me stranded at the entrance, feeling awkward.

'Are you looking for anything in particular?' the sales assistant asked from behind the counter. Her voice, although warm and crisp, was unmistakably foreign.

'I'm waiting on my friend, in lieu of a husband,' I laughed, indicating to the finger where a sizeable diamond once used to sit. It was best to quickly change the subject. 'Oh, where are you from?'

'Romania!' she said, beaming.

'Oooooh, I've been there. Bucharest, Brașov and Transylvania.' I admitted that Dracula's castle hadn't been quite my kind of destination.

Animatedly, we talked about its unsettling collection of torture devices, grimly engineered to annihilate witches, warlocks and hapless warmongers.

She smiled and beckoned me to follow her towards the back of the store, where I could feel more comfortable in a private lounge area.

'Would you like a chilled glass of champagne while you wait?'

How could I possibly say no at eleven in the morning? Champagne has a way of softening the edges of the world. Especially before lunchtime. After the cork popped, conversation bubbled over, effervescent and unrestrained. Occasionally we would glance out into the store to see my starry-eyed friend still pointing to items she'd like to try.

'Are you a dancer? Or did you do gymnastics?' the shop assistant asked. It was a familiar question.

'One hundred years ago I did classical ballet. And you?'

I was about to find out Danielle had clearly been brushing up against some serious talent.

'I used to love Nadia Comăneci; she was everything when I was growing up. The Olympics and all.' I was gushing again.

'Well, Kristina,' Danielle said almost in a whisper as she leaned forward, 'I used to train with Nadia.'

I had to catch my breath. Twice. We clinked glasses in a quiet salute to greatness, and I listened intently as she let me into the training secrets forged behind the Iron Curtain – the kind you only hear about if you're sitting with someone who went through it all.

Nadia, once the emblem of perfection and silent resistance, had somehow threaded herself back into my story.

This time she had returned through someone with a deep interest in spiritualism, working in Bulgari. It felt less like a coincidence and more like a signpost.

It wasn't only about Nadia. Not this time. Answers about where I'd come from, and who I'd once been, were getting strangely closer.

What I was about to find out was that I was now sitting opposite a Romanian-Greek past-life regressionist. It was an unexpected path for a former diplomat, trading geopolitics for the unseen.

I knew how to skim the edges of past lives through astrology, and over the years a few psychics had offered messages from 'the other side'. But unless they delivered a detail so precise it could only have come from there, I still had my doubts. Which is why what happened next caught me completely off guard.

Danielle lived five minutes from Dad's place, in a neat, unassuming home. I was welcomed at the door by her husband, tall, elegant and German by temperament as much as descent. He then ushered me inside to a life that appeared, at first glance, to be ordinary enough.

'Tea?' he enquired as we walked towards the smell of baking biscuits coming from the kitchen at the back of the house. It was delightful to see a man of presence so comfortable in the kitchen, as Danielle emerged from her regression room.

'I've just been preparing my space for you. I told my husband about our immediate connection, as it's so hard to trust people these days. There are so many charlatans.'

Off to the right of the kitchen, away from the warmth and sweetness of the biscuits, her sunroom greeted me with a disorienting rush of energy.

At first I didn't know where to look. I'm sure it hadn't been designed to disarm, but I felt like I had entered another era. Heavy lace curtains softened the afternoon light into pale, floating shards, and every crystal on the windowsill and bookshelf caught it, scattering small flashes of brilliance across the walls.

The bed sat at the centre of it all, ringed with talismans arranged with quiet intention, as if the space had been mapped for safe passage. Somewhere above the rhythm of my own breathing, classical music threaded through the air – delicate, steadying – until it suddenly felt like I'd arrived at the threshold of something completely unknown.

Danielle settled me onto the bed with practised ease, tucking a blanket around me for warmth, which struck me as odd. Summer had already arrived, and I wouldn't have normally needed it.

'Close your eyes. Relax. Trust the process.'

With one eye slightly open, I could see her hands working feverishly up and down, down and up, and all over above my body. Her eyes were open but not quite present. I quickly shut my eyes again for fear of being caught with a secret known only to Danielle.

She began to chant, spiralling into a trance-like state. I didn't recognise the words that poured out of her like a forgotten dialect from somewhere long ago. Whatever she was saying, something now spoke *through her,* and as I started to drift I could feel another energy enter the room. One thousand per cent, the two of us weren't alone behind a locked door that day.

I cannot be sure how long I was under her spell. She gently woke me with a tap and a whisper, which stirred me to half-life.

I was immediately distracted by the volume of classical music that filled the room. Dazed and confused, I couldn't fathom where I was.

'Can you turn the music down? It's very loud.' I had woken irritated.

'It's barely on but let me turn it off.' She patted the lounge beside her as I rolled off the bed.

Alongside the wall a small settee was plumped with cushions, a pleasant place to spend the afternoon reading with a cup of tea. It was where I now sat as Danielle placed her hand on my forearm to soothe my ruffled state.

'Are you okay? We had a powerful session today.'

Words escaped me as she started to speak.

'Who is Lotta? Lotta. Oh, your mother. Flo. Florence. Your name is Florence. Florence Lawrence. You were a very famous movie star. The first. You liked to drive. And ride horses. You liked the countryside. They gave you film roles because you could ride a horse. You were very famous for a while, then you grew old, and work stopped. They didn't want you. A new era had come. They wanted new stars, for the talking pictures.'

As Danielle spoke she gestured, vaguely at times, as if reaching back or collecting the spirit energy around her. Was someone still in the room? Were they still talking to her? It was as if she was speaking through someone who was telling her what to say. Her accent stumbled across English words she didn't know. At those times she gestured until I helped her with a word.

'You had a problem with your skin. It's sensitive, I think it's your bone marrow.' Danielle scratched her arm in long sweeping strokes as if to soothe her skin. She winced as if it caused her discomfort, but didn't pause.

'You danced. You were on stage as a little girl, with Lotta. Canada. Then New York. She was always on the road with you. Your father isn't around anymore. He died. An accident. You were little.'

Her hands flickered to indicate blinking motions and made the sweep of the old-fashioned side arm indicator, repeating the motion twice.

'You liked to drive cars.'

Then: 'Oh, did you know you were an inventor? Brakes. You invented the brake light, so people knew there was a star driving the car as the brake light lit. It's why you didn't put your hand out the window. A star wouldn't do that. They stole your invention. Your businesses all failed. You were terrible at business and had a lot of bad luck. You had an accident, your back, and depression.'

Danielle paused, then exhaled slowly, as if releasing whatever burden she had been carrying.

'Your marriages all failed. You didn't choose well. You killed yourself ... and the world moved on. You were forgotten.'

Initially I thought she must have stumbled across my spirit energy on the internet. It seemed the most rational explanation. Yet the coincidences were unnervingly specific. My failures echoed her failures. How could so many details align? Was it possible there were still traces of her in me? How did she reach the parts of my life I'd kept sealed since childhood?

She couldn't have known I rode, let alone that I'd injured my spine. I remembered an endurance race when I felt certain a film crew was following me through the desert. A déjà vu so vivid, it was as if I was actually in a movie.

I'd never told a soul.

I needed to speak to Dad. His mind was scientific, but he'd always been open to what ifs.

If anyone could help me separate possibility from delusion, it was him. That day I hurried home with more questions than any of us could have answers to.

'How was it?' His old eyes were now bright with curiosity as he switched on the kettle.

'There were things she couldn't possibly have known. Do you think she Googled me?'

Dad smiled with the patient look he saves for those times when I'm overthinking things.

'There are eight billion people in the world. She doesn't know you. And she doesn't have time to research every client and magically land on details only you know. It's the same with your astrology. You just prepare your notes based on a time, date and place, and get on with it.'

He had a point.

I couldn't help myself. I tapped in her name. *Florence Lawrence.*

Born Florence Annie Bridgwood on January 2, 1886, in Hamilton, Ontario, Canada. Canadian-American actress and inventor, often called the 'first movie star'.

Dad booked a session with Danielle. He wanted to see what she'd pick up from him; some small confirmation of his quiet belief that in another life, he'd been a healer. She picked it without prompting.

As much as it was strangely fascinating, I still wasn't finished with my story, so I wrote to a world-renowned evolutionary astrologer, author and academic. As an evolutionary astrologer, he would have the answers.

I would need a headline that grabbed his immediate attention. Something like: *Am I a famous movie star?*

It worked. An email was waiting for me the very next morning.

With respect to your questions … It is not only entirely probable, but likely inevitable, that you are, in some way, the same person.

Steven Forrest has never claimed past lives can be proven by science. He has, however, heard thousands of stories and unmistakable patterns of incarnations. People, he said, are living proof that they exist.

Maybe Florence was still on a mission to right the wrongs of men.

SURVIVAL IS OPTIONAL

CAIRNS IS A PLACE WHERE, IF YOU'RE not careful, the most unsuspecting things can kill you. A casual swim could be out of the question even if you're dying from the heat, as box jellyfish drift like ghosts, waiting for their moment. Crocodiles lie in wait in the water, sly in its shallows.

Spiders and snakes are always lurking too, as is the infamous Suicide Bush. A stinging tree so potent it can drop a grown man to his knees. It is sinister in the way it bides its time until the unaccustomed brush past it.

The most venomous creatures don't only lurk beside waterfalls; they wait in beautiful bars and well-lit rooms too, charming, articulate, perfectly at ease. They strike just as fast, and the paralysis lasts far longer.

For a long time I mistook that kind of danger for love, excitement and possibility. If there was anything left to know about survival, it could also be found waiting for me in tourist-free Far North Queensland during COVID lockdown.

With the state borders still closed, I flew north from the Gold Coast to see Tina. We had worked together on the Sydney Olympic Games and she was the very first person I had met from Mount Isa, a place shaped by heat, distance and resilience. The right friendships survive time, geography and all those different choices in between.

In Cairns, nature would teach me what life had been trying to say all along: never linger in the habitats of known predators.

The local park offered me one last benediction, though not in the way I expected. At the entrance to the Catania Wetlands, bright yellow DANGER: CROCODILES signs were nailed to the posts and scattered along the path. I'd planned a leisurely stroll around the lake while my friend Tina and her husband ran ahead, but the moment they disappeared, reality settled in.

Being croc-wise isn't a suggestion. It's how you make it home.

By Monday, the danger of the weekend had given way to something far more surreal. Clouds of butterflies, almost twelve hundred of them, lifted, floated and fluttered past. I felt the world lean in, inviting me to be still, to inhale, as they settled for a heartbeat then drifted off again.

They reminded me that life is shorter than we imagine, and so astonishingly fragile that we must pause to appreciate the fleetingly beautiful moments.

SISTERHOOD

WOMEN WHO OPEN THEIR DOOR, put the kettle on, and wrap you in a blanket while you cry through *The Holiday* and *Love Actually* are everything. They listen to the same heartbreak ad infinitum without flinching. They lend you clothes, give you their bed, feed you when you've forgotten to eat, and turn up your favourite song when their words fall on deaf ears.

They travel beside you, recognise the career opening before you do, and quietly warn you about the man who will break your heart. Often weeks in advance. They blow-dry your hair before first dates and help piece you back together after the last one.

This is not grand love or performative love. It is practical, steady, uncelebrated sisterly love. The kind that saves lives. I've been blessed to have so many fleetingly beautiful moments with those women who have lifted me up throughout my life.

Michele is like that. After Sharon died, she quietly paid for my trip to Turkey. She simply said, when I was struggling, *You need to do this. I'll help you get there.*

Annie and I first met Michele in a maid's quarters in Dubai, where she was shaping brows and quietly undoing our heavily tattooed mistakes.

A Virgo, Michele was modest, kind, and softly ethereal. A self-made beauty mogul, for want of a better phrase. Her home was serene and designer-scented, its corners anchored by oversized crystals. Hermès flats and body-skimming maxis felt less like fashion and more like a philosophy. Her candles were always lit as soul music drifted through her Sonos while sage wafted through the air.

After two marriages and two children, she was done funding men's lives. She chose instead to invest in women, one brow, one conversation, one quiet restoration at a time.

For us, it was always coffee before six in the morning. If I wasn't riding, I'd join her in the loungeroom she had reinvented as a private reformer studio. It was a ritual sustained by a woman who understood that reinvention is a discipline.

We bonded over astrology, clean eating, divorce and spiritual philosophies. That expanded to champagne at our favourite bars and our shared talent for guessing a man's star sign from where we sat. She swore we'd been sisters in another life. I believed her.

The call came the way it always seems to, unannounced but familiar. It carried the same quiet urgency as it had back in 2007.

'How quickly can you get here?'

It is a long flight to anywhere from Australia, as seasoned as we are as travellers. It's always nice to have the sisterhood and someone like Michele to come back to.

Outside waited a brand-new Range Rover, its mirrored windows concealing what the world wasn't meant to see. She had never used this airport before.

As the door was opened for me, her almond eyes lit up, her smile widening with unmistakable warmth.

Her white abaya, in unadorned silk, fell softly around her, every part of her fashion sense exquisite. The princess wore her diamonds the way some women wear their perfume: deliberately, and without apology. A constellation of piercings glittered in her ears, catching the light just as the fine lines of stones at her neck and wrists did. She was understated, exacting and quietly commanding.

'Welcome home. We're so happy to have you back in Dubai where you belong.'

ACKNOWLEDGEMENTS

Lewis. It is a lot to take in, I know. You encouraged me to write this book and lifted me up week after week. You are the centre of my universe. Thank you for choosing me as your mum.

Thank you, Dad, for driving to Auckland one Saturday morning to pick me up and welcome me into your family. You taught us to be kind and compassionate and to take care of our planet. You showed us how magical life is, especially when we look at it through the eyes of something greater than ourselves.

My brother Shaun, my half-brother Zak, and my cousins, Nick, Vali, Adelaide and Lexi: you kept it real as only Kiwis know how. Thank you for filling in the gaps, for showing up when I needed you, and for being my family.

Uncle Barry. Thank you for introducing me to a life more glamorous than anything I'd known and opening my mind up to the theatre of life that you knew was waiting for me.

To Olivia Morris, thank you for recognising the writer I was becoming, for believing in my work long before it had a title. You always knew when it was time to sharpen my narrative and when it was time to pour a drink and breathe.

And Neil Kalidas, thank you for refusing to let this story remain a conversation over coffee.

Jane Eddy, my Villa Maria nemesis. Thank you for illuminating that which we left behind so many years ago. Your laughter, care, and insight were a gift.

My deepest thanks to London-based Dr Claire Bassilious and Italian psychotherapist Francesca Gobessi. Your guidance, endless patience and emotional intelligence created a safe space where very difficult and triggering conversations could unfold naturally. Without you both, these pages wouldn't carry the honesty that may help other women recognise my journey in themselves and so they too can begin to heal.

Lindyn St. John: thank you for always being there and for bringing your Scorpionic editorial talent to those pages you knew needed more courage, less waffling, greater clarity and a few more well-placed (and much-dreaded) apostrophes.

Sally Ann Eddmenson, thank you for the belief, clarity, and the structure you offered when my future was so uncertain. Across continents and false starts, your coaching became the scaffolding for my growth, direction, and success.

Marc L., your formidable influence is matched equally by your warmth, concern and generosity of spirit. Because of you, I was able to start again. I remain deeply grateful.

To my darling Martina, thank you for forever picking up my broken bits. You stood beside me through chapters that never made it onto the page. You are the star of the show.

Susu, Paula, Annie O, Danielle, Emma, Kimberley, Kimi, Mariana, Mary Mumby, Micha, Michele, Myrna, Nicky McD, Sarah, Tallo, and Tina: a million thank-yous are not enough. All of you are the reason there was more of a story to tell.

To Cherine Ghali, Olga Pikina, Lynda and Maitha Al Qubaisi, Monique Dews, Tanja Bernards and Tiffany Johns. I honestly couldn't ask for a better ride-or-die crew. Thank you for everything that kept me going. Wherever I am in the world, I feel your warmth, love and support.

Scientia Professor Gordon Parker AO, whose internationally recognised work in mood disorders and the Black Dog Institute has changed the landscape of mental health not only for people like me, but for so many in Australia.

To my New Zealand award-winning structural editor and author, Caroline Barron. You so bravely endured my messy, confusing, and complicated manuscript! Without you, my book would never have found its shape and I never would have kept going.

Patricia Bell, my Irish–New Zealand copy editor – thank you for the care and diligence you brought to my manuscript, for catching what needed catching and for helping me get my story to the finish line.

Stan Carey, my Irish proofreader. Saving the day with your extraordinary understanding and insight into English as a universal language.

Laura Duffy, my fabulous book designer in New York: you became an unexpected guiding star. Your artistry and grace gave my cover its first true voice.

And finally, to Dubai-based Iranian creative, Kian Kanani. Your talent as a sought-after international fashion photographer graces my cover but not as a fashion model. Thank you for seeing into my soul and translating my story into such a powerful image.

www.ingramcontent.com/pod-product-compliance
Lightning Source LLC
Chambersburg PA
CBHW021230060726
47590CB00005B/1702